Published by The Tech Buzz Press, Sheridan, Wyoming | press.techbuzz.ai

The information in this book is for educational purposes only and does not constitute financial, investment, or legal advice.

ISBN 979-8-9955191-0-2 (hardcover)

ISBN 979-8-9955191-1-9 (paperback)

ISBN 979-8-9955191-2-6 (ebook)

ISBN 979-8-9955191-3-3 (audiobook)

LCCN: 2026908393

First Edition, March 2026 | Printed in the United States of America

Contents

INTRODUCTION: THE $100 BILL THAT LEARNED TO THINK

The first EAT trade was entirely anticlimactic. I remember staring at my screen, watching numbers shift. That was it. No fireworks, no celebration, no dramatic moment where the heavens parted and the future of philanthropy revealed itself. Just a transaction on a decentralized exchange. Numbers moving from one line to another. We didn't even have the meal tracker up yet. We just knew, based on the treasury balance, that the fees had been collected and the meals were funded. It could have been funding anything. The software was completely agnostic. A smart contract collecting fees and routing them to a wallet. The code didn't know about hunger. It didn't know about the 47 million Americans facing food insecurity, or the distribution networks that needed funding, or the children who would eat because of what just happened on a screen in an office in Irvine, California. The code just ran. The fee was collected. The money moved. But I knew what it meant.

And that knowledge was a turning point. It shifted something fundamental in how I thought about what I was doing and what I wanted every day of my working life to be about. Everything I did from that point forward could be funding meals. And once you see that, once you feel the weight of it, regular business starts to feel less. Any money I could make that didn't fund meals seemed smaller. Not worthless. Just smaller. The mission was too powerful for anything else to compete. From that moment forward, every trade on the EAT token funded meals. Not sometimes. Not when the price went up. Not when someone decided to be generous. Every trade. Buy or sell, bull market or bear market, panic selling or speculative buying. The smart contract doesn't care about your motivation. It collects the fee regardless. And as of this writing, that mechanism has funded nearly 10,000 meals. 10,000 times, a person facing food insecurity received food because someone, somewhere, made a trade on a decentralized exchange. Most of those traders weren't thinking about hunger. They were thinking about their portfolio. It didn't matter.

On launch day, December 10th, 2025, EAT surged 600%. Every crypto outlet ran that number as the headline. Here's the part that mattered more: on that same day, trading activity generated enough fees to fund dozens of meals. Not from a viral campaign. Not from a celebrity endorsement. Just from people trading a token, doing what crypto participants do every single day, and meals appearing at food banks as a direct result. Then, weeks later, the broader crypto market crashed. Bitcoin dropped. Altcoins bled out. The social feeds filled with red candles and panic. And EAT kept funding meals. Because people trade in down markets too. They sell, they buy the dip, they rebalance, they panic. Every one of those trades generated fees. Every fee funded impact. Markets crash. Meals don't stop.

That's the idea at the center of this book. Not that people should be more generous.

Not that technology will save us. But that money itself is changing in ways that allow it to carry purpose, follow instructions, and create outcomes that were impossible when money was just a number in a bank's database. Money is becoming software. And software can be programmed to do things that money never could.

The Path Nobody Plans

I didn't set out to build financial infrastructure. I set out to understand why people stay poor. My background is in research. I spent years in academia studying the questions that most people only encounter as headlines: why do disparities in health and wealth persist even when resources exist to close them, what actually prevents people from improving their circumstances, and where do food insecurity, poverty, and technology intersect in ways that create or solve real problems. I published research in those areas. I was good at it. And the work was deeply personal in ways that academic papers never convey.

During my PhD, I did an enormous amount of in-person fieldwork. Long drives out to sites. Late nights running programs. Evaluating interventions for childhood health, for adults in crisis, for communities that had been forgotten by the systems that were supposed to serve them. I sat with families. I visited food banks. I watched programs try to close gaps that had been widening for decades. The boots-on-the-ground work taught me something that no paper ever captured: I could help the people I was physically present with. I could make a real difference during the time I was there. That was the clincher.

Being with people, seeing their faces, understanding their circumstances, that did so much. But I could only be in one place at a time. And every hour I spent driving to a site, running a program, and then going home to write about it was an hour I could have spent building something that might reach a thousand times more people. All of that time, I always felt I could be doing more. I knew where technology was going. I had been an avid investor in blockchain for years. I couldn't help but think that my time could be leveraged better elsewhere. That tension became unbearable. Not because the research didn't matter. It did. It still does. But after one of my longer studies, when I finally went back to write the paper, which was one in a scheme of hundreds of similar papers about similar subjects, I realized this was not the path for me. It wasn't disruptive enough. It wasn't moving the needle.

The tools to build actual solutions were sitting right there, and I was spending my time documenting problems. Academia is great. There's a lot of validity to it. But if you're actually trying to help people and create change at scale, you eventually face a choice. You can create systems that meet people where they are, which requires an enormous investment of time just to understand, or you can create systems that automatically uplift, which requires money, energy, technology, and a cultural shift that researchers will never be the ones to create. I wanted to be the person who created that shift. The last study I did was in 2019, using an AI application to help people, years before ChatGPT made the technology a household word. That was the last straw. I knew I could never go back to academia. I would be on this path for the rest of my life. I chose the technology route because it was more tangible and more scalable. Research without infrastructure is observation without intervention. I needed to build the intervention.

But the research didn't disappear. It became the invisible architecture of everything I've built since. The Tech Buzz, the media company I co-founded that now reaches over a million subscribers, came from understanding information asymmetry, how the gap between what insiders know and what regular people know creates disadvantage. Standard, the AI venture studio, came from understanding that the tools to build solutions are now accessible to anyone willing to learn them. And WYDE and the EAT token came directly from years of studying why the nonprofit sector's infrastructure is fundamentally broken and how market mechanisms could be redirected toward impact. Every piece traces back to the same question I started with in academia: why do systems that should help people fail to do so, and what would it take to build systems that don't?

The idea that became WYDE and the EAT token started the way half the good ideas in tech start: on something close to a napkin. My co-founder Martin and I were in our office on the 19th floor of the WeWork in Irvine, the 400 Spectrum building, looking out at the city below us and working through the economics of cause-driven tokens. The question was almost absurdly simple. What if every trade funded a meal? Not every profitable trade. Not every trade above a certain threshold. Not trades on special charity days or during awareness campaigns. Every single trade. The idea was that if you designed the fee structure of a token correctly, market activity itself, the buying and selling that happens billions of times a day across crypto, could become the permanent funding mechanism for a cause. The trading doesn't stop. So the funding doesn't stop.

But before we got to the mechanism, we had to choose the cause. That decision took longer than you'd think. We considered everything. Cancer research, specifically childhood leukemia, working with organizations like St. Jude's. Dog shelters. Homelessness. Poverty broadly. There are a lot of reasons people will trade something. Look at Dogecoin. Look at all the tokens that do absolutely nothing except sustain a community around a meme. People love the community. They love the meme of the thing. Our thesis was simple: imagine if that same energy actually helped something. Imagine if the meme did help dogs. Or children. Or anyone at all. When we dove into cancer, the math was sobering. The cost of meaningfully contributing to treatment for childhood leukemia was around $400,000 per case. That would require enormous trading volume. By the end of a year, we might fund treatment for one to five children. An extraordinary milestone by any human measure. But it wasn't going to demonstrate the model's potential fast enough.

We needed something tangible, something where the impact-per-dollar was immediately visible and undeniable. So we asked a different question: what is the cost of a meal? At scale, purchasing and preparing food from scratch runs somewhere between one and five dollars. But then we discovered something that changed the entire calculus. The biggest hunger relief organizations in the country, groups like Feeding America, already have the food. Grocery chains donate surplus inventory. Farms contribute excess harvest. The meals exist. What these organizations desperately need is funding for distribution: the trucks, the cold chains, the logistics of getting food from where it is to where it's needed. And that distribution cost? About twenty cents per meal.

We used ten cents as our base calculation and twenty cents as our conservative estimate. That meant roughly $40 in trading volume on the EAT token would *generate enough fees to fund one meal. Not a pledged meal. Not a promised meal. An actual meal, funded, recorded on the blockchain, irreversible. The timing was right too. SNAP benefits were being defunded. Food insecurity was in the news. And hunger is a universal language, something every person on earth understands in their body, not just their mind. We looked at each other. We looked at the numbers. We looked out at the city from the 19th floor. And we knew we had it.*

The $100 Bill That Learned to Think

I want you to hold a $100 bill in your mind. Not a metaphorical one. The physical object. Cotton and linen blend. Green ink. Benjamin Franklin's face. That $100 bill is one of the most successful pieces of technology ever created. It is portable, universally recognized, requires no electricity, and has been a reliable store of value for the better part of a century.

It is also profoundly stupid.

That bill doesn't know who holds it. It doesn't know where it's been. It can't enforce conditions on how it gets spent. It can't split itself into smaller pieces automatically. It can't send a portion of itself to a food bank every time it changes hands. It can't verify that the person spending it has the right to spend it, or that the person receiving it will use it for its intended purpose. It sits in your wallet, inert, waiting for a human to decide what to do with it.

Now imagine a $100 bill that carries instructions.

Imagine money that, every time it moves, automatically routes a fraction to hunger relief. Not because the sender chose to donate. Because the money itself was programmed to. Imagine money that knows the conditions under which it can be transferred: only after a contract is fulfilled, only to verified recipients, only in amounts that match an agreed-upon schedule. Imagine money that can report its own transaction history to anyone who asks, in real time, without requiring a bank or a government to look it up.

That's not money anymore. That's software. Software that happens to carry value.

This transformation is happening right now. Stablecoins, digital dollars that live on the blockchain, settle $1.39 trillion per month. BlackRock, the largest asset manager on earth, has tokenized treasury bonds on a public blockchain and built a fund that crossed $2.9 billion in assets. JPMorgan has issued programmable deposit tokens on a public network. Smart contracts on Ethereum and its Layer 2 networks execute billions of dollars in automated financial transactions every day, with no banker, no broker, and no middleman involved. The $100 bill didn't just go digital. It learned to think.

And it's not just financial institutions seeing this. The GENIUS Act, signed into law in July 2025, established the first major federal framework for stablecoins. Wyoming created the DUNA, a legal structure that gives decentralized organizations the same standing as a corporation. Europe enacted MiCA, the world's first comprehensive crypto regulatory framework. For the first time in history, governments are building regulatory infrastructure specifically for programmable money. Not cracking down on it. Building for it. That's a signal that the people who make the rules believe this is permanent.

The same transformation that turned communication into email, publishing into the internet, and commerce into e-commerce is now happening to money itself. And just as those earlier transformations didn't merely digitize the old thing but created entirely new possibilities, programmable money isn't just faster dollars. It's a new kind of money that can carry logic, embed purpose, compose with other financial instruments like software APIs, and operate autonomously through AI agents that never sleep.

Think about that. Compare it to what happens after the Super Bowl. In 2026, Kalshi ran a one-day free grocery event. Polymarket spent a million dollars on a five-day popup "free market" giving away groceries. Clever marketing. Generated headlines. And then it was over. The confetti hit the field and the feeding stopped. EAT's mechanism doesn't depend on a Super Bowl, a crisis, or a marketing budget. It runs because markets run. Every day. Permanently. That's the difference between a promotion and infrastructure. Between an event and a system.

There's a thread that runs through everything in this book, and I want to introduce it now because once you see it, you can't unsee it.

Money is energy.

Every phase change in money's history was an energy efficiency upgrade. Shells were portable energy: light enough to carry, scarce enough to hold value, limited by geography. Coins were durable energy: standardized by weight, stamped by authorities, expandable across trade routes. Paper was lightweight energy: a promise backed by gold you didn't have to carry. Digital money was instant energy: numbers in databases that moved at the speed of wire transfers and credit card swipes. Each upgrade reduced the friction, reduced the energy lost in transit, and allowed value to flow faster and farther.

Programmable money is intelligent energy. Money that doesn't just move but thinks. Money that carries conditions, follows rules, executes logic, and reports its own behavior. Like every previous upgrade, it doesn't merely make the old thing faster. It creates entirely new possibilities that the old system couldn't imagine.

Bitcoin is the clearest proof of this. Its mining infrastructure is an energy grid. Miners around the world convert raw electrical power, often from sources that would otherwise be wasted, into digital scarcity. In El Salvador, they mine Bitcoin with geothermal energy from volcanoes, literally converting the heat of the earth into monetary value. That global mining network represents the largest dedicated energy-to-value conversion system ever built. Michael Saylor, who has staked over $33 billion of his company on Bitcoin, puts it more bluntly than anyone: Bitcoin is digital energy. He isn't theorizing. He's betting the company.

And as you'll see later in this book, that same mining infrastructure is now being evaluated for a second purpose: powering the artificial intelligence revolution. The data centers, the GPU clusters, the energy contracts, the cooling systems. They already exist. Built for Bitcoin. Repurposable for AI. Meanwhile, the five largest technology companies on earth are collectively spending over $600 billion per year building new AI infrastructure. Their free cash flow is going negative. They are issuing the largest corporate bond deals in history to fund the buildout. This is not a product bet. This is an energy infrastructure project, and it mirrors every previous industrial revolution.

Two technological revolutions are reaching their deployment phases at the same time. Crypto and blockchain spent the years from 2009 to 2022 in their installation phase: speculation, ICOs, DeFi summer, the FTX crash. AI has been in its installation phase since 2022: ChatGPT, massive capital expenditure, billion-dollar valuations, uncertain business models. Both are now crossing into deployment. Regulation is arriving. Institutions are entering. The speculation is cooling and real utility is emerging. Every previous technological revolution, from canals to railways to the internet, followed this same pattern. But two revolutions reaching deployment simultaneously? That has never happened before. And the opportunities at their intersection are the largest and least contested.

This is also why cause coins matter at a level deeper than charity. The EAT token converts one form of energy, market activity, into another form of energy, meals for people who need them. Attention energy from traders becomes metabolic energy in human bodies. The smart contract is the converter. The blockchain is the grid. From a click on a screen to calories in a person's body, the conversion happens in seconds. That's not a metaphor. That's thermodynamics.

Money, software, compute, attention, and capital are all the same substrate expressed at different layers of abstraction. The people who understand this are building the future. Everyone else is still thinking in ledgers.

Why This Book. Why Now.

Here is what I can tell you that nobody else can: I built pieces of this system. I built a media company with over a million subscribers. I built an AI venture studio generating real revenue. I built the first Impact Exchange on a legally recognized decentralized framework in Wyoming. I built a token that funds meals through trading activity. I watched some of it work and some of it break. I know what the inside looks like.

And I know this: the transformation is accelerating faster than almost anyone realizes. Trust in the federal government has been in free fall since 1960. The financial system excludes billions. Two technological revolutions, artificial intelligence and programmable money, are reaching their deployment phases simultaneously. That has never happened before in the history of technology. Not once.

The monetary order that has governed the world since a group of bankers met in secret on Jekyll Island in 1910 is ending. Not collapsing overnight. Ending the way every monetary order ends: slowly, then all at once. What replaces it is already being built, in open-source code, on public blockchains, by thousands of builders instead of seven men on a private island. Ray Dalio diagnosed the changing world order. This book is about what replaces it. The new money order.

Here's where we're going. Part I is called Energy. It covers how money actually works today, why it's breaking, the trust crisis that makes programmable money inevitable, and the energy theory that connects everything in this book. Part II is Infrastructure: blockchain, smart contracts, stablecoins, central bank digital currencies, and DeFi, explained so that every reader can follow regardless of technical background. Part III is Convergence: institutions entering the space, tokens bridging crypto and AI, AI agents that need financial rails, cause coins directing market energy toward human good, prediction markets pricing belief, and the regulatory renaissance that's building guardrails so all of it can scale. Part IV is The Golden Era: who wins, who loses, what can go wrong, and the mental models you'll need to navigate a financial system that runs on logic instead of ledgers.

I want you to finish this book feeling like you've uncovered what's actually happening versus what everyone thinks is happening. The people behind the scenes know what's going on, and it looks a lot more complex from the outside than it really is. All of this is zeros and ones multiplied over and over until you have systems so intricate they seem impenetrable. But they all start with simple frameworks. That's all that money is. That's all the economy is. That's what our world runs on. Simplicity first.

But before we can see where this is going, we need to see what we are leaving behind. The architecture of trust that holds the current system together. How it was built, who it was built for, and what happens when it starts to crack. Because it is cracking. And the cracks have names.

This book starts with a trade. Numbers on a screen. And a meal that funded itself.

PART I: ENERGY

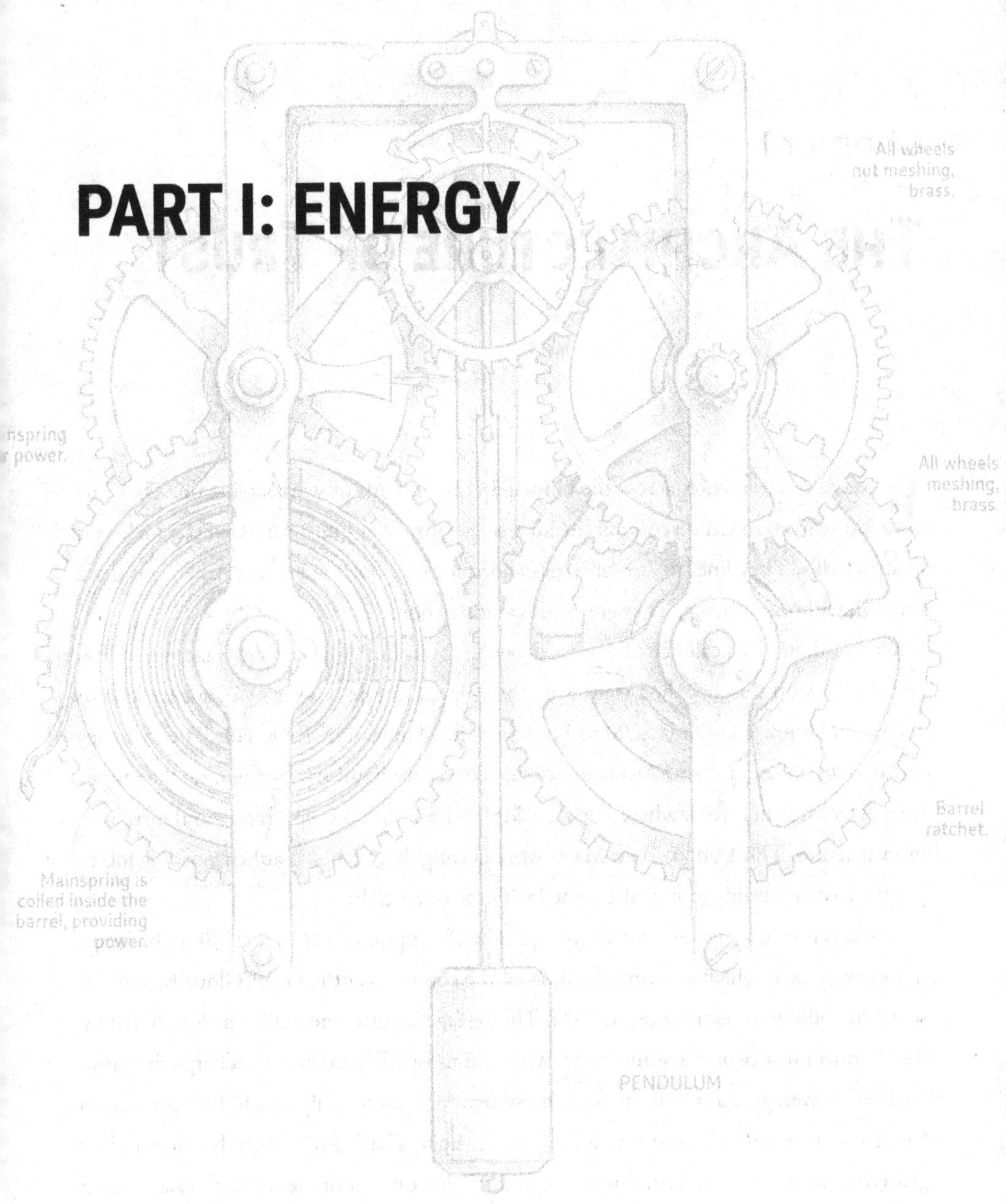

Chapter 1

THE ARCHITECTURE OF TRUST

Every Friday, in cities across the United States, millions of workers line up. They line up at Western Union counters inside gas stations. They line up at MoneyGram kiosks in strip malls. They line up at remittance shops in neighborhoods most Americans drive through without noticing. They are sending money home.

One of them, let's call her Maria, works two jobs in Los Angeles. She wakes up at five, cleans offices until noon, then waitresses until nine. On Friday afternoon, she walks into a Western Union and sends $200 to her family in Manila. The fee is $12. The exchange rate markup takes another $7 to $10 that she'll never see itemized. By the time the money reaches her mother, somewhere between $19 and $22 has disappeared into the transfer infrastructure. Think about that. Maria worked roughly two hours at her morning job to pay the cost of sending money she earned with the other eight.

Maria is not unusual. She is the average. The Philippines receives $40 billion in remittances every year, which accounts for 8.5% of the country's entire GDP. Globally, workers sent $905 billion in remittances in 2024. The average cost to send $200 was 6.49%. Banks, the channel most people assume is the safest and most efficient, actually charge the most: 14.55% on average. Add it all up and the system extracts roughly $48 billion per year in fees from the people who can least afford to pay them. That's $48 billion that doesn't buy groceries, doesn't pay tuition, doesn't keep the lights on in a home seven thousand miles away.

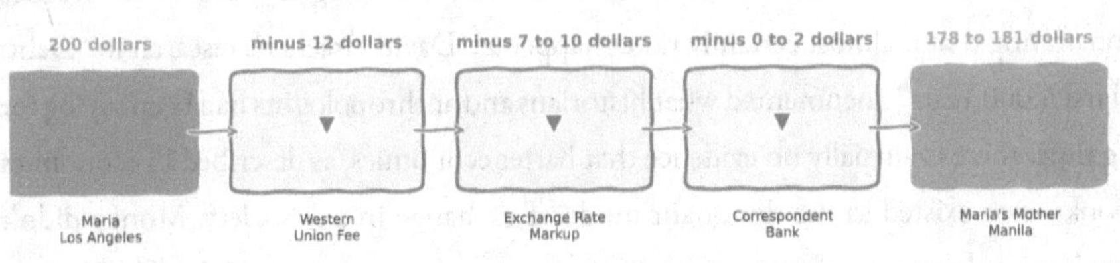

Figure 1.1: Where Maria's $200 goes. Three intermediaries extract fees before the money reaches Manila.

I didn't learn any of this in a textbook. I learned it by paying contractors at Standard Labs the venture studio Martin and I built after I got tired of studying problems. We hired developers in the Philippines because the talent was excellent and the cost structure made sense for a startup with limited capital. The first time we tried to pay a Filipino contractor through the traditional banking system, I watched the fees and delays compound in real time. Wire transfer fees on both ends. Correspondent bank charges in the middle. A three-day wait for "settlement." The developer needed money to pay his rent that week. Our money was in transit, sitting in some intermediary's ledger, earning interest for someone who didn't build anything.

That experience rewired how I thought about financial infrastructure. The system was not designed for Maria. It was not designed for our developer in Manila. It was designed for the institutions that operate it. Everyone else got the interface. Nobody got the infrastructure.

What Money Actually Is

Before we can talk about where money is going, we need to talk about what money is. And most of what you were taught about it is wrong.

The standard story goes like this: once upon a time, people bartered. A farmer with wheat wanted fish. A fisherman wanted wheat. But what if the fisherman didn't want wheat today? Barter was inefficient, so humans invented money as a medium of exchange. Shells, beads, precious metals. Problem solved.

It's a clean story. It makes intuitive sense. And anthropologists have spent decades demonstrating that it almost certainly never happened. David Graeber's research in "Debt: The First 5,000 Years" documented what historians and anthropologists had been saying for a long time: there is virtually no evidence that barter economies, as described in economics textbooks, ever existed as the dominant mode of exchange in any society. Money didn't emerge because barter was inconvenient. Money emerged from systems of debt, obligation, and trust. You kept track of who owed what to whom. The community remembered. The temple recorded it.

This distinction matters more than it sounds. If money evolved from barter, then money is fundamentally about the physical object: the coin, the bill, the gold bar. But if money evolved from trust networks, then money is fundamentally about the system underneath the object. The ledger. The record. The agreement between people about what counts.

Every major upgrade in money's history was actually an upgrade in the trust technology underneath it. Temples in ancient Mesopotamia were the first trust institutions. They stored grain, kept records, and managed debts between farmers and merchants. The temple didn't just hold your wheat. It held your trust. When medieval banks emerged in Florence and Venice, they didn't invent a new form of money. They invented a new form of trust. You could deposit gold with a Medici bank in Florence and withdraw it in Bruges because the bank's reputation was the trust layer that made the transaction work across distance. Central banks took the next step: they centralized trust at the national level. You didn't need to trust your individual bank. You trusted the Bank of England, the Federal Reserve, the institution behind the institution.

Each upgrade followed the same pattern. The trust technology got bigger, more centralized, and more abstract. From your neighbor's memory, to the temple's clay tablet, to the bank's ledger, to the central bank's reserve system. At every step, the promise was the same: trust us. We'll keep the records straight.

And for a long time, that promise held.

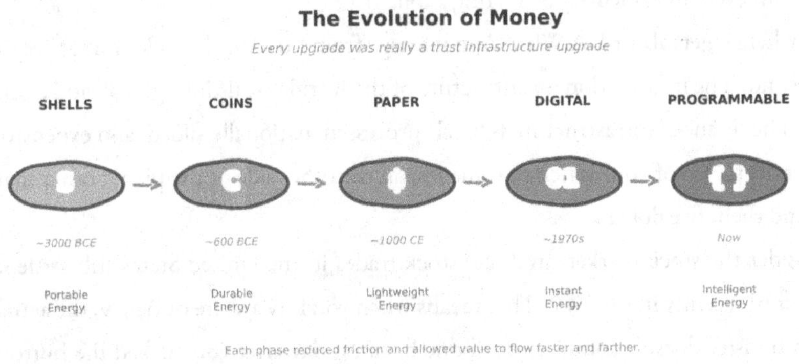

Figure 1.2: Every upgrade in money's history was really a trust infrastructure upgrade.

How Your Money Actually Moves

Here's something nobody thinks about. When you send a Venmo payment to split a dinner check, the money doesn't actually move. Not really. What happens is a series of promises get updated across multiple institutions' databases, and then, days later, the actual settlement occurs through a system built in the 1970s.

Most domestic transfers in the United States run through the Automated Clearing House, or ACH. ACH was developed in the early 1970s as a way to replace paper checks with electronic transactions. It processes transactions in batches, not in real time. When your employer deposits your paycheck via direct deposit, that money doesn't arrive the moment it's sent. The bank receives a batch instruction, credits your account, and then settles the actual transfer with the sending bank later. Sometimes same day. Often the next business day. If it's a Friday, you might be waiting until Monday.

International transfers are worse. The backbone of cross-border payments is SWIFT, the Society for Worldwide Interbank Financial Telecommunication. SWIFT is not a payment system. It is a messaging system. When Maria sends money to Manila, SWIFT doesn't move the money. It sends a message from her bank to a correspondent bank, which sends a message to another correspondent bank, which sends a message to the receiving bank in the Philippines. At each step, a fee is deducted. At each step, there is a delay. The whole chain can take three to five business days. The money doesn't travel. It gets re-promised from ledger to ledger, with every intermediary extracting a toll.

Here's where it gets absurd. A WhatsApp message from Los Angeles to Manila arrives in under a second. The information infrastructure of the world is real-time, global, and essentially free. The financial infrastructure is batch-processed, nationally siloed, and expensive. You can send a photo of your lunch to someone on the other side of the planet faster than you can send them five dollars.

Or consider the stock market. In 2026, stock trades in the United States still settle in T+1, and until recently it was T+2. That means when you buy a share of Apple, the actual ownership transfer doesn't complete until one business day after you clicked the button. For decades it was two days. The trade executes in milliseconds. The settlement takes a day. What fills that gap? Intermediaries. Clearinghouses. Custodians. Each one a layer of trust infrastructure that exists because the underlying system can't verify ownership in real time.

Every time you swipe your credit card at a coffee shop, five different companies take a cut before the money lands in the shop owner's account. The card network, the issuing bank, the acquiring bank, the payment processor, and sometimes a gateway provider. That 2 to 3% fee that the merchant pays isn't one fee. It's a bundle of tolls collected by a chain of intermediaries, each one extracting value for the service of saying "yes, the money is real, the buyer can pay, and we promise to settle this eventually." You drank the coffee in four minutes. The money is still making its way through the chain.

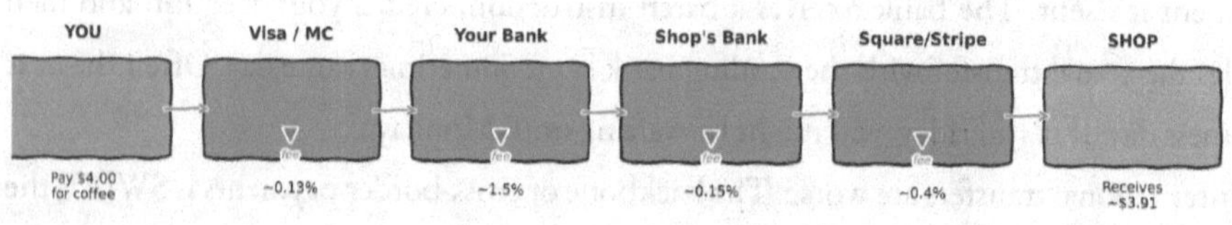

Figure 1.3: Five intermediaries split ~2.2% before the shop owner sees a dollar. Settlement: 1–2 days.

Every one of those intermediaries is a trust layer. And every trust layer has a cost. Not just in fees, but in time, in complexity, in friction. The more intermediaries, the more energy the system consumes to move the same unit of value from one person to another. Think of each middleman as a resistor in an electrical circuit. Useful energy goes in. Some of it converts to heat. What comes out the other end is always less than what went in.

When Trust Breaks

In 1958, when the Pew Research Center first measured trust in the federal government, 73% of Americans said they trusted the government to do the right thing always or most of the time. As of 2025, that number is 16%. A 78% relative decline over 67 years. The federal government now ranks as the least trusted institution in American life according to the Bentley-Gallup Force for Good report.

Figure 1.4: Trust in the U.S. federal government, 1958–2025. Source: Pew Research Center.

That number is not a political statistic. It is a structural one. And the financial system, built on a foundation of institutional trust, has experienced three escalating failures that tell you everything about where this is heading.

The first was slow. The 2008 financial crisis didn't happen overnight. It built for years inside layers of trust that nobody verified. Homeowners trusted brokers who told them they could afford the mortgage. Brokers trusted banks that packaged those mortgages into securities. Banks trusted rating agencies that stamped AAA on products nobody understood. Investors trusted the ratings. Regulators trusted the banks. Every layer of the system was operating on faith. When the bottom fell out, the U.S. government committed $700 billion in taxpayer money through the TARP bailout to keep the system from collapsing entirely. Trust had failed so completely that the government had to step in as the trust layer of last resort.

The second failure was fast. On March 9, 2023, depositors pulled $42 billion out of Silicon Valley Bank in roughly ten hours. The run didn't start with a line out the door. It started with a group chat. Venture capitalists texted each other. Founders called their CFOs. By the time the sun set on the West Coast, the bank was functionally dead. SVB had been operating on the same trust infrastructure as every other bank: the assumption that not everyone would want their money at the same time. But information now travels at digital speed, and trust collapses at digital speed too. The FDIC stepped in. The government backstopped deposits above the insured limit. Again.

The third failure is different from the first two, because it wasn't a sudden collapse. It was a slow reveal.

When the Department of Government Efficiency began its review of federal spending in early 2025, the stated goal was to identify waste and fraud across the federal government. What followed was contentious, politically charged, and far from straightforward. DOGE's own claims of savings were repeatedly disputed by independent analysts. NPR found that the organization's verifiable spending cuts amounted to roughly $2 billion, a fraction of the hundreds of billions claimed. Congressional investigators from both parties found different versions of the problem. A Senate subcommittee report estimated that DOGE itself had generated $21.7 billion in new waste through mass buyouts and workforce disruptions.

But here's the thing that matters for this book, and it has nothing to do with which side of the political aisle you sit on: the underlying problem that DOGE exposed was not new. The Government Accountability Office has tracked improper payments, meaning payments that should not have been made or were made in incorrect amounts, since 2003. The cumulative total through fiscal year 2024 is $2.8 trillion. In fiscal year 2024 alone, sixteen federal agencies reported $162 billion in improper payments across sixty-eight programs. The GAO estimates that the federal government loses between $233 billion and $521 billion annually to fraud.

Read those numbers again. $2.8 trillion in cumulative improper payments. Up to $521 billion lost to fraud per year. And the GAO has been publishing these findings every year for over two decades. These are not secrets. They are publicly available reports that nobody acts on because the system was never designed for verification. It was designed for trust.

This is not about DOGE as an organization. It is not about any administration. It is about what happens when you build systems on the assumption that trust is sufficient and then run those systems for decades without verifying whether the trust was warranted. The black hole exists regardless of who decided to look into it. The money was "trusted" to flow correctly. It didn't. Nobody checked because the architecture assumed checking wasn't necessary.

Ray Dalio has documented this pattern across civilizations. In "Principles for Dealing with the Changing World Order," he traces the roughly 150-year cycle of rising and declining empires, and one of the consistent markers of the declining phase is the erosion of internal trust, institutional effectiveness, and financial discipline. The United States is exhibiting those markers now. I'm not a doom-and-gloom thinker. I'm a builder. But builders need to understand the full picture: trust is a depleting resource. Every fraud uncovered, every institution that fails, every headline about billions unaccounted for erodes whatever trust remains. And you cannot rebuild trust faster than it's being spent.

Unless you build systems that don't require it.

The Leapfrog

In 2007, a telecom company in Kenya launched a service called M-Pesa. The premise was simple: let people send money to each other using their mobile phones. No bank account required. Just a phone number and a network of local agents, usually shopkeepers, who could convert between digital balances and cash.

At the time, fewer than 20% of Kenyans had a bank account. But mobile phone penetration was skyrocketing. The banks hadn't reached the population because extending branch infrastructure to rural Kenya wasn't profitable. The roads were bad. The distances were long. The individual transaction sizes were tiny. From the bank's perspective, the math didn't work.

M-Pesa didn't try to fix the banks. It didn't lobby for better branch networks or financial inclusion programs. It just built around them. Within two years, M-Pesa had more users than every Kenyan bank combined. By 2012, a quarter of Kenya's GDP was flowing through the platform. Today, mobile money accounts in Sub-Saharan Africa are held by 40% of adults, up from 27% in 2021. Globally, 1.3 billion adults still have no financial account of any kind (I will expand on this in Chapter 2). But 900 million of those people own a mobile phone. The infrastructure problem is not that we can't reach these people. It's that the existing financial system was never designed to.

That same leapfrog pattern is happening right now in the United States. Not in rural areas without banks, but in the legal infrastructure for new kinds of organizations.

When my team and I launched WYDE, the first Impact Exchange built on blockchain, we chose Wyoming for a reason. Wyoming had created the DUNA framework, the Decentralized Unincorporated Nonprofit Association, the first state-level legal structure specifically designed for crypto-native organizations. It was the most forward-looking regulatory framework in the country. The DUNA gave us articles of incorporation, a recognized legal structure, and a path to 501(c)(4) tax-exempt status. The IRS accepted it.

The banks did not.

We could not get a bank account. Coinbase wouldn't open one. Mercury wouldn't open one. We went to banks that specifically market to nonprofits. None of them recognized the DUNA structure. The most progressive legal framework in the country, designed by state legislators to enable exactly the kind of organization we were building, and the existing banking infrastructure literally could not process it. The systems did not speak to each other.

We solved it eventually by creating a subsidiary LLC, which the banks understood. But that's beside the point. The point is that the trust architecture of American finance is failing not through malice, but through incompatibility. Wyoming built the road. The banks don't have vehicles that drive on it. M-Pesa proved in 2007 that when the infrastructure won't serve you, you build around it. We proved the same thing in 2025. Same pattern. Different continent. Different century. Same conclusion.

And then there's the story that made verification real for me in a way that no research paper ever could.

In 2021, Martin and I were just getting Standard Labs off the ground. We hadn't raised any outside capital yet. Every dollar was coming from our own

pockets. We hired a developer based in Russia to build smart contracts for us. He was talented, affordable, and available. He insisted on being paid in USDC, a stablecoin pegged to the US dollar, which ran on the Ethereum blockchain. We agreed. We sent $19,000. The following week, when we expected the first code delivery, the developer told us he never received the money. My stomach dropped. $19,000 was an enormous amount for us at that stage. A US-based developer would have cost three times as much. If the money was gone, we were starting over. I ran through the scenarios in my head. Did we send it to the wrong wallet address? Was it lost in some blockchain void? Had we just made the most expensive mistake of the company's short life? Then it hit me. This wasn't a wire transfer. This was the blockchain. I pulled up Etherscan, the public blockchain explorer. Anyone can use it. Every transaction that has ever occurred on the Ethereum network is recorded there, permanently, with timestamps and wallet addresses visible to the world. I searched for our transaction hash. There it was. $19,000 in USDC, sent from our wallet, sitting in his wallet. Hadn't moved. I verified the receiving address against the one he had given us. It matched. He was lying. And we could prove it. It was Martin who played it exactly right. Instead of calling the developer a liar, which would have given him a reason to disappear with the money and end the chat, Martin sent a calm message: "We can see that the $19,000 is in the wallet you confirmed as yours, received from our wallet. Here's the transaction hash. Please use those funds and get the work done." The developer's response was one word: "Ok." No apology. No explanation. No "you caught me." Just ok. And he delivered the code by Friday of that same week.

On the old system, that $19,000 disappears. Wire transfers don't have public receipts. Bank transfers can be disputed, delayed, obscured. If someone on the other side of the planet tells you the money never arrived, your options are to file a claim, hire a lawyer, or eat the loss. On the blockchain, the lie was visible to anyone who cared to look. The money didn't hide because it couldn't hide. That is the difference between faith-based trust and verification-based trust. One depends on believing the other person. The other depends on math.

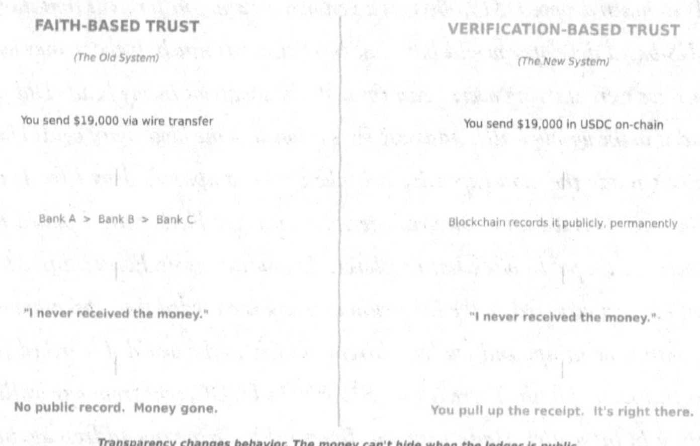

Figure 1.5: Faith-based trust vs. verification-based trust. The money can't hide when the ledger is public.

Designed for Whom

I met Ben in Dallas at a conference where half the room was in tech and the other half was running nonprofits. He is the chief development officer at one of the largest food-related nonprofits in Texas. When I asked him what his days actually look like, he did not sugarcoat it. He spends the majority of his year, his words, whining and dining and building a repository of information to convince someone, whether that is an individual donor, an institution, or an enterprise, to write a check in the fourth quarter. That is the business model. Months of relationship-building and case-making compressed into a fundraising window that opens in October and closes in December.

We talked about the state of technology. About blockchain-based funding. About AI and how everything is accelerating. He saw it. He understood the massive lift it could provide for his organization and his industry. But then he said something that I have not stopped thinking about. He said it is almost impossible to conceptualize how any of this gets implemented in the nonprofit sector. Not because the technology does not work. Because his organization is a human-centered operation. They promote dignity for people. People-to-people is how that dignity is substantiated. The minute you automate the funding, you risk automating away the very thing that makes the work meaningful. He could see the future. He just could not see how to get there without losing the part that matters most.

Ben's problem is not a funding problem. It is an architecture problem. The infrastructure he depends on was not designed for what he is trying to do with it.

I keep coming back to this question. Every system is designed for someone. The question is who.

I saw this pattern before I ever touched financial infrastructure. I saw it in academia. The research pipeline is supposed to work like this: study a problem, write a paper, publish it, inform policy, help people. Here's how it actually works. You spend a year conducting a study. You write the paper. You wait months to a year for peer review. You pay to submit it to a private journal so that the public can read research that was funded with public money. If your study isn't read or cited enough, you lose the government funding that supports your next study. That funding then goes to the same private publishers who charge other researchers to access the work that taxpayers already paid for. And the entire academic establishment treats open-source alternatives as less prestigious, which means less funding, which means less research, which means fewer solutions.

That system was not designed for the people the research is supposed to help. It was designed for journals, tenure committees, and grant agencies. The people at the end of the chain, the ones living with the health disparities and food insecurity and poverty that the research documents, they are an afterthought. An impact statement in the appendix.

The pattern is the same everywhere. SWIFT was designed for banks. ACH was designed for payroll processors. Credit card networks were designed for issuers. Publishing was designed for publishers. Healthcare billing was designed for insurers. The nonprofit sector, all $3.7 trillion of it, has never had access to public capital markets while every corporation in America can issue stock to millions of investors. In every case, the people the system is supposed to serve get the interface: a website, an app, a customer service number. The actual infrastructure, the rails that money rides on, the protocols that determine who gets access and at what cost, those were built for someone else.

I left academia because I couldn't keep documenting the problems from within a system that was itself part of the problem. My soul wanted another route. The pace of technology was accelerating. The tools to build actual solutions were available. And I was spending my years in a system designed for prestige accumulation, not for impact. Somewhere between my last study and my first startup, I decided that research without infrastructure is observation without intervention. I needed to build the intervention.

Everything I've built since has been aimed at the same gap: the distance between the people a system is supposed to serve and the people it actually serves. The Tech Buzz exists because information asymmetry is a designed-in feature of insider economies. WYDE exists because the nonprofit sector was locked out of market infrastructure by default, not because someone decided to exclude it, but because nobody designed the on-ramp. The EAT token exists because charitable giving depends on a trust architecture that is structurally identical to the one losing $2.8 trillion in improper payments. Every donor is asked to trust that their money reaches its purpose. Most never verify. Most can't.

Here's what I want you to take from this chapter. The system is not just slow, expensive, and inconvenient. Those are symptoms. The underlying condition is architectural. The financial infrastructure of the world was built on the assumption that institutional trust would always be sufficient. That assumption held for a long time. It is no longer holding.

Trust in the federal government has collapsed. The GAO documents hundreds of billions in annual fraud that nobody fixes. Banks cannot interface with legal structures created by their own country's state legislatures. Stock trades take a full day to settle. Sending money across a border costs more than a meal. The system isn't broken because bad people run it. The system is broken because it was designed for a world that no longer exists: a world where information moved slowly, where institutions were broadly trusted, where the friction of distance and time justified layers of intermediaries extracting fees for the privilege of saying "trust us."

That world is gone. Information moves at the speed of light. Trust has been spent. And the system that depends on both is cracking in ways that patches cannot fix.

The question is not whether the current system will be replaced. The question is what replaces it, who builds it, and whether the new architecture will repeat the same mistake.

Because the old architecture was built on three things. Trust that the people running the system would be honest. Institutions powerful enough to enforce the rules when they weren't. And gatekeepers who controlled access, deciding who got to participate and who got locked out. Every layer of the financial system, from the Fed to your local bank to the accredited investor threshold that keeps 81% of American households out of the best investment opportunities, runs on that same architecture. Trust, institutions, gatekeepers.

All three are under pressure. The trust numbers speak for themselves. The institutions are struggling to keep pace with a world that moves at the speed of information. And the gatekeepers are looking increasingly like the problem they were supposed to prevent. The cracks are too wide to ignore. And they are getting wider.

Chapter 2

THE BREAKING POINT

In the fall of 2021, my team pitched First Republic Bank on a blockchain solution. We had built something we believed in. A system that could bring transparency and speed to processes that First Republic was still running on infrastructure from the previous decade. This was during COVID, so everything was on Zoom. We prepared the deck, walked them through the technology, answered their questions. They were polite. They asked good questions. They seemed genuinely interested in what blockchain could do for their operations.

Then they ghosted us.

No rejection email. No follow-up call. Just silence. We sent one check-in, then another. Nothing. At the time, my co-founders and I went through the usual post-mortem. What did we get wrong? Was the pitch too technical? Did we misread the room? We knew more about blockchain than anyone in that building, and we were offering to bring that expertise to their doorstep. The ghosting stung because we couldn't figure out what we did wrong.

Two years later, First Republic didn't exist. In March 2023, depositors pulled $100 billion in a matter of days. The FDIC seized what was left. JPMorgan bought the carcass. The bank that couldn't be bothered to return our emails was gone, and we understood why they had ghosted us. They weren't evaluating our technology. They were using us for a free education session while their balance sheet was already rotting from the inside. They had bigger problems than blockchain adoption. They just couldn't tell anyone, including us, what those problems were.

That same year, Silvergate Bank went down. Silvergate was right down the street from us in San Diego. We had pitched them too. Same result. Different flavor of the same disease.

Silvergate had positioned itself as the crypto-friendly bank, the bridge between traditional finance and the digital asset world, and when FTX collapsed in late 2022, the contagion spread through Silvergate's deposit base like a virus. Signature Bank followed. Silicon Valley Bank followed. The 2023 regional banking crisis wasn't one bank failing. It was a category failing. The common thread was not crypto exposure or interest rate risk or any of the specific causes that analysts pointed to in each case. The common thread was that these were trust-based institutions, and when trust evaporated, they had nothing underneath.

I keep coming back to this. The financial system we inherited is not only slow, not only expensive, not only exclusionary. It is structurally incapable of serving the world we actually live in. It is banks that ghosted me disappearing two years later. It is institutions I pitched crumbling under the weight of problems that transparency would have caught years earlier. The breaking point is not a future event. We are living in it.

Chapter 1 mapped the plumbing. The two-day settlement times. The 3% card fees that most people never notice because they're baked into prices. The billions in annual remittance fees that function as a tax on being poor and far from home. All of that is real, and all of it represents energy lost to friction in a system designed for a slower world.

But the speed and cost problems are the easy critique. Everyone in fintech has made them. Every pitch deck for every payment startup since 2010 has included a slide about how long it takes to settle a stock trade versus send a text message. The deeper failures are structural, and they go beyond plumbing.

The financial system has five fractures. Speed and cost are two. The other three are the ones that matter more, because they aren't fixable with faster rails or cheaper transactions. They require a fundamentally different architecture.

Access. Transparency. Programmability.

Access: the system was built for people already inside it. If you have a bank account, a credit score, and a mailing address, it works for you. If you lack any of those, you are locked out. Not temporarily. Structurally.

Transparency: the system operates on trust, and trust means opacity. Give us your money and trust us to handle it correctly. At every layer, that trust is periodically betrayed in spectacular fashion, because opacity is not a bug. It is the system.

Programmability: money is dumb. A dollar in your bank account has no instructions, no conditions, no logic. It cannot execute a contract, verify a condition, or route itself anywhere. Money, in its current form, is a passive store of value in a world that increasingly demands active, intelligent, self-executing financial instruments.

Every instruction requires an intermediary, and every intermediary extracts a fee and introduces a delay. These are not three separate problems. They are three expressions of the same underlying failure: a financial system designed for physical proximity, institutional trust, and human-speed transactions, operating in a world of digital distance, institutional skepticism, and machine-speed information.

I want to show you what all three fractures look like at once, because they do not arrive separately. They compound.

In early 2023, Martin and I flew to Connecticut for a meeting about a remittance problem. A government contact from a country I am intentionally not naming had reached out because their citizens were losing up to ten percent every time money moved across borders. Ten percent. A farmer sends money to pay a supplier, and a tenth of it disappears into the clearing system before it arrives. A merchant takes out a loan, and the fees embedded in the trust network that processes the transaction eat into the principal before the first payment is due. This was not a crypto problem or a fintech problem. This was an architecture problem. The entire financial clearing system for this country ran on a trust network that was more archaic than the existing banking system in the United States, and the cost landed on the citizens. We sat in that meeting and heard the full picture. Access: the banking network did not extend to where most of the country's economic activity actually happens. Transparency: nobody could trace where the fees were accumulating or who was extracting what. Programmability: there was no mechanism to automate any part of the clearing process. The money moved through human hands at every step, and every pair of hands took a cut. Three fractures, one country, one Tuesday afternoon in a conference room in Connecticut. On the red-eye home, Martin

and I stayed up the entire flight building a proposal. ChatGPT had just come out. We were iterating on the solution in the earliest version of the tool, feeding it the problem, getting back frameworks, refining, rebuilding. It is genuinely funny now to look at what we produced with that first version compared to what we could build today. The gap between what that tool could do in January 2023 and what it can do now is its own kind of proof that the deployment phase is real. But the problem we were trying to solve has not changed. The architecture is still extracting ten percent from people who cannot afford it. The tools to fix it exist. The infrastructure does not. Not yet.

The Year Everything Fell

FTX collapsed in November 2022, and if you were in the blockchain space, it felt like the floor dropped out.

Here's what most people don't understand about the FTX story, the part that the Netflix documentaries and the courtroom drama never quite capture. For a lot of people building in crypto, Sam Bankman-Fried wasn't a villain. He was proof of concept. He was a young founder who had built something massive, who was getting meetings with senators and regulators, who was being profiled in every major publication as the future of finance. His effective altruism pitch was compelling. His exchange worked. The infrastructure he built was real. For founders like me, watching SBF succeed felt like validation that what we were all building had a future.

Then the story shifted. The overleveraged positions at Alameda. The commingled customer funds. The guaranteed minimum returns in the early pitch decks, which is a massive red flag that somehow didn't stop the money from flowing in. It turned out that the infrastructure was real, but the integrity underneath it was hollow.

Here's my take on what happened, and I say this as someone who has sat in those early fundraising meetings, who knows the pressure of being a young founder trying to convince someone to take a bet on you. In the very earliest stages, when you are under thirty and running your first real company, you will say almost anything to not blow the meeting. You will stretch projections. You will frame risks as opportunities. You will project a confidence you don't fully feel, because if you don't, nobody writes the check. Every founder knows this territory. The line between aggressive optimism and fraud is not as bright as it looks from the outside.

Alameda Research's early pitch decks effectively guaranteed minimum returns. That's a massive red flag. Any regulated fund manager would have been shut down by the SEC before the ink dried. But in the crypto world of 2019, there was no SEC watching. There was just a young team with quantitative credentials and a story that sounded smart, pitching to investors who wanted to believe that crypto had its own Goldman Sachs. The money flowed in, and once it was flowing, the incentive to keep it flowing overrode whatever internal alarm bells might have been ringing.

I am not excusing what SBF did. The fraud was real, the conviction was justified, and the people who lost money deserved better. But the founder empathy is real too. Jensen Huang has said that nobody in their right mind would start a company if they knew what it actually entailed. The superpower of an entrepreneur, he says, is their ignorance. You trick your brain into asking "How hard can it be?" because if you actually knew the answer, you would never begin. Entrepreneurship runs on a kind of stupid optimism. You don't know the risks. You don't know the issues. That's typically how you start a company.

Jeff Bezos frames it from the other direction. He says it's human nature to overestimate risk and underestimate opportunity, which is why most people never take the leap. Most aspiring founders are too cautious, not too reckless. They see the danger and miss the upside. The people who actually build things are the ones who bias against that caution.

SBF and Elizabeth Holmes are what happens at the extreme other end. They didn't just bias against caution. They obliterated the line between optimism and fabrication. Holmes at Theranos. Neumann at WeWork. SBF at FTX. The pattern is uncomfortably familiar to anyone who has pitched for their livelihood. They clearly were not estimating the risks of going too far. Most founders live somewhere in the middle: scared enough to be honest, optimistic enough to keep going. The ones who end up in courtrooms are the ones who lost the fear entirely.

What FTX revealed was not that crypto is a scam. It revealed that centralized control pretending to be decentralized is worse than either centralized or decentralized alone. FTX failed because it was a traditional financial institution wearing blockchain clothes. Customer funds were held in centralized wallets controlled by a small group of people with no external oversight. The exchange ran on trust, the same trust model that every bank uses, but without any of the regulatory guardrails that banks are required to maintain. When the trust broke, there was nothing underneath. No transparency, no on-chain verification, no way for customers to confirm that their assets existed.

The biggest failure in crypto history was not a failure of decentralization. It was a failure of centralization.

Four months later, Silicon Valley Bank proved the same principle in traditional banking. SVB's collapse in March 2023 was the fastest bank run in history. Depositors withdrew $42 billion in a single day. Not because SVB was running a fraud. Because SVB had made a straightforward bet on interest rates that went wrong, and when word got out, the information traveled faster than the institution could respond. Twitter threads. Group chats. Slack channels. Founders texting each other: get your money out. By the time SVB's leadership could draft a reassuring statement, the deposits were already gone.

SVB was a trust failure at a different speed. In previous generations, a bank run required people to physically line up outside a branch. The speed of information was limited by the speed of human movement. By 2023, information moved at the speed of a tweet, and the trust infrastructure of a 40-year-old bank couldn't survive contact with that velocity. The institution's energy, its credibility, its depositor confidence, drained faster than it could be replenished. I was watching it happen in real time in group chats with other founders. The message was the same everywhere: move your money. Nobody waited for official communications. Nobody trusted the bank's reassurances. By the time the CEO released a statement saying the bank was sound, the deposits were already out. The statement itself became evidence of desperation, which accelerated the withdrawal. Information energy exceeded institutional energy, and the institution collapsed.

First Republic was next. Then Silvergate. Then Signature. Each one a different business model, a different set of exposures, a different proximate cause. But the root failure was identical: trust-based systems, operating on opacity, collapsing when transparency arrived uninvited. The system was still carrying bad debt from FTX the year before. You could see it if you looked, and eventually everybody looked at the same time.

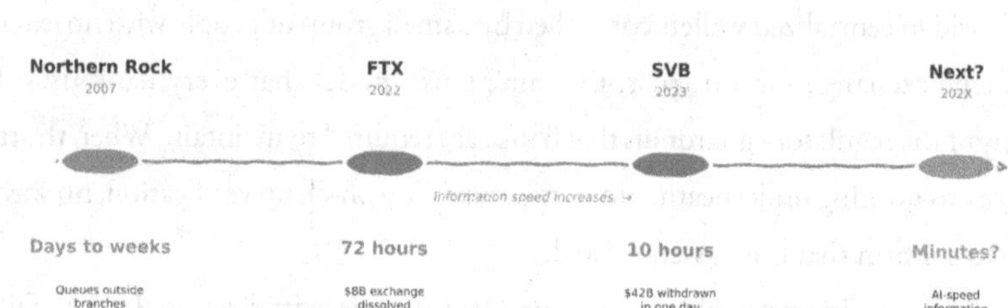

Figure 2.1. The Speed of Collapse

My company, Standard, had started in the blockchain space. After FTX, we pivoted to AI, like a lot of builders did. Not because we stopped believing in the technology, but because the market's trust in anything associated with crypto evaporated overnight, and we had a team to feed and a business to run. The pivot worked. Standard grew. But the experience of watching the institutions I had personally pitched disappear within two years left a mark. It wasn't abstract. These were banks I had sat across a Zoom call from. Silvergate was down the street.

The Black Hole

FTX was a private-sector trust failure. SVB was a banking-sector trust failure. In 2025, a third sector got its turn.

The Department of Government Efficiency, known by the acronym most people either love or hate depending on their politics, began pulling back the curtain on where federal money actually goes. I'm going to set the politics aside entirely, because the structural finding transcends any administration or ideology: when you actually look at how government money flows, what you find is a black hole.

Billions of dollars in payments that cannot be traced to verified recipients. Contracts awarded to entities that appear to exist only on paper. Duplicate payments, phantom vendors, programs that continued receiving funding years after they were supposed to have ended. The specific numbers are still being tabulated at this writing, and they will likely be contested and debated for years. But the pattern is not in dispute, because it is the same pattern we saw with FTX and SVB: trust-based systems without verification create the conditions for failure to compound invisibly.

The mechanism is worth understanding because it applies everywhere, not just in government. When money flows through opaque channels with no automated verification, errors compound. A duplicate payment goes unnoticed. A contract gets renewed by default. A vendor submits an invoice for work that was never performed, and nobody flags it because the system was not designed to flag it. Each individual failure might be small. But compounded over years, across thousands of programs and millions of transactions, small failures become systemic fraud. Not because bad actors planned it, though some did, but because the system's architecture made fraud the path of least resistance.

This is not a claim that every government employee is corrupt or that every program is wasteful. It is a structural observation. When money is opaque, analog, and trust-dependent, fraud doesn't require a conspiracy. It just requires nobody checking. The money was trusted to flow correctly. It didn't. Nobody checked because the system was designed around the assumption that trust was sufficient. For decades, that assumption held, not because it was true, but because nobody had the tools or the incentive to test it at scale.

The Pew Research Center has tracked trust in the federal government since 1958. That year, 73% of Americans said they trusted the government to do what is right most of the time. By 2025, that number was 16%. Not a dip. Not a cycle. A 78% relative decline over 67 years. And it cuts across party lines. Republican trust in government surges when a Republican is in office and collapses under a Democrat. Democratic trust does the same in reverse. The lowest trust ever recorded for any party was Democrats in 2025 at 9%. Opposition party trust in the executive branch has fallen from 49% to 7%.

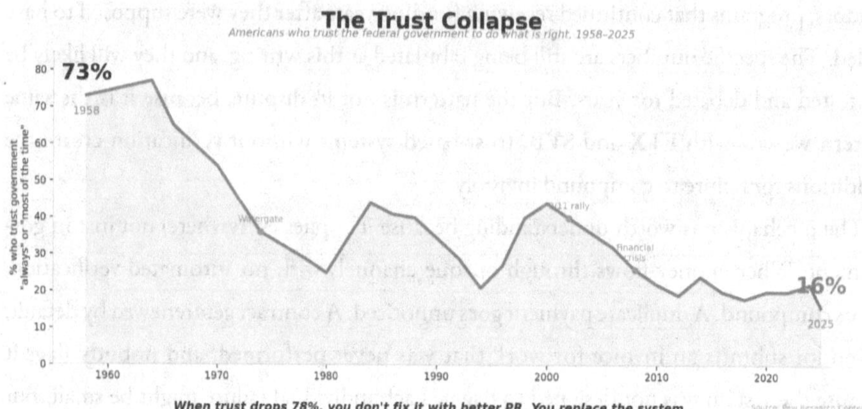

Figure 2.2. The Trust Collapse

Ray Dalio has documented this pattern across civilizations. In his framework, the decline of internal trust, institutional effectiveness, and financial discipline are hallmarks of a declining phase in the roughly 150-year cycle that empires follow. The United States, by Dalio's metrics, exhibits many of these markers. I don't cite this to be alarmist. I cite it because Dalio's framework, like Carlotta Perez's technology framework that I'll get to later, describes the pattern without prescribing the solution.

The solution is what this book is about. Not eliminating trust. Humans need trust for society to function. But replacing blind trust, trust-without-verification, with systems that enforce rules regardless of who is operating them. A smart contract on a public blockchain doesn't care who you are or what political party you belong to. It runs the same for everyone. The ledger is public. The flows are traceable. You don't need to trust the operator because you can verify the operation.

Three sectors. Private finance, banking, government. Three different institutions. Three different proximate causes. One structural diagnosis: trust-based systems without verification fail, and they fail at the speed of the information environment they operate in. In 2022, that speed was fast enough to destroy an $8 billion crypto exchange overnight. In 2023, it was fast enough to collapse a $200 billion bank in a weekend. In 2025, it is fast enough to expose decades of government waste in months. The speed is only going to increase. The trust infrastructure is not going to get stronger. Something has to change, and the only question is whether the change is designed or whether it is forced.

Three sectors. Three different failures. But the same architecture underneath every one of them. FTX was trust failing: opacity enabling fraud because the system assumed honesty. SVB was institutions failing: a regulated bank collapsing because institutional safeguards couldn't keep pace with information velocity. The unbanked, the locked-out investors, the nonprofit sector with no public market, those are gatekeepers failing: billions of people and trillions of dollars excluded by design, not by accident. The old system didn't just have a trust problem. It had an architecture problem. And the architecture was cracking at every load-bearing wall simultaneously.

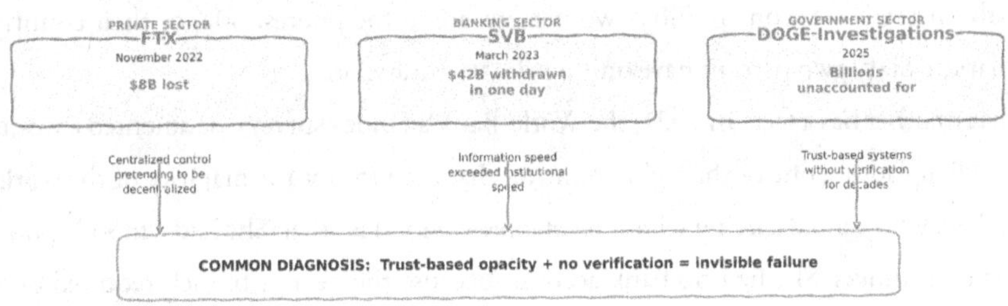

Figure 2.3. *Three Sectors, One Root Cause.*

The Locked-Out Billion

Everything I've described so far is a trust problem. The failures of FTX, SVB, and government transparency are failures of systems that assumed trust would hold. But there is a different kind of breaking point, one that doesn't make headlines because it has been true for so long that it feels like a permanent condition rather than a crisis.

1.3 billion adults on earth have no financial account. No bank. No credit union. No digital wallet. No way to save, borrow, invest, insure, or transfer money through any formal channel. They are locked out of the energy grid of finance entirely.

What does that look like in practice? It looks like a migrant worker in the Philippines earning $400 a month and paying $28 in fees to send money home to their family. It looks like a smallholder farmer in Nigeria who can't get a loan to buy seed because she has no credit history, not because she's not creditworthy, but because the system that would assess her creditworthiness doesn't extend to her village. It looks like a market vendor in Indonesia keeping his life savings in cash under a mattress because the nearest bank branch is a two-hour bus ride away and requires documentation he doesn't have. These are not edge cases. These are the default experience for more than a billion people.

The World Bank tracks this through the Global Findex database, and the numbers are worth sitting with. Globally, 79% of adults now have a financial account, up from 51% in 2011. That's real progress. But the 21% who don't are concentrated in exactly the places where financial access would matter most: Bangladesh, China, Egypt, India, Indonesia, Mexico, Nigeria, Pakistan. Eight countries account for more than 650 million of the unbanked. Fifty-five percent are women. Fifty-two percent are in the poorest 40% of their country's population. Sixty-two percent have only a primary education.

That number has a face. In 2021, the World Bank's Findex survey documented a woman in rural Bangladesh, one of the eight countries that account for the majority of the world's unbanked, who earned a living selling vegetables at a local market. She had a mobile phone. She had customers. She had no bank account because the nearest branch required documentation she did not have and charged minimum balance fees she could not maintain. Every transaction she conducted was in cash. Every time she needed to send money to her daughter in Dhaka, she paid a courier. Every time the courier took a percentage. She is not an edge case. She is the median.

Here's the number that should reframe everything: 900 million of those unbanked adults own a mobile phone. 530 million of them own a smartphone. The infrastructure problem isn't that we can't reach these people. It's that the current financial system wasn't designed to. The rails don't extend there. The compliance costs don't justify the account sizes. The identity verification requirements assume documentation that many people in developing economies simply don't have.

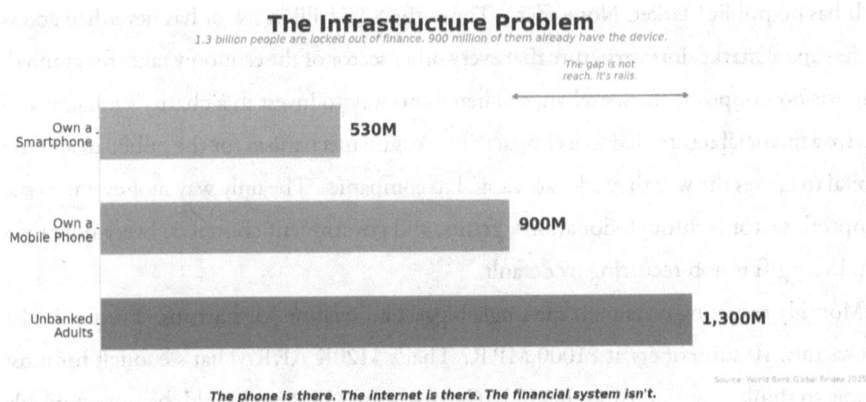

Figure 2.4. The Infrastructure Problem

Kenya proved this doesn't have to be permanent. M-Pesa launched in 2007 and turned mobile phones into bank accounts. By 2023, 40% of adults in sub-Saharan Africa had mobile money accounts, up from 27% in 2021. Digital payments in low and middle-income countries reached 62% of adults. The gender gap in financial access narrowed from nine percentage points to five. A phone call became a payment became a savings mechanism became a loan application. No bank branch required.

M-Pesa was the proof of concept. But it was built on proprietary rails controlled by a telecom company. The next phase, the one this book is about, runs on open protocols that anyone can build on. When money becomes software running on public infrastructure, the question of financial access stops being about whether a bank decides to open a branch in your village. It becomes about whether you have a phone and an internet connection. For 900 million people, the answer is already yes.

The $3.7 Trillion Orphan

There is one more breaking point, and it's the one that eventually led me to build what I built.

The US nonprofit sector generates $3.7 trillion in annual revenue. That's larger than the GDP of the United Kingdom. There are 1.5 million registered 501(c)(3) organizations. Americans gave $592.5 billion to charity in 2024, a new all-time record. By every measure, this is an enormous, vital, indispensable sector of the economy.

It has no public market. None. Zero. The entire $3.7 trillion sector has never had access to the capital market infrastructure that every other sector of the economy takes for granted. There is no nonprofit stock exchange. There is no way to invest in a charity's mission and receive a financial return tied to its impact. There is no mechanism for the public to allocate capital to causes the way they allocate capital to companies. The only way money enters the nonprofit sector is through donations, grants, and government contracts. Every dollar is a gift. Every gift is non-recurring by default.

Monthly recurring revenue is the single biggest innovation for startups. Every founder knows this. 10 subscribers at $1000 MRR? That's $120K ARR. That's enough for most people to think about quitting their job. Getting your MRR up is gold, because monthly recurring revenue compounds into annual recurring revenue. MRR means you can plan. You can hire. You can invest in infrastructure instead of spending every month wondering whether the money will be there next month.

Nonprofits don't have MRR. They have annual fundraising campaigns. They have galas and bake sales and direct mail and digital ads. They have the ASPCA spending $57 million a year on advertising to generate $390 million in donations, which is an incredible return, but it's still $57 million that could have gone to actual animals. Smaller nonprofits spend 20 to 30 cents of every dollar raised on the machinery of raising the next dollar. Forty percent of a typical nonprofit's time and energy goes to fundraising, not to the mission. That's not a funding model. That's a treadmill.

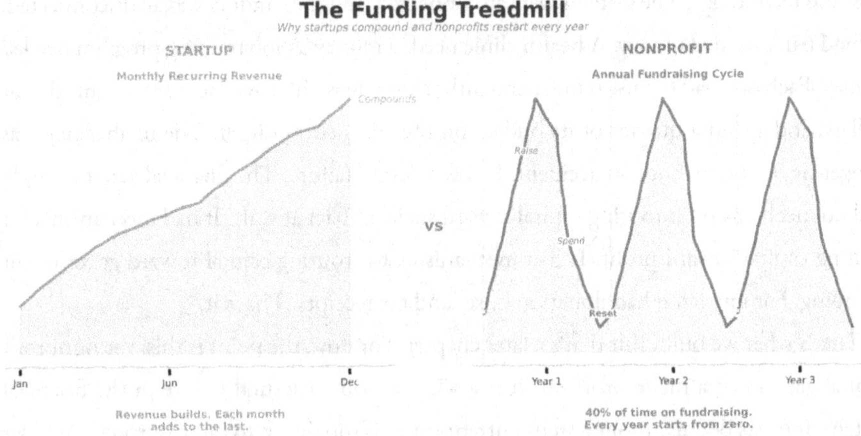

Figure 2.5. The Funding Treadmill

I've lived on both sides of this. As a researcher, I learned how to write grants and raise money for the good I could do in the world. That came naturally. The startup fundraising was harder, more uncomfortable, more rejection, more cold calls and cold emails and saying whatever it took to find a problem that someone cared about enough to fund. Forty companies later, we had our first profitable venture, The Tech Buzz. But the nonprofit funding problem stayed with me because I had seen it from the inside. The researchers doing the work, the organizations delivering the services, they were spending as much energy on fundraising as they were on the actual mission. And unlike a startup that eventually hits product-market fit and grows its revenue organically, a nonprofit has to re-raise its entire budget every single year.

This was the recognition that led to WYDE: the $3.7 trillion nonprofit sector needs a public market. Not a donation platform. Not a GoFundMe. A market, the kind of capital infrastructure that channels ongoing financial energy toward impact the way stock exchanges channel financial energy toward companies. If the mechanism existed, if trading activity in a public market automatically generated funding for verified causes, then the treadmill stops. The fundraising burden drops. The nonprofits can spend their energy on the mission instead of on the machinery of asking for money.

I saw this first as a researcher studying the intersections between health, poverty, food access, and technology. The systems were all connected, and the funding was all disconnected. A food bank needed money. A health clinic needed money. A job training program needed money. Each one had to raise it independently, compete with each other for the same donor dollars, and spend a quarter of its budget on the competition itself. The inefficiency was staggering, and it was not an accident. It was a design failure. The financial system simply had no mechanism for routing capital toward social impact at scale. It had mechanisms for routing capital toward profit. It had mechanisms for routing capital toward government spending. For impact, it had donation boxes and tax receipts. That's it.

That's what we built. But that's a later chapter. For now, the point is this: the nonprofit capital gap is not a niche problem. It is a $3.7 trillion structural failure in the financial system. It exists because money, in its current form, is too dumb to carry purpose. A dollar donated to a food bank and a dollar spent on a stock trade are the same dollar. Neither one carries instructions. Neither one can execute logic. Neither one can automatically route itself toward a defined outcome. The technology to change that now exists. The infrastructure is being built. The question is whether the system upgrades before the breaking point becomes a collapse.

The Substrate Underneath

FTX. SVB. First Republic. Silvergate. Signature. DOGE. Billions locked out. $3.7 trillion with no market. These are not separate problems. They are symptoms of the same underlying condition: the financial system was built on trust, and trust is a depleting resource. Every fraud uncovered, every institution that fails, every headline that reveals money disappearing into a black hole, erodes the remaining trust further. The spiral is downward, and the spiral is accelerating.

But here's what I keep coming back to. Every breaking point in history has been a building point. The 2008 financial crisis created the conditions for Bitcoin. The FTX collapse accelerated the push for regulation that now makes compliant token infrastructure possible. The SVB run demonstrated, in the starkest possible terms, that trust-based banking cannot survive the information velocity of the modern world. Each failure is a proof point for the thesis that the old system cannot hold.

The people I know who are building the next financial infrastructure, the ones writing smart contracts and designing token economics and constructing the regulatory frameworks for programmable money, they don't look at the breaking points and see doom. They see demand. Every failure is a signal: the market wants something different. The market wants transparency. The market wants verification. The market wants money that carries its own instructions instead of relying on institutions that may or may not be trustworthy.

The question underneath all of these failures, the one that connects the trust crisis to the access crisis to the nonprofit capital gap to everything else in this book, is a question about energy. What is money, really? What is it made of? What gives it value? Why does a Bitcoin miner in Wyoming consume as much electricity as a small city to produce something that has no physical form? Why does a dollar earned through eight hours of labor feel different from a dollar earned through a lucky trade? Why does the entire global financial system, trillions of dollars of daily activity, ultimately rest on nothing more substantial than collective belief?

The next chapter answers those questions. And the answer changes everything.

Chapter 3

THE ENERGY THEORY OF VALUE

S omewhere in the oil fields of the American West, around 2018, two guys named Cully Cavness and Chase Lochmiller noticed something that had been hiding in plain sight for decades.

Natural gas. Enormous quantities of it, venting straight into the atmosphere. Oil companies were pulling crude out of the ground across Wyoming, Montana, North Dakota, and Colorado, and the natural gas that came with it was a byproduct they couldn't economically capture. No pipeline nearby. No refinery close enough to justify the cost. So they did what the industry had always done: they burned it off. Flared it. Billions of cubic feet of energy, lit on fire and wasted, because nobody could figure out a use for it.

Cavness came from a third-generation oil and gas family. Lochmiller came from quantitative trading and high-frequency finance. They looked at the flares and had the same thought from different angles: what if you didn't need to move the gas? What if you brought the computation to the energy instead of the energy to the computation?

They started hauling shipping containers full of Bitcoin mining rigs out to flare sites across the Powder River Basin in Wyoming, the Williston Basin in Montana and North Dakota, and the DJ Basin in Colorado. Plugged them into generators running on gas that would otherwise be wasted. The miners consumed the energy, converted the electricity into computational work, and that work produced Bitcoin. Energy that was literally being thrown away, set on fire as waste, was now being converted into the most talked-about store of value on earth.

The company they co-founded, Crusoe, is now valued at over $10 billion. It has pivoted from Bitcoin mining into AI cloud infrastructure, co-developing the first hyperscale sites for OpenAI's $500 billion Stargate project, with a 1.2-gigawatt campus in Abilene, Texas and a planned 1.8-gigawatt facility in Wyoming. Revenue went from $276 million in 2024 to a projected $1 billion in 2025. The same fundamental insight, bring the computation to the stranded energy, now powers artificial intelligence workloads at a scale that rivals the hyperscalers. Oil companies that used to pay fines for excess flaring now have a customer for their waste product.

This story has a predecessor that most people don't connect. In the 1860s, John D. Rockefeller standardized the refining of crude oil into kerosene for lamps. His operation, Standard Oil, produced an enormous amount of gasoline as a byproduct. For years, refiners literally dumped it. Gasoline was waste energy. Then the internal combustion engine arrived, Henry Ford mass-produced automobiles, and that waste product became the fuel that powered the twentieth century. Rockefeller's kerosene refining also produced lighter fractions that were initially discarded, which were eventually refined further into jet fuel, powering another industry that didn't exist yet. And when it came time to distribute the oil, Rockefeller initially relied on Cornelius Vanderbilt's railroads, until the pricing became so punishing that Rockefeller laid his own pipelines across the country, building an entirely new energy infrastructure layer out of competitive necessity.

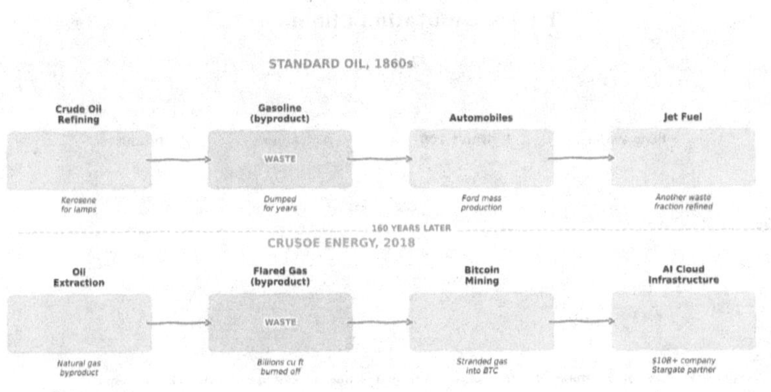

Figure 3.1: The Waste-to-Value Pattern

The pattern repeats across centuries. A contractor looks at a beach and sees sand for concrete. A plumber sees refined silica and thinks ceramic fixtures. But a semiconductor manufacturer takes that same sand, purifies the silicon, etches transistors at the nanometer scale, and produces the most valuable objects per gram humans have ever manufactured. An NVIDIA H100 GPU weighs about five pounds and sells for $25,000 or more. The raw silicon in it is worth pennies. The difference between pennies and $25,000 is energy transformation: the manufacturing energy, the engineering knowledge embedded in the design, decades of research energy that made fabrication at that scale possible.

And that very same chip, once it exists, transmutes further. Plug it into a data center running an AI model and it turns electrical energy into tokens. Those tokens turn into knowledge, images, video, code, and new products. Solo entrepreneurs are building six-figure businesses using Claude and GPT, trading their human energy, time, creativity, judgment, for compute energy, and converting the output into economic energy: revenue, customers, products that exist because a chip turned sand into intelligence. The conversion chain runs from a beach to a billion-dollar company, and every link is an energy transformation.

Flared gas into Bitcoin. Crude oil waste into gasoline. Sand into chips into AI. Every story is the same story: stranded energy that someone else overlooked, converted through infrastructure into massive economic value.

That is the story of money. It always has been. And once you see money through the lens of energy, everything in this book clicks into place.

The Transmutation Chain
How pennies of sand become billion-dollar companies

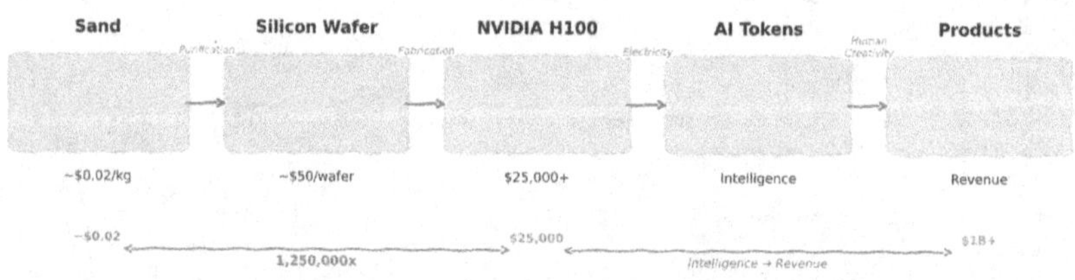

"Every link is an energy transformation. The conversion chain runs from a beach to a billion-dollar company."

Figure 3.2: The Transmutation Chain

The Oldest Technology

There is a version of monetary history that almost everyone learns, and it goes something like this: first there was barter, then shells and beads, then coins, then paper, then bank accounts, then credit cards, then Venmo. Each step made transactions more convenient. Money got faster, lighter, more portable. Progress.

That version is not wrong, but it misses the essential point. Every one of those transitions was an energy efficiency upgrade.

Think about what gold actually is in terms of energy. Someone had to find it, dig it out of the earth, refine it, transport it, stamp it into a standardized weight, and guard it. All of that required enormous expenditure of human and physical energy. A gold coin is a container for the energy that went into producing it. That is why it has value. Not because gold is pretty, though it is. Not because it is scarce, though it is. Because the energy cost of producing it creates a floor beneath its worth. You cannot fake the energy expenditure. You cannot counterfeit the work.

The Roman Empire understood this intuitively. The gold solidus, stamped with the emperor's face, was accepted across Europe and into Asia because people trusted that the coin contained a specific weight of gold, which represented a specific energy expenditure to produce. The system worked for centuries.

Then they started clipping the coins. Shaving tiny amounts of gold from the edges, melting the clippings, and minting new coins with slightly less gold in each one. Inflation in its most physical form: diluting the energy content of the monetary unit while pretending the unit was unchanged. People noticed. Trust eroded. The currency weakened. The empire, eventually, fell. You can debate the causes for years, and historians do. But the monetary debasement is always in the conversation. When you reduce the energy content of the money, you reduce the trust in the system, and when trust goes, everything built on it follows.

You have experienced debasement. Every time you have noticed that the same grocery cart costs more than it did last year, and your salary has not kept pace, you have felt it. But here is the piece most people miss: the debasement is not just in the price. It is in the energy. You are working the same hours, producing the same output, converting the same human energy into labor, and the system is returning less stored energy back to you. The dollar in your account represents less purchasing power, which means less stored energy, which means your conversion rate, the rate at which your work becomes your life, has been quietly degraded. That is not inflation. That is energy theft. And it has been happening, in one form or another, since the first Roman emperor figured out he could shave the edges off a gold coin and nobody would notice until it was too late.

Paper money was the next upgrade. Instead of carrying heavy gold coins across a continent, you carried a piece of paper that represented a claim on gold sitting in a vault somewhere. Same stored energy, dramatically less friction. The promise note was a compression algorithm for value. It reduced the energy cost of transporting wealth from enormous to nearly zero, at the expense of requiring trust in whoever issued the paper. That trust, initially backed by gold reserves, gradually became trust in governments and central banks. The gold standard ended in 1971 when Nixon closed the gold window and from that point forward the dollar was backed by the productive energy of the American economy, the military that protected it, and the institutional trust that the world placed in both.

Digital money compressed further. Numbers in a database. Wire transfers. Credit card swipes. Your entire financial life reduced to electrons moving through copper wire and silicon chips. The energy cost of a transaction dropped from days of horseback travel to milliseconds of electrical current. Remarkable. Revolutionary. And still profoundly limited, because those digital numbers lived inside institutional databases that required armies of intermediaries to maintain, reconcile, and secure.

Every phase change in money's history solved one energy problem and created another. Gold solved the problem of portable, trustworthy value but was heavy and expensive to move. Paper solved the weight problem but required trusted institutions to back the promise. Digital solved the speed problem but centralized control in banks and payment processors who extracted enormous fees for the privilege of moving numbers between databases. Each solution was an energy efficiency upgrade that hit a new ceiling.

Programmable money breaks through that ceiling. And Bitcoin is the proof.

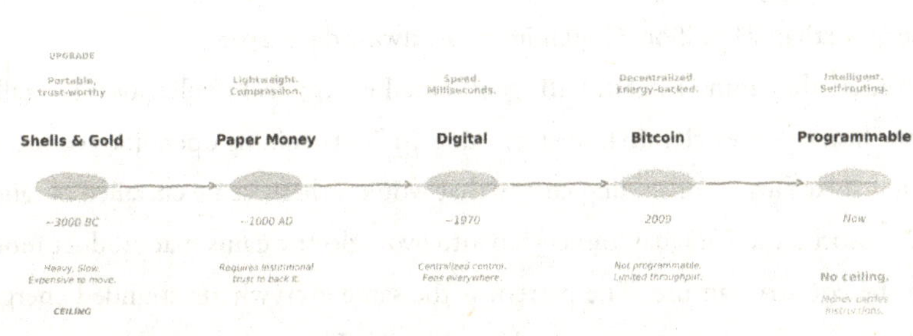

Figure 3.3: Money's Energy Phases

Digital Energy

Michael Saylor has a way of saying things that makes you rethink everything you assumed.

He calls Bitcoin digital energy. Not a currency. Not a commodity. Not even an investment. Energy. The purest form of energy storage that humans have ever created. When I first heard him frame it that way, during one of his marathon podcast appearances where he builds the argument brick by brick for three hours, I thought he was being hyperbolic. He has staked over $54 billion of his company on this thesis. 714,644 Bitcoin, acquired at an average cost of roughly $76,000 each. 3.4% of all the Bitcoin that will ever exist, held by a single company, with a public plan to push past 1.4 million coins, over 6.7% of total supply, by 2027. That tends to make people skeptical of your objectivity.

But sit with the argument for a while and it starts to feel less like salesmanship and more like physics.

Here is what Bitcoin mining actually does, stripped of all the jargon and ideology. Miners around the world operate specialized computers that consume electricity and perform a specific kind of mathematical computation. That computation is deliberately, almost absurdly, energy-intensive. It has to be. The difficulty is the point. The energy expenditure is the mechanism that creates scarcity. You cannot fake the work because the work is verified by the entire network. This is not a metaphor for gold mining. It is gold mining. The same fundamental principle, energy expenditure creating verifiable scarcity, expressed in a digital substrate instead of a physical one. The difference is that Bitcoin's scarcity is absolute. There will never be more than 21 million. Gold miners can always dig deeper.

In El Salvador, they mine Bitcoin with geothermal energy from volcanoes. Literally converting the heat of the earth into monetary value. In Texas, mining operations co-locate with wind and solar farms, consuming energy that would otherwise be curtailed because the grid can't absorb it. In Paraguay, miners tap into hydroelectric dams that produce more power than the country can use. The pattern is the same everywhere: stranded energy, power that has no other buyer, gets converted into Bitcoin. The total mining infrastructure consumes roughly 150 terawatt-hours of electricity per year, operating in facilities on every inhabited continent. Critics see waste. I see the largest dedicated energy-to-value conversion system ever built. A grid purpose-built for transforming raw electrical power into a globally recognized store of value, running 24 hours a day, 365 days a year, with no central operator and no off switch.

People are starting to notice. Not only the crypto crowd. Jordan Peterson, of all people, has spoken publicly about Bitcoin's energy dimension with what I can only describe as genuine awe. Watching a public intellectual who built his career on psychology and philosophy grapple with the implications of energy-backed digital scarcity in real time is fascinating. It signals that this argument is crossing from niche to mainstream in a way that the technology narrative never quite managed. People who don't care about blockchain care very much about energy. And Bitcoin, when you frame it correctly, is an energy story.

There is another correlation that almost nobody discusses, but the data is hard to ignore. Plot the energy production of a nation against the strength of its currency over long time horizons and the relationship is striking. Countries that produce more energy per capita tend to have stronger, more stable currencies. Countries whose energy production declines tend to see their currencies weaken. The United States, Russia, Saudi Arabia, Norway: energy-producing nations with currencies that punch above their weight. This is not a perfect correlation and economists will argue about confounding variables forever. But the directional relationship makes sense through the energy lens. A currency is a claim on the productive capacity of its issuing nation. More energy in, more value out, stronger currency. The logic holds.

And here is the part that connects this chapter to everything else in the book: that entire mining grid, all the facilities, the cooling systems, the power contracts, the networking infrastructure, the physical space, can be repurposed. The same hardware architecture that mines Bitcoin can run AI workloads. Cavness and Lochmiller proved it at Crusoe. They started with flared gas and Bitcoin and became a $10 billion AI infrastructure company because the underlying energy systems are transferable. A grid built for one purpose turns out to be useful for another. That is not an accident. That is what happens when you build energy infrastructure at scale. It compounds.

The $700 Billion Signal

I want to tell you what those numbers feel like from the inside, because from the outside they read like a press release.

In 2023, I was in a development meeting at Standard. A potential client was pitching us on a project, and to show his credentials he walked us through something his team had done in the telecom industry. He pulled up a walkthrough of buildings in downtown Los Angeles. High-rises. Glass and steel. The kind of towers you walk past every day assuming they are full of offices and people. They were not. The floors were gutted. No desks, no cubicles, no humans. Just servers and wiring. Entire buildings converted into data centers for the telecom backbone, and you would never know it from the street.

What struck me was not the buildings themselves. It was the scale of the conversion. These were not purpose-built data centers in the desert. These were commercial real estate assets in one of the most expensive cities in the country that had been quietly repurposed because the economics of housing data had surpassed the economics of housing people. And this was 2023. Before the AI infrastructure buildout hit full speed. Before the hyperscalers committed hundreds of billions to new capacity. The buildings in downtown LA were the early signal. The construction that is happening now, the purpose-built campuses and the converted industrial sites and the power contracts being signed at scales that would have seemed fictional three years ago, is going to make those downtown towers look like a rehearsal.

Now zoom out from Bitcoin mining and look at what the largest technology companies on earth are doing right now. They are building energy infrastructure at a scale that has no precedent in the history of corporate spending.

In 2025, Google spent $91.4 billion on capital expenditure. Amazon committed $125 billion. Microsoft deployed roughly $80 billion. Meta spent around $72 billion. In total, the four largest hyperscalers plus the Stargate Project, a $500 billion multi-year initiative by SoftBank, OpenAI, and Oracle, poured well over $450 billion into AI infrastructure in a single year. Crusoe is co-developing the Stargate project's first hyperscale sites, with $12 billion in capital spend through 2026.

And they are accelerating. Google's guidance for 2026 landed at $175 to $185 billion, nearly double what they spent in 2025 and far above the $120 billion Wall Street was expecting. Meta projected $115 to $135 billion. Amazon is expected to approach $200 billion. The four hyperscalers combined are approaching $700 billion in AI infrastructure spending for 2026 alone. That number is so large it almost stops meaning anything, so let me make it concrete.

These companies are spending more on AI infrastructure in a single year than the GDP of most developed nations. Their aggregate capital expenditure now exceeds their projected free cash flow. They are going cash flow negative to fund the buildout. Google's free cash flow is projected to plummet from $73.3 billion to $8.2 billion. Meta's drops roughly 90%. Amazon is projected to go negative by $17 to $28 billion. To cover the gap, they are issuing debt at unprecedented scale. Meta's $30 billion bond offering in 2025 was the largest investment-grade corporate deal of the year. Google issued $25 billion in bonds and quadrupled its long-term debt to $46.5 billion.

Read that again. The most profitable companies in the history of capitalism are voluntarily going cash flow negative and issuing the largest corporate bond deals in history. This is not a product bet. Nobody spends $700 billion on a product. This is an energy infrastructure buildout. Data centers are the new power plants. GPU clusters are the new generators. Electricity contracts are the new mineral rights. The companies funding this buildout are not buying software. They are buying energy transformation capacity: the ability to convert raw electricity into intelligence.

And this should sound familiar. Because it is exactly what Bitcoin miners have been doing since 2009, at a smaller scale, with less institutional polish, but with the same fundamental logic. Convert energy into something valuable. Build the infrastructure to do it at scale. Compound.

The parallel to previous industrial energy revolutions is exact. The railroad boom of the 1860s and 1870s was not a transportation bet. It was an energy infrastructure buildout. Rockefeller needed those rails to move oil, then laid his own pipes when the pricing turned hostile. The companies that built track went bankrupt at extraordinary rates, but the track remained, and the energy economy that grew on top of it dwarfed the original investment. The electrification of American cities in the 1890s and 1900s followed the same pattern. Massive energy capital expenditure, uncertain returns, plenty of failures, and then an explosion of value creation that nobody could have predicted when the first wires were strung.

We are in that phase right now. Twice over. Because two technological revolutions are building their energy infrastructure simultaneously.

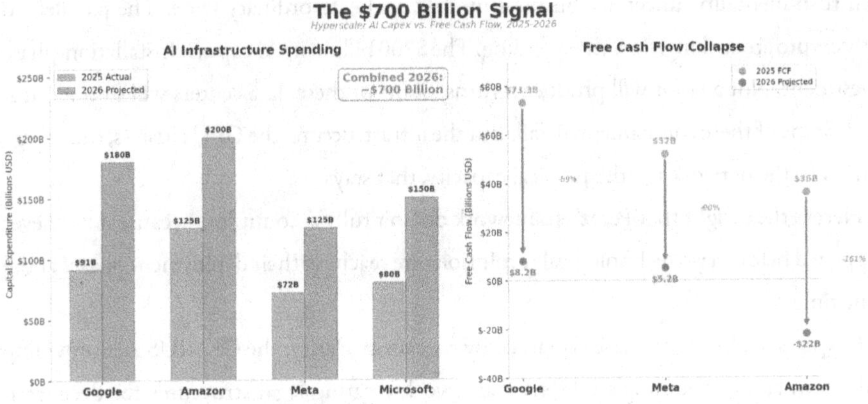

Figure 3.4: The $700 Billion Signal

Two Revolutions, One Grid

Crypto and blockchain spent the years from 2009 to 2022 in what Carlotta Perez would call the installation phase. Perez is an economist who mapped the pattern that every major technological revolution follows: first a frenzy of speculative investment builds the infrastructure (canals, railways, telegraph lines, fiber optic cables), then a crash separates the real from the fake, and then a deployment phase begins where the surviving infrastructure gets put to productive use. The dot-com crash of 2000 was the turning point for the internet. The surviving infrastructure, the fiber optic cables, the server farms, the protocols, became the foundation for Google, Amazon, Facebook, and everything else that followed.

Bitcoin's 2022 moment was FTX. The crash that separated the frauds from the builders. The ICO mania of 2017, the DeFi summer of 2020, the NFT bubble of 2021, and the spectacular implosion of FTX in November 2022 were all installation-phase phenomena.

Speculative, chaotic, sometimes criminal, and absolutely necessary. Because they funded the infrastructure. The blockchain networks, the smart contract platforms, the mining grid, the developer tools, the exchanges, and the wallets all got built during the frenzy. Most of the money was lost. The infrastructure remained.

AI entered its own installation phase in late 2022 with the launch of ChatGPT. Massive capital flooding in, billion-dollar valuations for companies with minimal revenue, a gold-rush mentality, uncertain business models, and extraordinary hype. The parallels to early crypto are striking. So is the spending. The $700 billion in AI capex is installation-phase investment. Not all of it will produce returns. Some of these data centers will sit underutilized. Some of these companies will fail. But the infrastructure, the GPU clusters, the energy contracts, the networking, the physical capacity, that stays.

Here is the insight that Perez's framework doesn't fully account for, because it has never happened before: two technological revolutions are reaching their deployment phases at the same time.

Crypto's deployment phase is marked by regulatory clarity: the GENIUS Act providing stablecoin rules, Wyoming's DUNA framework creating legal structures for decentralized organizations, Europe's MiCA regulation, the SEC shifting from enforcement-first to frameworks. It is marked by institutional adoption: BlackRock's Bitcoin ETF reaching $97 billion faster than any ETF in history, JPMorgan issuing programmable deposit tokens on a public blockchain, sovereign wealth funds taking Bitcoin positions. Speculation is cooling. Utility is emerging.

AI's deployment phase is marked by the same signals. Business models are forming. Revenue is materializing. The technology is moving from impressive demo to indispensable tool. Companies are building AI into every product, every workflow, every decision process. The question has shifted from "is this real" to "how fast can we adopt it."

And the two revolutions need each other. AI agents need financial rails that operate at machine speed, 24 hours a day, without human approval for each transaction. Blockchain provides those rails. Crypto needs intelligent applications that create real economic value beyond trading. AI provides that intelligence. The intersection is where the most valuable infrastructure of the next decade will be built, and it is the least contested space because most people still think these are separate industries.

The Bitcoin mining grid is the physical proof that these two revolutions share the same energy substrate. Crusoe's transformation from flare-gas Bitcoin miner to $10 billion AI factory company is the proof of concept. The data centers going up for AI training could, in theory, mine Bitcoin during off-peak hours. The mining facilities could run AI inference when profitability dips. The hardware, the energy contracts, the cooling systems, the physical locations, they are interchangeable. Because at the bottom of both revolutions is the same thing: converting electrical energy into something the world needs.

The Energy Multiplier

There is one person who seems to understand this convergence intuitively, even if he has never framed it in exactly these terms. And regardless of what you think of his politics, his management style, or his social media habits, the pattern in what he has built is undeniable.

Elon Musk started with PayPal: financial energy. Moving money frictionlessly was the original thesis. Then Tesla: literal energy. Building the infrastructure to generate, store, and distribute electrical power. Then SpaceX: escape energy, the thrust required to leave Earth's gravity well, optimized relentlessly until the cost per kilogram to orbit dropped by an order of magnitude. Then X, the platform formerly known as Twitter: attention energy, the infrastructure through which hundreds of millions of people direct their focus, their time, their engagement. Then xAI: compute energy, the data centers and models that convert electricity into artificial intelligence.

The conventional read is that Musk is a serial entrepreneur with a short attention span, jumping from industry to industry because he gets bored. The energy read is different. Each company is an energy conversion system. Each one feeds energy to the others. Tesla's batteries and solar infrastructure can power xAI's data centers. xAI's intelligence can optimize Tesla's autonomous driving. X provides the distribution network, the attention energy infrastructure, that all the other companies need. SpaceX provides the satellite connectivity that makes the whole system global. These are not separate bets. They are nodes in an energy network where each node amplifies the others.

Infrastructure stacking, not diversification. Energy multipliers, not investments.

But there is something else happening in that stack that most people miss entirely. Every company Musk builds produces two things: the intended product and everything else. Tesla's product is cars. But the byproducts, the battery technology, the solar infrastructure, the Supercharger network, the energy storage systems, the driving data, those feed xAI's data centers and SpaceX's operations. X's product is a social platform. But the byproduct, the largest real-time human sentiment dataset on Earth, is what made xAI possible in the first place. He didn't buy Twitter to build an AI company. The AI company was the byproduct of owning the data. The product is what everyone sees. The byproduct is where the real value hides. And this is not unique to Musk. It is a pattern that runs through every major wealth creation event in history.

Rockefeller refined crude oil into kerosene. Gasoline was waste. He threw it away. The waste product powered the twentieth century. Edison built a power grid to sell light bulbs. The grid became the substrate for everything that followed. Vanderbilt built railroads to move freight. The byproduct was a national market that created the modern economy. In every case, the byproduct was worth more than the product. And the people who saw the byproduct built empires. The people who only saw the product built careers.

I will come back to this idea later in the book, because when AI enters the equation, the number of byproducts that can be identified and captured explodes by orders of magnitude. But for now, remember it. The product is what everyone competes for. The byproduct is where the real value hides. The energy lens lets you see both.

I am not saying Musk consciously designed this network as an energy strategy. I am saying the pattern is there, and it maps precisely onto the thesis of this book. The people who build energy infrastructure, who see the conversion mechanisms between different forms of energy and build the systems that make those conversions efficient, end up controlling disproportionate amounts of value. Not because they are smarter. Because energy compounds in ways that individual products do not.

Everything Runs on Energy

Now let me take this argument somewhere most people don't expect it to go.

Money is a form of energy. We have established that. Bitcoin proved it in the starkest terms possible: raw electricity converted into digital scarcity. But money is not the only form of energy in the economy. It is not even the most fundamental one.

Labor is energy. When you go to work, you are converting metabolic energy, the food you ate for breakfast, into productive output. Your employer pays you money for that output. The money is a receipt for the energy you expended. When you save that money, you are storing your expended energy for future use. When you spend it, you are releasing that stored energy into the economy. Every paycheck is an energy transfer. Every purchase is an energy release. Every savings account is an energy reservoir.

Attention is energy. When a hundred million people watch the Super Bowl, they are directing their attention, their time, their cognitive energy, toward a single event. That concentrated attention has monetary value because advertisers will pay to redirect a fraction of it toward their products. A thirty-second Super Bowl ad costs $7 million not because of the airtime. It costs $7 million because of what happens after. Once you have appeared in the Super Bowl, the validation compounds. You hit every American in one concentrated burst. The trust gets built in that moment, when families gather on Sunday and talk about the ads together. Every ad campaign you run afterward is easier and cheaper because the convincing already happened. The conversion cycle shortens permanently. That is why the premium is astronomical: you are not buying thirty seconds of screen time. You are buying compounding trust energy that makes every future conversion more efficient.

Compute is energy. Every query you send to ChatGPT or Claude consumes electricity, measured in the tokens processed. AI companies price their services in tokens, literally atomic units of compute energy. The more tokens a task requires, the more energy it consumes, the more it costs. When a solo entrepreneur uses Claude to write code that generates revenue, they are converting compute energy, electricity running through GPUs, into economic energy, revenue from the product they built. The entire AI economy is an energy conversion system with tokens as the unit of measurement.

The key unit across all of these is the transaction. Not the account balance. Not the market cap. The transaction. Because transactions are where energy actually flows. A dollar sitting in a savings account is potential energy. A dollar being spent is kinetic energy. The volume of transactions in an economy tells you how much energy is in motion, and the friction in those transactions tells you how much is being wasted.

Think about what happened when Bitcoin introduced peer-to-peer, frictionless transactions. For the first time, monetary energy could flow directly from one person to another without passing through an intermediary. No bank extracting a fee. No payment processor taking a percentage. No three-day settlement window where someone else earns interest on your money in transit. The transaction cost dropped from 2-3% to fractions of a penny. The settlement time dropped from days to minutes. The energy loss in transit went from substantial to nearly zero. That is an efficiency gain on the same order of magnitude as replacing horse-drawn carriages with automobiles. Not an incremental improvement. A phase change.

And every time you reduce friction in transactions, you increase the total number of transactions that can occur. More transactions means more energy flowing through the system. More energy flowing means more value being created, more connections being made, more problems being solved. An economy with a billion frictionless transactions per day is fundamentally more productive than one with a million high-friction transactions per day, even if the total dollars involved are the same. The energy throughput is higher. The system does more work.

This is not a metaphor. I want to be clear about that. I am not saying money is like energy in some poetic sense. I am saying that the economic system is an energy system. It obeys energy principles. It follows energy logic. And once you see it that way, things that seem confusing become simple.

Why does currency debasement destroy economies? Because it dilutes the energy content of the monetary unit. In 2020, the United States printed roughly $4 trillion in new money with no corresponding increase in economic energy. The value of every existing dollar fell because the energy was spread across more units. People's savings lost purchasing power. Their stored energy was diluted without their consent. The national debt has risen to $38.7 trillion, which means the government has borrowed against future energy production at a scale that dwarfs anything in history. That is what debt is: a claim on energy that hasn't been produced yet.

Why do banks charge 3% on credit card transactions? Because they are intermediaries in the energy transfer process, and intermediaries extract energy. Every middleman in the financial system is a resistor, converting useful energy into waste: fees, delays, friction. The 2-3 day settlement time for stock trades is not a technological limitation. It is an energy extraction opportunity for the institutions that sit between buyer and seller.

Why does it cost $48 billion a year to send remittances to developing countries? Because the energy transfer network for international money movement was designed by and for the institutions that profit from inefficiency. A migrant worker in Los Angeles converting their labor energy into dollars and sending those dollars to their family in Guatemala loses 6.49% of the energy to intermediaries along the way. That is not a bug. It is a business model.

The Latent Energy Nobody Sees

Here is where the energy argument gets personal for me.

Before I built WYDE, before I launched EAT, before I co-founded Standard or The Tech Buzz, I was a researcher studying the systems that keep people poor and hungry. I spent years looking at data on food insecurity, health disparities, and the intersection of poverty and technology. And the thing that academic research could never quite capture, the thing that drove me out of the university and into building, was this: we don't know how to value what poverty actually costs us.

Think about that for a moment. We can calculate GDP to the decimal point. We can price a derivative on a derivative. We can model the exact cost of a thirty-second Super Bowl ad and its compounding return over twenty years. But the cost of poverty? Food insecurity? Obesity? Chronic noncommunicable disease? Mental health crises? These are staggeringly expensive to society, and nobody has a real number. Not a confident one. Not one that policy moves on.

Today it feels less like math and more like an intuition problem. Everyone knows it is wrong. Everyone senses the scale. But we cannot force people to do something they don't want to do, and so the problem compounds in the background, invisible and enormous, like inflation on the things that matter most. The same currency debasement that erodes the dollar's purchasing power has a parallel in how we deliver basic human needs. As the currency weakens, companies and politicians seek the cheapest options to solve basic needs: cheaper food that is less nutritious, cheaper housing that is further from opportunity, cheaper healthcare that treats symptoms instead of causes. The debasement flows downhill and lands on the people who can least absorb it.

A person facing food insecurity is energy-deficient in the most literal sense. They lack the caloric energy to fuel their body optimally, which reduces their productive energy, which reduces their earning capacity, which reduces their monetary energy, which reduces their ability to acquire food. It is a downward spiral of energy depletion, and every point of friction in the system, every food desert, every bureaucratic hurdle, every inefficient distribution network, bleeds energy out of people who have none to spare.

The United States produces enough food to feed every person in the country several times over. The energy exists. What is missing is the conversion mechanism: the infrastructure that efficiently routes food energy from where it is produced to where it is needed. The nonprofit sector, which handles much of this routing, operates on infrastructure that is decades behind the for-profit economy. No public market. No programmable funding. No real-time allocation. Just donations, grants, and fundraising campaigns that restart from zero every fiscal year.

The $3.7 trillion nonprofit sector is not a charity problem. It is an energy infrastructure problem. And the 47 million Americans facing food insecurity are not suffering from a lack of generosity. They are suffering from a failure to correctly value the gap, to understand the latent energy of human disparities and the draw down on our entire economy, and to build the conversion infrastructure that routes available resources to the people who need them.

That is what cause coins are, at their most fundamental level. Energy converters. They take the kinetic energy of financial markets, trading activity that happens billions of times a day regardless of anyone's charitable intentions, and convert a portion of it into directed social impact. The smart contract is the conversion mechanism. The blockchain is the energy grid it runs on. The output is measurable in the most basic energy unit of human survival: calories delivered to people who need them.

I will spend all of Chapter 11 on how this works in practice. For now, the point is this: the energy theory of value is not an abstract framework for understanding Bitcoin. It is a practical framework for understanding why the financial system fails the people who need it most, and what programmable money can do about it.

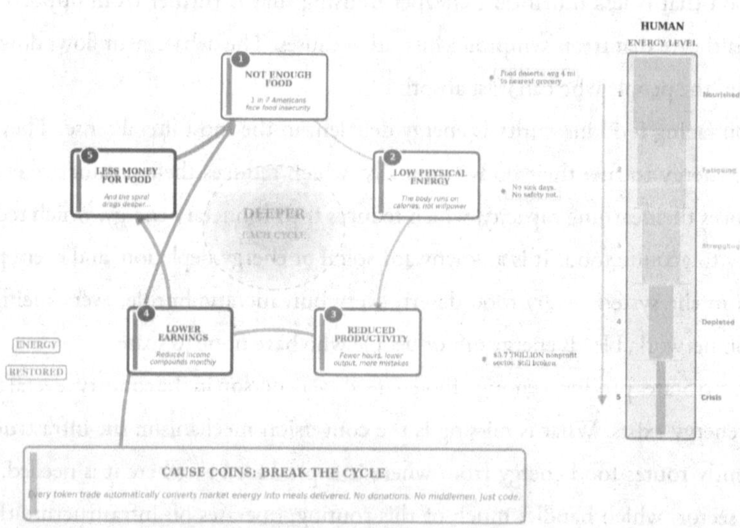

Figure 3.5 — The Energy Depletion Spiral

The Unified Field

Let me pull this together.

Money is energy. It always has been, from the first shell traded for grain to the last Bitcoin mined on a volcano. Every phase change in monetary history was an energy efficiency upgrade, reducing the friction in how energy moves from one person to another.

Bitcoin proved this by building the largest energy-to-value conversion system in history. Its mining grid consumes more electricity than many nations, producing digital scarcity that the world's largest financial institutions now treat as legitimate. That same grid is already being repurposed for AI compute, because the infrastructure is transferable. Crusoe's journey from flared gas to a $10 billion AI factory company is the proof of concept.

The $700 billion in AI capital expenditure is the same phenomenon at corporate scale. Data centers are energy infrastructure. GPU clusters are energy conversion systems. The companies spending themselves into negative free cash flow are not making product bets. They are investing in the ability to transform electricity into intelligence, which is the most valuable energy conversion available today.

Attention is energy. Labor is energy. Compute is energy. Capital is stored energy. They all convert into one another through infrastructure, and the mechanisms that make those energy conversions most efficient capture the most value.

Programmable money is the next energy upgrade. It doesn't just reduce friction. It adds intelligence to the energy flow. Smart contracts route monetary energy according to programmed logic: automatically, transparently, without intermediaries extracting energy at every step. A dollar that carries instructions is more energy-efficient than a dollar that doesn't, because the instructions eliminate the need for humans and institutions to provide direction at every transfer.

Think about why those intermediaries exist in the first place. Every fee, every delay, every middleman in the financial system is there because the old architecture required trust at every handoff, institutions to enforce each transfer, and gatekeepers to control who could access the system. Those layers were not arbitrary. They were the energy cost of running a financial system on human promises instead of code. Remove the need for trust at each step, replace the institutional enforcement with protocol logic, open the gates to anyone with an internet connection, and the energy cost drops by orders of magnitude. That is not an incremental improvement. That is a new architecture.

The poverty problem, the hunger problem, the cause problem is not a generosity problem. It is an energy routing problem. The energy exists. The conversion mechanisms have been broken, or more accurately, they were never built. The financial system was designed to route energy efficiently for the people and institutions that built it. Everyone else got the scraps.

Programmable money changes that. Not because the technology is magic, but because it allows anyone to build energy conversion mechanisms that were previously available only to those with access to the existing financial energy infrastructure. A smart contract on a public blockchain doesn't care who you are, where you live, or how much money you have. It runs for everyone. The energy flows according to the code.

That's the thesis. And everything that follows in this book, the blockchain layer, the smart contracts, the stablecoins, the institutional stampede, the AI agents, the cause coins, the regulatory renaissance, all of it is an application of this energy principle. Energy in, value out. The substrate varies. The principle holds.

The question is not whether money will become software. It already is. The question is what we build with it. And that depends on whether you see the energy underneath or whether you are still thinking in ledgers.

The next chapter maps the pattern that makes all of this predictable. Every technological revolution follows the same arc. Installation, crash, deployment, golden era. Crypto has been through its crash. AI is in the middle of its frenzy. And for the first time in the history of technology, two revolutions are converging at the deployment phase simultaneously. The pattern repeats. But this time it doubles.

That's where we're going next.

Chapter 4

Installation to Deployment: The Pattern That Repeats

In early March 2025, Martin and I flew to Reno for the day. A CPA with a radio show wanted to talk about scaling his company, potentially partnering with us, maybe even investing in our business. We had eight hours in the city. The meeting itself was scheduled for an hour and a half. We spent the other six and a half hours in his conference room losing our minds on a whiteboard. The idea had hit us that week. Attention, we called it. A token launchpad where anyone could reply to any post and create a token, earn money when it traded, and the reply would in theory go viral. It wasn't a product yet. It was ideas. But we knew how to build it, and something about the regulatory shift that had just happened made the whole thing feel urgent. So there we were, in the most boring CPA office in northern Nevada, filling whiteboards with token mechanics and launch sequences while this man's conference room slowly transformed into our war room. The actual meeting finally happened. Halfway through,

we couldn't help ourselves. We told him we had just unlocked one of the biggest products we were going to build. We said it had major implications for the very things we were discussing with him that day. We were cocky about it. A little arrogant, honestly. And he had absolutely no idea what we were talking about. His director of marketing stared at us. The CPA nodded politely. They could not have been more lost. That was the crazy and really funny part, two guys vibrating at a frequency that the room couldn't receive. What we sketched on that whiteboard is built today. It became the foundation for WYDE. On the Uber ride to that meeting, our driver told us about his life. He was an immigrant, supporting family back home. His parents had recently passed. His son was heading off to the Marines. He talked about the famous people he'd picked up at the Reno airport over the years, the conversations he'd had, the stories he carried from one passenger to the next. And in our heads, Martin and I were doing the math on what we'd just conceived, because in theory, this man's conversations, the ones he was having with passengers every single day, could generate income for him. Not because someone decided to tip him. Not because an algorithm chose to surface his content. Because the interaction itself could create a token, and the token could trade, and the trading activity could flow back to the person who started the conversation.

We didn't tell the Uber driver about the token. It would have sounded insane and wasn't built yet. But that car ride crystallized something I keep coming back to: the gap between what's now possible and what ordinary people believe is possible has never been wider. And that gap is the story of this chapter.

The Breath of Fresh Air

To understand why Martin and I were building under a conference table in Reno, you have to understand what the previous four years felt like for anyone building in crypto in the United States.

It felt like building with a gun to your head. The SEC under the Biden administration pursued an enforcement-first strategy against the crypto industry that was breathtaking in its scope. Coinbase, the largest US exchange, was sued. Ripple fought a multi-year legal battle over whether XRP was a security. Kraken settled and shut down its staking program. Dozens of smaller projects received Wells notices, subpoenas, or informal warnings that amounted to the same message: we don't know what the rules are yet, but we're going to punish you for breaking them.

The effect on builders was devastating, not because the enforcement was always wrong, but because there was no framework to be right within. You could hire the best lawyers in Washington, structure your token as carefully as possible, and still wake up to a lawsuit. The rational response for many teams was to leave. Move to Singapore. Incorporate in the Cayman Islands. Build from Dubai. The United States was hemorrhaging crypto talent and infrastructure to jurisdictions that had figured out what we couldn't: that you can regulate an industry without trying to destroy it.

Then Trump took office in January 2025, and within weeks, the entire picture inverted.

The SEC began dropping enforcement actions. Not slowly, not quietly. Case after case, abandoned. The Coinbase suit. The Ripple case. Others that had been grinding through the courts for years. It felt like a dam breaking. In a matter of weeks, the legal cloud that had hung over every crypto company in America started to dissipate. The agency announced a meme coin moratorium, signaling that the era of regulation by ambush was over, at least for now.

And then there was the elephant in the room. Before he even took office, Trump launched his own meme coin. I have mixed feelings about this, and so does everyone I know in the industry. The motivations are debatable. The optics are complicated. But the practical effect was unmistakable: if the president of the United States launches a token, no regulator is coming after yours. Whatever you think about why he did it, that single act did more for the legal clarity of crypto in America than four years of lobbying, lawsuits, and Congressional testimony combined. It set a floor under the entire industry. And for anyone building something real, something that was genuinely better with blockchain technology rather than just extractive, it was the best possible signal.

That's when we started launching products again. March 2025. The conversations with Martin weren't tentative. They were urgent. We were all-in on AI and had been building there, but the crypto side had been on pause because the regulatory risk was existential. Now the risk was gone, or at least manageable, and we couldn't move fast enough.

I want to be precise about this moment because it matters for the larger argument of this book. The regulatory shift was a phase transition. It marked the beginning of crypto's deployment era in the United States. And understanding what that means requires understanding the pattern that every technological revolution follows.

The Pattern

I referenced Carlotta Perez in the previous chapter, and I want to go deeper here because her framework is the single most useful lens I've found for understanding where we are and what comes next.

Perez is an economist who studied every major technological revolution of the past 250 years and found that they all follow the same arc. It doesn't matter whether you're talking about canals in the 1770s, railways in the 1840s, steel and electricity in the 1890s, automobiles and mass production in the 1920s, or the internet in the 1990s. The pattern repeats with eerie consistency.

First comes the installation phase. A new technology appears. Early believers pour money into it. Speculation runs wild. Infrastructure gets built, often wastefully, often by people who don't fully understand what they're building. Fortunes are made and lost. The mania attracts fraud. The fraud attracts regulators. And then the whole thing crashes.

Then comes the turning point. The crash separates the real from the fake. The frauds go to prison or disappear. The tourists leave. But the infrastructure remains. The canals are still there. The railroad tracks are still there. The fiber optic cables are still there. And the people who survived the crash, the builders who were in it for the technology and not just the money, start putting that infrastructure to productive use.

That's the deployment phase. Regulation arrives, not to kill the industry but to standardize it. Institutions enter, not as speculators but as operators. The technology moves from the fringes to the center of economic life. And then something remarkable happens: a golden era emerges where the installed infrastructure produces returns that dwarf the original speculative investment. The dot-com crash wiped out $5 trillion in market value.

The deployment phase that followed created Google, Amazon, Facebook, and the entire modern internet economy. The infrastructure that the speculation funded became the foundation for everything.

This is not a metaphor. It is a map. And we are standing at the turning point.

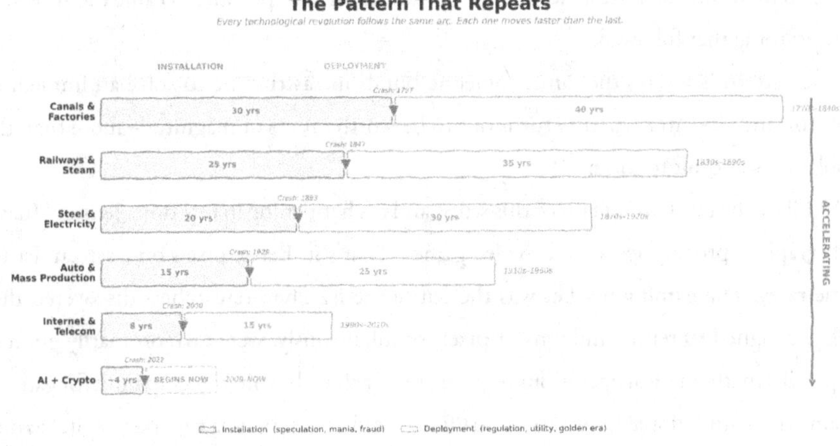

Figure 4.1. The Perez Framework Visualized, a Pattern That Repeats

Byproducts and Breakthroughs

The thing about technological revolutions that Perez maps cleanly but that most people miss in real time is that the biggest winners are almost never doing what they set out to do.

I talked about Rockefeller in the previous chapter, how Standard Oil produced gasoline as waste from kerosene refining, and that waste product ended up powering the twentieth century. But the pattern runs deeper than one company. The entire cast of characters from the first Industrial Revolution followed the same trajectory: they built infrastructure for one purpose and unlocked value they never anticipated.

Cornelius Vanderbilt built railroads to move freight. Those railroads created the national market that made mass production possible, which made Henry Ford's assembly line economically viable, which created the middle class, which created consumer demand, which created the modern economy. Vanderbilt didn't set out to create the middle class. He set out to move cargo faster than canals could. The rest was a byproduct of the infrastructure he installed.

Thomas Edison built a power generation system to sell light bulbs. The electrical grid he created as a distribution mechanism ended up powering factories, appliances, communication systems, and eventually computers. Edison didn't envision the internet. He wanted to sell a product. But the infrastructure he built to deliver that product became the substrate for everything that followed.

The pattern is always the same: someone builds infrastructure to solve an immediate problem, and the infrastructure turns out to be worth orders of magnitude more than the problem it was built to solve.

Nvidia is the modern version of this story, and it's happening in real time. Jensen Huang built graphics processing units for video games. That's it. Better pixels on a screen. Faster frame rates. The gaming market was the entire thesis. Then researchers discovered that GPUs, designed to render millions of pixels simultaneously, were extraordinarily good at the parallel mathematical operations required for machine learning. A chip built for gaming became the foundational hardware for artificial intelligence. Nvidia's market capitalization went from $150 billion in early 2023 to over $3 trillion by 2025. The gaming chip became the AI chip, and the company that made it became one of the most valuable on earth. Not because Huang planned it. Because the infrastructure he built for one purpose turned out to be essential for another.

This is exactly what is happening with blockchain infrastructure right now. Bitcoin's mining network was built to secure a digital currency. That network, the data centers, the energy contracts, the cooling systems, the GPU clusters, is now being repurposed for AI compute. Ethereum was built as a programmable ledger. Its smart contract infrastructure is becoming the financial operating system for AI agents that need to transact autonomously. The crypto infrastructure that speculators funded during the installation phase is being redeployed for purposes its original builders never imagined.

Rockefeller didn't know about automobiles. Edison didn't know about computers. Huang didn't know about AI. The builders of crypto infrastructure in 2017 and 2020 didn't know about AI agents. But they built the rails. And the rails are what matter.

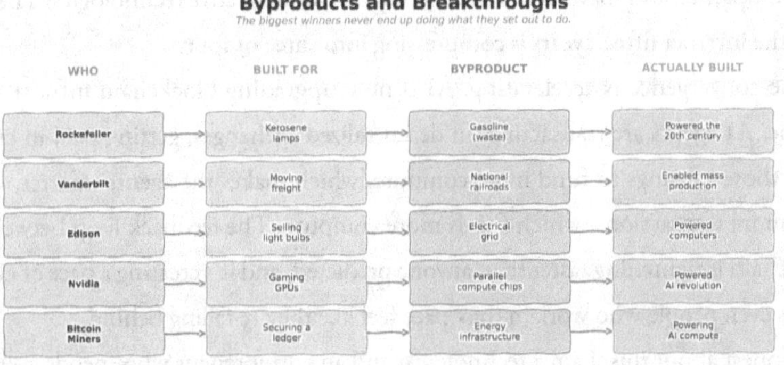

Figure 4.2. Byproducts and Breakthroughs

The Fastest Thing in Our World

Here is what makes this moment different from every previous technological revolution, and why Perez's framework, as useful as it is, doesn't fully account for what's happening.

Nothing has ever moved this fast.

The canal era played out over decades. Railways took a generation to install and another generation to deploy. Even the internet, which felt breathtakingly fast at the time, took roughly fifteen years from the invention of the World Wide Web in 1991 to the point where it had fundamentally restructured commerce, communication, and media. The installation phase of the internet lasted from roughly 1994 to 2001. The deployment phase ran from about 2003 to 2015. Call it twenty years from start to maturity.

AI is operating on a completely different clock. OpenAI released ChatGPT in November 2022. Within eighteen months, every major technology company on earth had reorganized around AI. And as I mapped in Chapter 3, within two years, the capital expenditure cycle had reached $700 billion. By the time you read this, the number will be higher. Anthropic, the company behind Claude, raised $30 billion. xAI, which didn't even exist until March 2023, acquired X, formerly Twitter, in early 2025, and was then itself acquired by SpaceX in February 2026 in a $1.25 trillion deal, the largest merger of all time, ahead of a planned IPO. A company that didn't exist three years ago is now part of the most valuable private entity in history. OpenAI has released multiple generations of upgrades, launched agents, acquired companies, and spawned an entire ecosystem of derivative technologies. The cycle that took the internet fifteen years is compressing into three or four.

And the convergence is accelerating. AI is now upgrading blockchain infrastructure in real time. AI agents are transacting on decentralized exchanges, getting paid in crypto, and using those earnings to fund more compute, which makes the agents smarter, which generates more transactions, which funds more compute. The feedback loop between AI and blockchain is tightening faster than anyone predicted, and it's creating a pace of change that makes even people who work in this space feel like they're falling behind.

I'll be honest about this. I am a technologist and an entrepreneur who spends every day in AI and blockchain, and the speed of new launches has outpaced my ability to bring our customers up to speed on what's possible. The products and capabilities emerging are so nuanced, so far beyond what most people imagine, that when we describe them to clients, they don't believe us. It sounds fanciful. Like novelty. Like something from a science fiction movie that hasn't been made yet. Most people don't even understand that the videos they're seeing online today are ninety percent AI-generated. The gap between the frontier and the mainstream understanding of it has never been wider.

This speed is why the convergence of AI and blockchain is qualitatively different from any previous overlap of technological revolutions. Someone could reasonably argue that electricity and the automobile were concurrent, or that railroads and the telegraph overlapped. They did. But those technologies moved at human speed. They required physical infrastructure that took years to lay down. The deployment of the telegraph required stringing wire across a continent. The deployment of electricity required building power plants and running lines to every home and factory. These were massive, slow, physical projects constrained by the speed of construction.

AI and blockchain are software. Their deployment speed is constrained only by compute, capital, and code. A new AI model can be trained in weeks. A new blockchain protocol can be deployed in days. A smart contract can be written, tested, and launched in hours. The iteration cycles are measured in months, not decades. And because both technologies are digital, they compound: each improvement in one feeds directly into the capability of the other, creating a feedback loop that accelerates faster than any physical infrastructure buildout ever could.

This is why I believe we're standing at the precipice of the fourth Industrial Revolution, and why the abundance it creates will be unlike anything previous generations experienced.

The first three industrial revolutions were constrained by atoms: coal, steel, oil, concrete. This one runs on bits. And bits scale in ways that atoms never could.

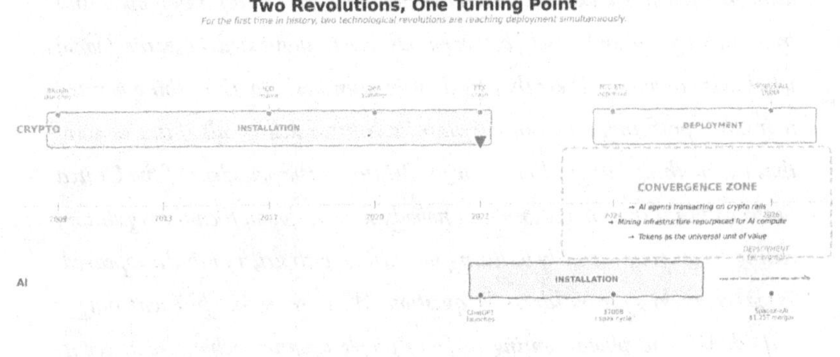

Figure 4.3. Two Revolutions, One Turning Point

The Signals of Deployment

I know what the turning point felt like in my own work, and it did not come from a piece of legislation. It came from a token launch. The months leading up to the Trump inauguration were surreal. Polymarket was going haywire. The entire world was pricing the outcome of the election in real time: voting fraud odds, cabinet picks, policy predictions, everything. I was watching it all from the office. And then Trump launched his token. Chart goes up. Chart goes down. Then Melania launched hers. Then Hayden Adams got indicted (and then got off). All of this was happening in a compressed timeline that felt like someone had hit fast-forward on the entire industry. Here is what I

saw that most people missed in the chaos. Trump did all of this strategically, right before he took office. He had already won his lawsuit against the Biden administration. He was not scared of being sued. He loved suing people. And by launching a token himself, before he was even inaugurated, he set the floor of what was acceptable. Were they good token launches? No. Everything pointed to insiders profiting, meme coin dynamics, limited utility, all of it. But all of that was nothing but good news for us. Because if the president of the United States can launch a meme coin and nobody shuts it down, then the regulatory ceiling for anyone actually building something with utility just disappeared. It was clear skies for builders. No question. We were in the office watching it unfold. We had photos coming in from people we knew who were at events in Washington that Trump was hosting right before the token launched. The whole thing had a surreal quality, like watching the future arrive in a way nobody had scripted but everybody could feel. 'He just won the presidency, and now he launches a token before going into office?!' That was the moment, even before he took the oath, where you knew the regulatory shift was real and it was going full tilt toward crypto. For us, that meant one thing: build faster.

Perez's framework gives us specific markers to look for when an installation phase transitions into deployment. The crash has happened. Regulation is arriving. Institutions are entering. The speculation is cooling and real utility is emerging. Check every box.

Crypto's crash was FTX in November 2022. The fraud was spectacular, the damage was real, and the aftermath was exactly what Perez would predict: the tourists left, the frauds were prosecuted, and the builders who remained started the unglamorous work of building for the long term. That crash was painful. It was also necessary. It cleared the field.

The signals that followed were unmistakable. The GENIUS Act is providing a framework for stablecoins. Wyoming's DUNA legislation created a legal structure for decentralized organizations that didn't exist anywhere in the world before. Europe's MiCA regulation established the first comprehensive crypto regulatory framework for a major economic bloc. The SEC pivoted from enforcement-first to frameworks. And the institutions followed: BlackRock's Bitcoin ETF reached $97 billion faster than any ETF in history, JPMorgan issuing programmable deposit tokens on public blockchains, sovereign wealth funds taking Bitcoin positions, and Fidelity launched crypto products. These are not crypto-native startups gambling on the future. These are the largest, most conservative financial institutions on earth building blockchain infrastructure because they have concluded, after years of resistance, that the deployment phase is here.

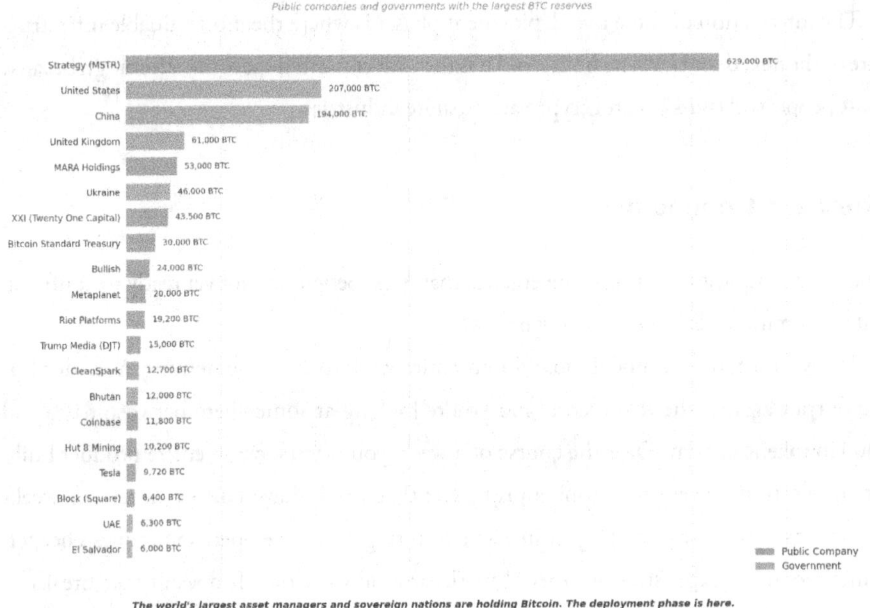

Figure 4.4. Crypto Treasuries

AI's installation phase is further behind, but the same markers are emerging. The speculative mania is extraordinary, yes. Not every company with "AI" in its pitch deck will survive. Not every data center being built will be fully utilized. But the revenue is materializing. The business models are forming. The technology is moving from impressive demonstration to indispensable tool. The $700 billion in capex is installation-phase investment, and much of it will not produce returns. But the infrastructure will remain, just as it always does, and the deployment phase will put it to work in ways that the current speculators cannot imagine.

And here is the insight that changes everything: the two deployment phases are converging into each other. Crypto's infrastructure gives AI agents financial rails that operate at machine speed, twenty-four hours a day, without human approval for each transaction. AI's intelligence gives blockchain applications the capacity to create real economic value beyond trading. It's becoming increasingly clear, based on the open networks that Ethereum and others have built, that cryptocurrency is the natural transaction layer for AI. Not because someone designed it that way. Because the infrastructure requirements align. AI agents need programmable, permissionless, always-on financial infrastructure. That is exactly what blockchain provides.

The intersection of these two deployment phases is where the most valuable infrastructure of the next decade will be built. And it is the least contested space in technology, because most people still think AI and crypto are separate industries.

Work as a Commodity

There is an implication of this convergence that most people are not yet ready to confront, but it's coming whether we're ready or not.

Today, you can let a model loose for an entire week to create something. You monitor the output against the token cost, and you're looking at somewhere between $100 and $300 in tokens per day. Over the course of a week, you often have an entire product built. An application, a website, a tool, a prototype that would have taken a developer weeks or months. The cost is roughly equivalent to hiring that developer, sometimes cheaper, sometimes more expensive. But the AI works around the clock. It doesn't take breaks. It doesn't have meetings. It doesn't context-switch between Slack messages.

I run these models every day. At Standard, we've built entire products this way. Not prototypes. Products. Revenue-generating tools that clients pay for. And every month, the cost drops. Every month, the output gets better. The models iterate on a cycle that no human workforce can match, because the models improve while they work. A junior developer you hire today is roughly the same junior developer six months from now, maybe marginally better. An AI model you deploy today is categorically different from the one you'll deploy in six months. It's not learning on the job. The entire architecture upgrades underneath it.

That changes the math on labor in ways that most business leaders have not yet internalized. When the cost of commodity work approaches zero, the question is no longer "can I afford to build this?" The question becomes "what should I build?" Every idea that was previously too expensive to prototype becomes viable. Every experiment that couldn't justify a team gets run by a model over a weekend. The bottleneck moves from execution to imagination. And that shift, from a world where labor is the scarce resource to a world where good ideas are the scarce resource, is a bigger deal than most people realize. It means the value of a human being in the economy is no longer primarily determined by their ability to execute tasks. It's determined by their ability to identify which tasks matter.

Here's my take on what happens when that cost curve continues to drop, which it will. If you're running an AI model twenty-four hours a day to do the same tasks a human does during eight, you're using the AI wrong. The eight-hour equivalence is a trap. It's thinking about AI through the lens of the old system, the same way early automobile buyers thought about cars as faster horses. The question is not whether the AI can do a human's job cheaper. The question is what work looks like when the constraint of human time is removed from the equation.

Elon Musk talks about this in terms of what he calls universal high income, not universal basic income, becoming the norm as AI and robotics eliminate traditional labor categories. At the Viva Technology conference in 2024, he put it bluntly: in a benign scenario, probably none of us will have a job, and there will be no shortage of goods or services. I think he's directionally right, but the framing misses something. Universal high income is a safety net for a world where work has been taken away. The more interesting question is what happens when work is redefined, when the commodity version of labor, the tasks that can be automated, is handled by machines, and humans are freed to do the things that machines cannot: create meaning, build relationships, make judgment calls that require wisdom rather than data, and direct energy toward problems that matter.

Because that's where the real disruption lives. Not in the job that gets automated. In the job that gets invented. Every technological revolution in the Perez pattern created more jobs than it destroyed, but the new jobs looked nothing like the old ones. The railway didn't just replace canal workers with train operators. It created an entire class of jobs that couldn't have existed before: telegraph operators, station managers, national logistics coordinators, mail-order catalog designers. The internet didn't just replace newspaper classifieds with Craigslist. It created social media managers, app developers, data scientists, influencers, and a million freelance categories that would have sounded absurd in 1995. The pattern is clear:

the installation phase destroys jobs. The deployment phase creates entirely new categories of work that the previous generation couldn't have imagined. We are at the hinge point of that transition right now.

The deployment phase of AI and crypto won't just automate commodity labor. It will create infrastructure that allows new forms of human contribution to be captured, priced, and compensated. Not because someone decides you deserve to be paid. Because the system is built to route value to wherever value is created. Smart contracts don't need a manager's approval to release payment. Token economics don't need a board of directors to decide who contributed. The infrastructure itself becomes the mechanism for recognizing work, broadly defined, wherever it happens.

Remember the Uber driver in Reno? Today, his value in the economy is defined by his ability to drive a car from point A to point B. That's commodity labor, and it will be automated. But his conversations, the stories he carries, the human connection he provides, those have value too. We just never had the infrastructure to capture it, price it, and route it back to him. The convergence of AI and blockchain starts to make that infrastructure possible. Not tomorrow. Not perfectly. But directionally, inevitably, the tools to value human energy more accurately and more broadly are being assembled right now.

The Infrastructure Underneath

I keep coming back to this idea: the pattern that Perez mapped is about energy. The installation phase is when energy is invested, often wastefully. Capital, attention, talent, and electricity flood into a new technology without clear direction. Most of it is lost. The deployment phase is when that invested energy starts producing returns. The infrastructure that survived the crash, the rails, the wires, the protocols, the data centers, becomes the substrate for a new economy. The golden era is when energy efficiency peaks and the whole system compounds.

We are at the turning point. Two technological revolutions are crossing from installation to deployment at the same time. The regulatory barriers are falling. The institutions are entering. The infrastructure from the speculative phase has survived and is being repurposed. The feedback loop between AI and blockchain is accelerating the pace of change beyond anything historical precedent would predict.

But knowing the pattern is one thing. Understanding the infrastructure is another.

That Uber driver in Reno is going to be fine. Not because someone is going to save him. Because the infrastructure that lets his actual value get captured and returned to him is being built right now. He does not know that yet. Most people do not. But the pattern says they will.

The pattern always delivers. It just makes you wait through the installation phase first.

That's where we're going next.

PART II: INFRASTRUCTURE

Chapter 5

THE PROGRAMMABLE LAYER

I f you have ever swapped a token on Uniswap, bridged assets to Base, or traded on Raydium, you can skip ahead to the next section. You already know what a blockchain does because you have used one. You have watched a transaction confirm in real time. You have seen a smart contract execute without asking anyone's permission. You live on the other side of a line that most people haven't crossed yet.

This section is for everyone else.

And by everyone else, I mean most people. I meet them constantly. At investor dinners, at conferences, at family gatherings where someone's nephew mentioned Bitcoin three years ago and now everybody has an opinion. They bought some crypto on Coinbase. Maybe Bitcoin, maybe Dogecoin, maybe something a friend told them about on a group chat. They watched the number go up and then watched it go down. Some made money. Most didn't. Some lost money they shouldn't have been risking in the first place. And through all of it, they have never opened a block explorer. They have never seen a transaction actually move across the network. They have no idea what a wallet address looks like or what happens between the moment they tap "buy" on an app and the moment their portfolio updates. The entire infrastructure layer is invisible to them. They are using the most transparent financial system ever built and they have never once looked at it.

I don't blame them. For years, nobody made it easy to look. The interfaces were terrible. The language was deliberately obscure, a tribal dialect designed more for insider signaling than for communication. And the headlines didn't help. Every time blockchain made the news, it was either a scam, a crash, or a Ponzi scheme. Reasonable people, busy people, people with actual jobs and families, looked at the whole thing and decided it wasn't worth their time.

But here's the thing. If you actually took ten minutes and opened a block explorer, something like Etherscan or Basescan, you would see something that would fundamentally change how you think about money. You would see every transaction that has ever happened on that network. Every single one. Amounts, addresses, timestamps, all of it, permanently recorded and publicly visible. You would see the smart contract that powers EAT and be able to read the code that automatically routes fees to hunger relief. You would see the exact moment BlackRock's tokenized fund received a deposit. You would see it all because the whole system is designed to be seen. The most transparent financial infrastructure in human history, and most people have never even glanced at it.

Here is why that is changing. And here is why this chapter might be the most important one in the book for you to actually sit with.

In December 2025, SEC Chairman Paul Atkins stood at the New York Stock Exchange and said something that would have been unthinkable five years earlier. He described blockchain technology as the foundation for the next generation of American capital markets. Not a speculative toy. Not a fringe experiment. The infrastructure that stocks, bonds, and every other financial instrument will eventually run on. He predicted the shift could happen within a couple of years. The head of the agency that spent the previous administration treating crypto companies like criminal enterprises was now saying the entire financial system should move onchain.

Think about that. The top securities regulator in the United States looked at blockchain and didn't see a scam. He saw the most open, transparent, auditable financial infrastructure that has ever existed. He saw every transaction recorded permanently, viewable by anyone, in real time. He saw something that makes the current system, with its two-day settlement times and its opaque intermediary chains and its periodic spectacular frauds, look primitive by comparison.

And here's the part that should get your attention. He's right. But most people don't know he's right because they have never actually looked at the thing he's describing.

So let's look at it.

I want you to forget everything you think you know about blockchain for the next few minutes. Forget the jargon, forget the memes, forget the guy at the party who told you to buy Shiba Inu. Start with the simplest possible image.

Imagine a spreadsheet. Not on your computer. Not on any single computer. A spreadsheet that exists simultaneously on thousands of computers around the world, and every single one of those copies is identical. When someone adds a new entry to the spreadsheet, every copy updates at the same time. Nobody owns the spreadsheet. Nobody can secretly edit it. Nobody can delete a row after the fact. Every entry that has ever been made is there permanently, visible to anyone who wants to look.

That's a blockchain. That's the whole concept at its most fundamental level.

The very first block ever created on the Bitcoin blockchain, Block 0, was mined by Satoshi Nakamoto on January 3, 2009. Embedded in its code was a message, a headline from that morning's Times of London: "Chancellor on brink of second bailout for banks." It was a timestamp and a statement of purpose. The entire system was built as an alternative to the institutions that had just failed catastrophically. And that message is still there, fifteen years later, permanently encoded in the first block of a chain that now secures trillions of dollars in value. Nobody can edit it. Nobody can remove it. The blockchain remembers.

When people say "blockchain" they are describing a specific way of organizing that spreadsheet. Instead of one long continuous document, the entries are grouped into blocks. Each block contains a batch of transactions, a timestamp, and a mathematical reference to the block that came before it. That reference is what makes the chain. Block 1 points to Block 0. Block 2 points to Block 1. Block 783,000 points to Block 782,999. Pull any block out of the sequence and the math breaks. The whole chain knows something is wrong.

This is not a metaphor. This is literally how it works. If you go to a block explorer, a website that lets you read a public blockchain the way you'd read a public database, you can see this in real time. Pick any Bitcoin or Ethereum transaction that has ever occurred, and you can trace it. The sender's address. The receiver's address. The exact amount. The exact time. The fee that was paid. The block it was included in. All of it, right there, permanently, for anyone on earth to verify.

Compare that to what happens when you send a wire transfer through your bank. Your money disappears into a black box. It passes through one, two, sometimes three intermediary banks, each of which charges a fee. You get a confirmation email that says "processing." Two to three business days later, the money shows up on the other end and you have no idea what happened in between. Nobody outside the banking system can audit that transaction. Nobody can verify in real time that the money went where it was supposed to go.

This is what the SEC chairman was talking about. Blockchain doesn't just digitize finance. It makes finance visible. Public blockchains are open-source, which means the code that runs them is available for anyone to read, audit, and verify. The transaction history is open. The rules are open. The entire system operates in daylight in a way that the traditional financial system never has and, structurally, never can.

There's an irony that most people in crypto enjoy pointing out. Many of the same companies that love to talk about transparency in their annual reports actually don't use public blockchains precisely because they are too transparent. They need some forms of privacy that public ledgers don't offer. That's a real limitation, and we'll get to it. But the core point stands. For the first time in the history of finance, we have infrastructure where the default setting is openness, not opacity. That is not a small thing. That is a fundamental inversion of how money has worked for centuries.

What Your Bank Shows You vs. What the Blockchain Shows Everyone

Same $500 transfer. Two completely different levels of transparency.

	YOUR BANK		THE BLOCKCHAIN
You see:	"Transfer Pending"	You see:	Tx hash, sender, receiver, amount
Timeline:	"2-3 Business Days"	Timeline:	Confirmed in 2-12 seconds
Route:	"Processing..."	Route:	Direct. Visible on block explorer.
Fees:	"See fee schedule"	Fees:	$0.001 (exact, shown before you send)
Audit trail:	"Contact customer service"	Audit trail:	Permanent. Public. Immutable.
Who verifies:	Nobody outside the bank	Who verifies:	Anyone on earth, right now
??? BLACK BOX ???		OPEN LEDGER — VERIFY IT YOURSELF	

The SEC chairman called blockchain the most open financial system we've ever seen. He's right. Most people just haven't looked yet.

Figure 5.1: Bank vs. Blockchain

The obvious question is: if nobody owns this spreadsheet, who stops someone from cheating?

In the traditional financial system, the answer is institutions. Banks verify transactions. Clearinghouses settle trades. Regulators audit the books. The whole apparatus runs on the assumption that these institutions will be honest, competent, and solvent. When they aren't, you get 2008. You get FTX. You get SVB. The system works right up until the moment someone you were supposed to trust turns out to be untrustworthy, and then everything built on that trust wobbles or collapses.

Blockchain replaces institutional trust with mathematical proof. The mechanism that makes this work is called a consensus algorithm, which is a fancy way of saying: the network has a method for all those thousands of computers to agree on what's true without any of them having to trust each other. That shift, from "trust the institution" to "verify the code," is not incremental. It is architectural. It replaces one of the oldest load-bearing walls in the financial system with something entirely different. And as you will see later in this book, it is just one of three walls being replaced.

Bitcoin uses a consensus method called Proof of Work. I covered this in Chapter 3 when we talked about Bitcoin mining as energy conversion, but here's the short version. To add a new block to the Bitcoin blockchain, a computer has to solve a computational puzzle that requires enormous amounts of electricity. The first computer to solve it gets to add the block and earns Bitcoin as a reward. This process is deliberately expensive. It costs real energy to participate. And because it costs energy, cheating costs energy too. To fake a transaction on Bitcoin, you would need to control more computational power than the rest of the entire network combined. As of today, that network consumes more electricity than many countries. The energy expenditure is the security.

Ethereum, the other blockchain that matters most for this book, used to run on Proof of Work too. In September 2022, it switched to a system called Proof of Stake in an event the community called "the Merge." Instead of spending electricity to validate transactions, Ethereum validators now lock up large quantities of ETH, the network's native token, as collateral. If they validate honestly, they earn rewards. If they try to cheat, they lose their stake. The security comes from having skin in the game rather than burning energy.

The Merge was a remarkable piece of engineering. Ethereum swapped out its consensus engine while the network was still running, processing billions of dollars in transactions daily. Imagine changing the engine on an airplane at 30,000 feet while the passengers keep watching their movies. The development took years of preparation. Multiple testnets. Months of coordination across a decentralized community of developers with no CEO and no corporate hierarchy directing the effort. When it went live on September 15, 2022, it reduced Ethereum's energy consumption by over 99% overnight. The network kept operating without a single second of downtime. It was one of the most complex software transitions in history, and most people outside crypto never heard about it.

Both approaches work. They just make different tradeoffs. Proof of Work is more energy-intensive but arguably more decentralized and battle-tested. Proof of Stake is more energy-efficient but concentrates influence among the wealthiest stakers. The debate over which is better is one of the oldest arguments in crypto. For our purposes, the key insight is the same either way: the blockchain stays honest not because anyone is morally compelled to be honest, but because the math makes cheating more expensive than playing by the rules. Trust is enforced by economics, not ethics.

That distinction hit me hardest when we were building EAT's smart contract. We did not have to convince the blockchain to be honest. We had to write the code correctly. The security was in the math, not in our reputation. For a first-time protocol builder, that was both liberating and terrifying. If the code was right, nobody could stop it from working. If the code was wrong, nobody could stop it from failing.

Layer 1, Layer 2, and Why It Matters

Here is where a lot of people's eyes start to glaze over, and I get it. But this is actually simpler than it sounds, and understanding it explains why different blockchains exist and why I built on the one I chose.

A Layer 1 is the base blockchain. Bitcoin is a Layer 1. Ethereum is a Layer 1. Solana is a Layer 1. Each one is a complete, independent network with its own validators, its own security model, and its own rules.

The problem is that base blockchains, especially popular ones, get congested. Ethereum, at the height of the 2021 NFT boom, was charging users fifty to a hundred dollars in fees for a single transaction. That's great if you're moving a million dollars. It's absurd if you're buying a coffee.

Layer 2s solve this. A Layer 2 is a network built on top of a Layer 1 that handles transactions faster and cheaper, then periodically settles the results back to the base chain. Think of it this way. Ethereum is the courthouse where the final legal record is kept. Layer 2s are the offices where the actual work happens. You don't go to the courthouse every time you sign a document. You do the work in the office and file the final record at the courthouse when you need to.

I spent months trying to explain this to investors on Zoom calls and they kept glazing over until I said: Ethereum is the Supreme Court, Base is the local court. Your case gets handled locally, fast and cheap. The ruling gets recorded at the top, permanent and secure. That was the version that stuck.

Here is what that architecture looks like when it touches a person's life.

Remember Maria from Chapter 1. Two jobs in Los Angeles. Sends $200 to her family in Manila every Friday. Pays $19 to $22 in fees through Western Union. The money takes one to three days to arrive. That is Layer 0: the legacy financial infrastructure, the one that was designed for the institutions that operate it.

Now picture Maria's daughter in Manila opening an app on her phone. Her mother sent $200 through a stablecoin transfer on Base. The fee was less than a penny. The money arrived in seconds. Not business days. Seconds. Her daughter did not need to know she was using a Layer 2. She did not need to understand rollups or settlement batches or Ethereum's security model. She needed her mother's money to arrive fast and cheap. It did. That is all she needs to know, and that is the whole point.

The difference between $22 in fees and less than a penny in fees is not a rounding error. For Maria, that is two hours of her morning job. Every week. Fifty-two weeks a year. The Layer 2 did not just save her money. It returned her energy. And it did it on infrastructure that settles back to Ethereum's base layer with the same security guarantees as a $10 million institutional transfer. That transaction happened on Base. Here is why I chose it.

Base is the Layer 2 I chose to build on, and it's the one that matters most for the WYDE and EAT story. Base is built by Coinbase, which is worth understanding in context. Coinbase has been through nearly every cycle this industry has produced. The 2017 ICO mania. The 2018 crash. The DeFi summer of 2020. The NFT explosion of 2021. The FTX implosion of 2022. And the institutional stampede that followed. Love them or take issue with them, Coinbase has the largest crypto distribution network in the United States. They have onboarded more Americans to cryptocurrency than any other company. When they decided to build a Layer 2, they weren't experimenting. They were extending their infrastructure into the decentralized world.

Base launched in August 2023 and within two years captured over 43% of the Layer 2 market by total value locked, with nearly $5 billion in assets. It's fast, it's cheap, transactions cost fractions of a penny, and it inherits Ethereum's security because it settles back to Ethereum's base layer. For a builder, that combination of low cost, high speed, and institutional-grade security is exactly what you want. Coinbase built Base with a deliberately builder-centric philosophy: make it easy for developers to deploy applications that real people actually use, not just applications that crypto insiders trade on. That philosophy is what attracted us. It's why EAT's smart contract lives on Base. Every trade, every fee routing, every meal funded, happens on Base and is ultimately secured by Ethereum.

And Coinbase is no longer alone in this. The list of companies building their own blockchains reads like a roster of the institutions that already run global finance. Robinhood launched its own Ethereum Layer 2 in February 2026, and within one week the testnet processed four million transactions, built specifically so the shares of Tesla and Amazon you buy on their app can settle in seconds instead of taking two days through the traditional clearinghouse system. Stripe, which processes more online payments than almost any company on earth, looked at existing blockchains and decided none were optimized for stablecoin payments, so they built their own Layer 1 called Tempo. Google is building one too. So is Circle, the company behind USDC.

And then, on February 11, 2026, something happened that would have been unthinkable even twelve months earlier. BlackRock, the largest asset manager on the planet, listed its $2.4 billion tokenized Treasury fund BUIDL on Uniswap, the decentralized exchange that started as 300 lines of code. And they didn't just list the fund. They bought Uniswap's governance token, UNI, putting a DeFi token on BlackRock's corporate balance sheet for the first time in history. The firm that manages $14 trillion in assets looked at a decentralized exchange built by a kid who taught himself to code, and decided that's where their Treasury fund should trade. Larry Fink, in a December 2025 column for The Economist, called tokenization the next major evolution in market infrastructure.

Read that list again. Stripe. Google. Visa. Deutsche Bank. Mastercard. CME Group. Robinhood. BlackRock. These are not crypto companies. These are the institutions that run the existing digital and financial systems. And they are building blockchains. Not buying Bitcoin as a speculative bet. Building the infrastructure. That tells you everything you need to know about where this is going.

Who's Building Blockchains Now

These are not crypto companies. These are the companies that run the existing financial system.

Company	Project	Type	Detail	Year
COINBASE	Base (L2)	Ethereum L2	43% L2 market share, $4.9B TVL	2023
ROBINHOOD	Robinhood Chain	Arbitrum L2	4M testnet txns in first week	2026
STRIPE	Tempo (L1)	New Layer 1	Visa, Deutsche Bank, Mastercard	2025
GOOGLE	GCUL (L1)	New Layer 1	Built with CME Group	2026
BLACKROCK	BUIDL on Uniswap	Ethereum DeFi	$2.4B fund on a DEX + bought UNI	2026
CIRCLE	Arc (L1)	New Layer 1	USDC-native payments chain	2026

If the companies that run the existing financial system are building blockchains, the question isn't whether the technology is real. It's what gets built on it.

Figure 5.2: Who's Building Blockchains Now

When Money Learns to Follow Instructions

Picture a rental agreement signed in 2027. The tenant sends a deposit. The smart contract holds it. When the tenancy ends, the contract checks the condition of the property using a connected inspection report. If there is no damage, the deposit returns to the tenant automatically. No landlord deciding to keep it. No dispute process. No thirty-day wait for a check that may or may not arrive. The deposit simply moves, because the conditions were met, and the code executed.

That is not a hypothetical. The components exist today. What does not exist yet is the integration layer that makes it feel as simple as signing a lease. But the architecture underneath is live, and it is the same architecture that routes EAT's transaction fees to food banks. The principle is identical: money that carries instructions. Whether those instructions say 'return this deposit when conditions are met' or 'route 1% of this trade to a meal fund,' the mechanism is the same. A smart contract.

Everything I just described, the ledger, the consensus, the layers, that's the plumbing. Important plumbing. Essential plumbing. But plumbing by itself doesn't change the world. What changes the world is what you build on top of it.

That's where smart contracts come in. And this is where money actually becomes software.

A smart contract is a program that lives on a blockchain and executes automatically when its conditions are met. That's it. No lawyer reviews it. No bank approves it. No intermediary decides whether to process it. The code runs, and the outcome happens.

The analogy I keep coming back to is a vending machine. You put in a dollar, you select B7, and the machine gives you a bag of chips. There is no negotiation. There is no counterparty risk. The machine doesn't decide halfway through that it doesn't feel like dispensing today. The logic is hardwired: input meets condition, output occurs. A smart contract works exactly the same way, except instead of chips, the output can be money, tokens, data, access rights, or any other digital asset, and instead of sitting in a break room, the machine lives on a global network that runs twenty-four hours a day, seven days a week, and cannot be turned off by any single person or company.

Nick Szabo first described this idea in the 1990s. It didn't become real until Ethereum launched in 2015 with a programming language that let anyone write and deploy smart contracts on a public blockchain. That was the moment money stopped being a static thing you move from place to place and started being a dynamic thing that can carry logic, execute conditions, and compose with other programs.

Compose is the key word. This is the part that separates blockchain from every previous financial technology. Smart contracts are composable, which means they can plug into each other like software APIs. A lending protocol can plug into a trading protocol which can plug into an insurance protocol, and the whole stack operates automatically. No integration meetings. No partnership agreements. No legal teams negotiating terms for six months. If the code is on the blockchain and it's public, anyone can build on top of it.

Uniswap is probably the clearest illustration. In 2018, Hayden Adams deployed a smart contract to Ethereum that was roughly 300 lines of code. That contract created an automated market maker, a system where anyone could trade one token for another without a centralized exchange, an order book, a broker, or a market maker. You connected your wallet, selected the tokens, and the smart contract executed the trade using a mathematical formula to determine the price. No middleman. No permission. No account application.

Three hundred lines of code. That's less than the login page of most banking websites. And it replaced the core function of an entire category of financial institution. Uniswap now processes billions of dollars in trading volume. The original contract still works exactly as it was written. Nobody can change it. Nobody can shut it down. The code runs.

And because Uniswap's code is public and composable, other developers built on top of it. Aggregators that check Uniswap's prices against other exchanges and route your trade to the cheapest one. Lending protocols that use Uniswap as a price reference. Yield strategies that automatically swap tokens and reinvest returns. Each new layer builds on the one below it without asking permission. This is what "money becomes software" literally means. Financial services are becoming composable code, snapping together like Lego blocks, and anyone with a laptop can assemble them into something new.

The traditional financial system cannot do this. If you want to build a product that combines lending, trading, and insurance, you need partnerships with a bank, a broker, and an insurance company. You need legal agreements with each one. You need regulatory approval for the combined product. You need integration work that takes months or years. On a public blockchain, you write a smart contract that calls three other smart contracts and you deploy it in an afternoon. The entire financial stack becomes an API.

What It Takes to Let People Trade

A centralized exchange vs. a smart contract that does the same job.

	TRADITIONAL EXCHANGE		UNISWAP SMART CONTRACT
Employees	6,000+	Employees	0 (code is autonomous)
Offices	Multiple countries	Offices	Lives on the blockchain
Legal team	Hundreds of lawyers	Legal team	The code IS the rules
Settlement	T+2 (two business days)	Settlement	Instant (same block)
Hours	Mon-Fri, 9:30–4:00 ET	Hours	24 / 7 / 365, forever
Codebase	Millions of lines	Codebase	~300 lines
Permission	Account application required	Permission	None. Connect wallet.
Billions in annual operating costs		Gas fees: fractions of a penny per trade	

**BlackRock just listed a $2.4 billion fund on the 300-line smart contract.
That's the whole story of this chapter in one sentence.**

Figure 5.3: What It Takes to Let People Trade

The Moment It Clicked

There is a reason I'm spending time on this. It's the thing that makes the rest of this book possible.

In November 2021, a group of strangers on the internet decided to buy the United States Constitution. Not a replica. An actual first-edition printing from 1787, one of only thirteen copies known to exist, heading to auction at Sotheby's. They called themselves ConstitutionDAO, and in less than a week, 17,437 people contributed a combined $46 million in cryptocurrency to a shared treasury controlled by a smart contract. No venture capital firm organized it. No bank enabled it. No legal entity existed when the money started flowing. People sent Ethereum to a contract address, received governance tokens in return, and collectively assembled the largest crowdfunding campaign for a physical object in history.

They lost the auction. A hedge fund billionaire outbid them. The DAO disbanded and contributors were refunded. By every conventional measure, it failed.

But here's what actually happened. Seventeen thousand people who mostly didn't know each other, spread across the world, pooled $46 million in days, governed by code, with complete transparency about where every dollar was and how it could be used. Try to do that through the existing financial system. Try to open a bank account for a nameless entity that doesn't exist yet, collect international deposits from thousands of unverified strangers, and place a bid at a major auction house, all in under a week. It's not possible. The infrastructure doesn't support it. The compliance requirements alone would take months.

The blockchain didn't just make this possible. It made it trivially easy. The hard part wasn't the technology. The hard part was winning the auction.

That's the shift. Blockchain removes the friction between intention and action in financial coordination. It makes things that were previously impossible become routine. ConstitutionDAO raised $46 million. Others have organized around anything from funding public goods to buying golf courses. These experiments are messy and half of them fail, but they demonstrate something fundamental about what programmable financial infrastructure enables: coordination at a speed and scale that the traditional system cannot match.

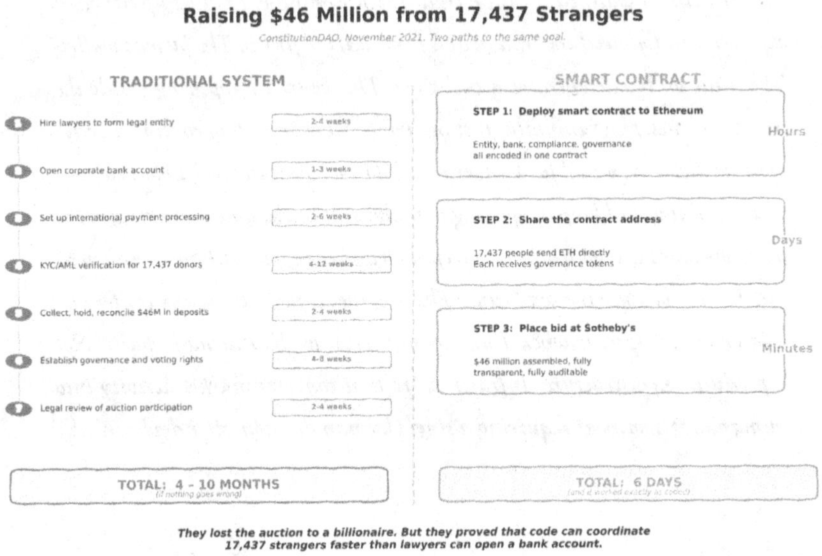

Figure 5.4: Raising $46 Million from 17,437 Strangers

The EAT smart contract works on the same principle, just aimed at a different target. Instead of coordinating a one-time purchase, it coordinates perpetual impact. Every trade triggers a fee. The fee routes automatically to hunger relief. The code enforces it forever. No board meeting. No annual fundraising gala. No middleman deciding whether to process the donation. The logic is in the contract, on the blockchain, running every second of every day.

That is what it means for money to become software. The money carries instructions.

The instructions execute automatically. The results are permanent and publicly verifiable. Every single part of that sentence was impossible before blockchain and smart contracts existed.

The first time I watched an EAT trade execute on Base, I pulled up the block explorer and followed the transaction from start to finish. The buyer's wallet. The trade on the decentralized exchange. The fee split happening inside the smart contract, programmatic, instant, irreversible. A portion routing directly to the wallet designated for hunger relief. The whole thing took about two seconds. And it would keep happening with the next trade, and the next, and the next, whether I was watching or asleep or on a plane. The machine doesn't need me. It runs because the code runs. That moment, more than any conference talk or whitepaper, is when I understood what we had actually built. Not a product. Infrastructure. Infrastructure that converts market activity into human meals without requiring a single human decision after deployment.

Take notes on this chapter if you need to. Re-read the parts that feel unfamiliar. Because everything that follows, the stablecoins, the DeFi protocols, the institutional products, the AI agents, the cause coins, all of it is built on the layer I just described. If the programmable layer doesn't click, the rest of the book is just stories about things that sound futuristic. If it does click, you'll start to see why the people building on this infrastructure believe they are building the next version of the financial system. And why they might be right.

The Bug That Can't Be Fixed

I need to be honest about the other side of this, because intellectual honesty is what separates a useful book from a sales pitch.

Smart contracts are immutable. That's the feature. Once deployed, nobody can change the code. That's also the risk. Because if the code has a bug, the bug is immutable too.

In June 2016, a smart contract called The DAO, one of the first major experiments in decentralized governance on Ethereum, held $150 million in contributed funds. A hacker found a flaw in the code, a recursive call vulnerability, and drained roughly $60 million before the community could respond. The money wasn't stolen in the traditional sense. Nobody broke into a safe. Nobody hacked a password. The hacker simply used the smart contract exactly as it was written. The code allowed the withdrawal. The blockchain executed it faithfully. The bug was in the instructions, and the machine followed the instructions perfectly.

The Ethereum community ultimately decided to rewrite the blockchain's history to reverse the theft, a hugely controversial decision that split the network into Ethereum and Ethereum Classic. The debate over whether that was the right call continues to this day. But the lesson was permanent: in a world of immutable code, the quality of that code is everything. You cannot call customer service. You cannot file a chargeback. You cannot ask a judge to reverse the transaction. The code is the law, and if the law has a loophole, someone will find it.

Since 2016, the industry has matured significantly. Smart contract auditing has become a multimillion-dollar industry. Firms like Trail of Bits, OpenZeppelin, and Certik review code before it goes live, looking for exactly the kind of vulnerability that sank The DAO. Formal verification methods, which use mathematical proofs to verify code correctness, are increasingly standard for high-value contracts. Bug bounty programs pay white-hat hackers millions to find vulnerabilities before malicious actors do. Immunefi, the largest crypto bug bounty platform, has paid out over $100 million in rewards. The tools are better. The practices are better. The stakes demanded it. But the fundamental tradeoff remains. Immutability is the source of both the power and the danger. You get permanent, trustless execution. You also get permanent bugs if you aren't careful.

I'll spend more time on this in Chapter 14 when I lay out the full risk landscape. For now, the point is this: the technology is real, it works, and it has genuine limitations that honest builders acknowledge and design around. Pretending smart contracts are perfect is as dishonest as pretending they are scams. They are powerful tools with sharp edges.

The Grid Is Live

Let me pull back to the energy thread that runs through this book.

In Chapter 3, I argued that money is energy. Every phase change in monetary history was an energy efficiency upgrade. Blockchain is the next upgrade. It is an energy grid for value. A network that moves monetary energy anywhere in the world, in seconds, with a permanent public record, and no requirement to trust any single institution or intermediary.

Smart contracts are the programs that run on that grid. They don't just move energy from point A to point B. They route it according to instructions. If this condition is met, send here. If that threshold is reached, execute this. Take 2% of every transaction and route it to a verified cause. The energy flows where the code directs it.

The transition from dumb money to smart money is the transition from passive energy storage to active energy routing. A dollar bill stores value. A dollar in a smart contract carries logic. The logic makes the energy intelligent. That intelligence is what makes every chapter that follows in this book possible: the stablecoins, the DeFi protocols, the institutional products, the AI agents, the cause coins. All of it runs on the programmable layer.

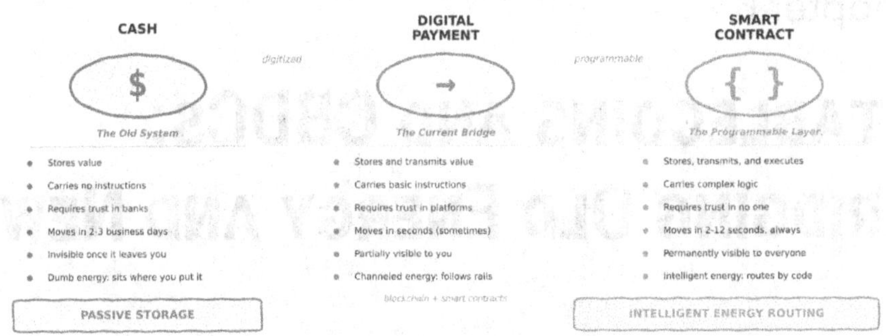

Figure 5.5: From Dumb Money to Smart Money

And that layer is no longer a niche experiment. When Stripe builds a blockchain for payments, when Google builds one for capital markets, when the SEC chairman says the entire American financial system could move onchain within years, the question of whether this technology is real has been answered. The only question left is what gets built on it.

The next chapter answers the first part of that question. Stablecoins and CBDCs: the bridge between the old energy system and the new one. Dollars that live on the internet. Government money that runs on code. Two competing visions for how traditional monetary energy gets converted into programmable form. The race is already underway.

That's where we're going next.

Chapter 6

Stablecoins and CBDCs: Bridging Old Energy and New

In the spring of 2022, everything was falling apart.

Luna had just collapsed, dragging the entire crypto market down with it. Forty billion dollars in value, gone in a week. The algorithmic stablecoin that was supposed to hold its peg through pure math turned out to be backed by nothing but confidence, and confidence evaporated overnight. People were panicking. Twitter was a funeral. And then something happened that most people missed in the chaos.

USDC dropped to ninety-seven cents.

Not because Circle was insolvent. Not because the reserves were fake. USDC dipped because Silicon Valley Bank, where Circle held a portion of its reserves, was in trouble, and the market got nervous. For about thirty-six hours, you could buy a dollar for ninety-seven cents.

I looked at that and thought: that is the best three percent you can make in a day. Because it is going back to a dollar. Sure enough, the next day it was sitting right at a dollar, and everything was fine. If you had put a million dollars into USDC at that moment, you would have cleared thirty thousand dollars in less than twenty-four hours on what was essentially a guaranteed trade.

That moment taught me something I keep coming back to. Most people in crypto lose money chasing volatile assets up and down, watching their portfolios swing 30 or 40 percent in a week, and they never think about stablecoins. The boring ones. The ones pegged to a dollar. They think stablecoins are just a parking lot, a place to sit while you wait for the next trade.

They are not a parking lot. They are the most important infrastructure in all of crypto. And most people, even most people who trade crypto every day, still do not understand why.

Here is the simplest way I can explain a stablecoin. It is a dollar that lives on the internet.

Not a digital approximation of a dollar. Not a token that tries to be worth a dollar through some complicated algorithm. A stablecoin, at its most basic, is backed one-to-one by actual dollars or dollar equivalents sitting in a reserve account. You put a dollar in, you get a token out. You send the token back, you get your dollar. The token moves on a blockchain, which means it settles in seconds instead of days, it works twenty-four hours a day including weekends and holidays, and it does not care what country you are in.

Your bank closes at five. It does not process transfers on Saturday. If you want to send money from New York to Manila, the transaction passes through correspondent banks that each take a cut and add a day. A stablecoin does all of that instantly, globally, for a fraction of a cent in gas fees. Same dollar. Completely different infrastructure.

The market reflects this. As of February 2026, the total stablecoin market cap is $307.6 billion. Monthly settlement volume hit $1.39 trillion in the first half of 2025. That is more than Visa and Mastercard process in cross-border volume combined. The majority of that activity, about 67 percent, flows through DeFi protocols and trading platforms. Another 15 percent is remittances, people sending money home across borders. About 10 percent is people in countries with unstable currencies using stablecoins as a hedge against inflation. The dollar is the world's reserve currency, and stablecoins are how the rest of the world accesses it without a U.S. bank account.

When I read that number, the 15 percent remittance share, I think about Maria from Chapter 1. Fifteen percent of $1.39 trillion in monthly volume is over $200 billion a year flowing through stablecoins as remittances. That is people sending money home. The same thing Maria does every Friday at Western Union, except without the $22 fee and without the three-day wait. The infrastructure is already doing what we said it would do. Most people just have not noticed yet.

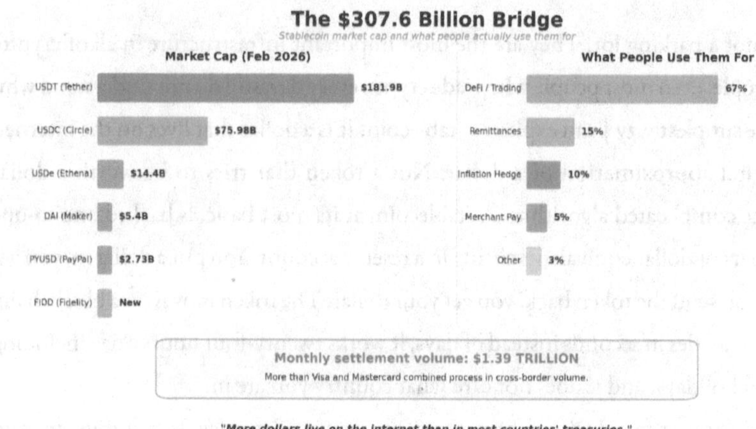

Figure 6.1: The $307.6 Billion Bridge

The territory is dominated by two players. Tether's USDT holds about 60 percent of the market at $181.9 billion. Circle's USDC holds about 25 percent at $76 billion. Everything else, from DAI to PayPal's PYUSD to the brand-new entrants, fights over the remaining 15 percent.

Here is the thing nobody talks about when they talk about stablecoins. The yield. If you buy stablecoins on Coinbase and similar exchanges today and hold them in your account, you are earning up to 4 percent. Right now. On a dollar-pegged asset. Imagine a mechanism where you can earn yield on the dollar sitting in your wallet, where your money works for you while you sleep, and you can pull it out instantly any time you want. That is what stablecoins enable. Most people do not get that. Even banks do not get that. Especially credit unions. It is only the biggest institutions that are starting to jump in now.

Nobody told me this when I started. I spent my first year in crypto watching Bitcoin and Ethereum charts, trying to time entries and exits, losing sleep over 10 percent swings. And the whole time, the smartest money in the room was sitting in stablecoins, earning yield, and waiting. The traders I know who have survived multiple cycles all say the same thing: stablecoins are not the boring part of crypto. They are the part that lets you stay in the game long enough for the interesting parts to play out.

You can also take collateral against a stablecoin position and make that yield again on the borrowed funds. That is looping, and I will come back to it in a moment, because it is both the most powerful and the most dangerous mechanic in all of decentralized finance. But at the basic level, the yield on stablecoins is real, it comes from the interest earned on the reserve assets backing them, and it represents a fundamental shift in what a dollar can do.

In the energy framework we have been building through this book, stablecoins are energy converters. They take the stored energy of the existing dollar system, all of its trust, its reserve currency status, its backing by the U.S. government, and they convert that energy into programmable form. The dollar does not change. What changes is the infrastructure it moves on. Old pipes replaced by new rails.

The Tether Paradox

The most controversial fact in crypto is also one of the most revealing.

Tether, the least transparent major stablecoin issuer, is by far the most used. USDT's $181.9 billion market cap dwarfs every competitor. It processes more daily volume than most stock exchanges. And for years, Tether has faced questions about whether its reserves are real, whether its audits are adequate, whether the whole thing is a house of cards.

And yet it keeps growing. Why?

Because the people who use Tether are not the people who read crypto Twitter debates about reserve attestations. They are the remittance sender in Lagos who needs to get dollars to a family member in Nairobi by tomorrow. They are the small business owner in Buenos Aires who watches the peso lose value every month and parks savings in USDT because it is the fastest way to hold dollars. They are the freelancer in Dhaka getting paid by a client in San Francisco and converting the payment instantly rather than waiting a week for a wire transfer and losing 5 percent to intermediaries.

Seventy-one percent of Latin American stablecoin activity is cross-border payments. That number tells you everything. Tether serves the people the banking system forgot, or never reached in the first place. It is ugly infrastructure, imperfect and opaque, but it works where nothing else does.

Circle represents the other path. USDC is fully audited, U.S.-based, playing by every rule regulators have written and several they have not written yet. Circle has positioned itself as the compliant on-ramp for institutions. And that bet is now being tested, because after the GENIUS Act passed in July 2025, banks started fighting to rewrite the rules in their favor. The same institutions that were too slow to build stablecoin infrastructure themselves are now lobbying to make sure the infrastructure built by companies like Circle operates on terms favorable to incumbent banks.

The tension between Tether's cowboy dominance and Circle's regulatory bet defines the stablecoin market right now. One serves the world's unbanked through sheer utility. The other is building the rails for institutional adoption. Both are necessary. Neither alone is sufficient.

When the Peg Breaks

There is a trick in crypto that sounds genius until it blows up. It is called looping, and it is what entire hedge funds build their positions on.

Here is how it works. You buy a stablecoin. You deposit it as collateral on a lending platform. You borrow against it. You take what you borrowed and buy more of the same stablecoin. You deposit that as collateral too. You borrow again. Each loop multiplies your yield. If the base rate is 4 percent, one loop gets you 8. Two loops get you 12. Three loops and you are advertising 24, 36, even 70 percent APY. It looks like free money. It feels like free money. The numbers on the screen keep going up.

The problem is that every loop also multiplies your risk. You are not earning yield on real value. You are manufacturing yield through leverage. And the entire structure depends on one thing: the stablecoin holding its peg. If it slips even a few percent, every loop unwinds at once. The collateral gets liquidated, the borrowing gets called, and the cascade starts.

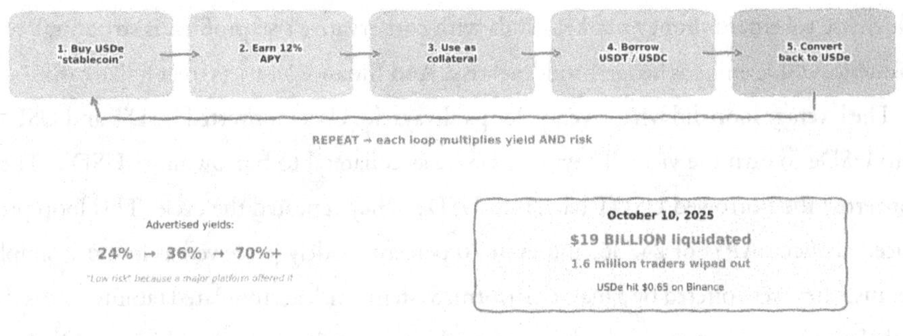

Figure 6.2: The Leverage Loop

Luna's UST was the first catastrophic lesson. It was not even a real stablecoin. It was algorithmic, meaning it maintained its peg through a mechanism involving its sister token Luna rather than through actual dollar reserves. It was, in the energy thesis of this book, fake energy. No real reserves, no real backing, just a mathematical model that worked until it did not. When UST lost its peg in May 2022, $40 billion evaporated. People lost everything. And the industry said: we learned our lesson.

We did not learn our lesson.

On October 10, 2025, Trump announced a new round of tariffs, and markets across the board got hit. But what happened in crypto was the largest liquidation event in the history of the industry. Nineteen billion dollars, gone in hours. 1.6 million traders liquidated. Bitcoin fell from $122,000 to $105,000 in a single session. Solana dropped 40 percent. Some tokens briefly traded near zero.

At the center of the wreckage was a product called USDe, issued by a company called Ethena. USDe was marketed as a stablecoin. It was listed alongside USDT and USDC on Binance, the world's largest exchange. Users could deposit it as collateral under the same terms as traditional stablecoins. Binance ran a promotional campaign offering 12 percent APY on USDe holdings. From a user's perspective, there was no visible difference between USDe and USDC.

But USDe was not a stablecoin. It was, as OKX CEO Star Xu later put it, a tokenized hedge fund. Ethena raises capital, deploys it into index arbitrage and algorithmic trading strategies, tokenizes the resulting fund, and calls the token a stablecoin. The difference between USDe and something like BlackRock's BUIDL or Franklin Templeton's BENJI, which are tokenized money market funds with conservative risk profiles, is structural, not cosmetic. USDe embeds hedge-fund-level risk. And Binance let users treat it like cash.

The leverage loop did what leverage loops always do. Users converted USDT and USDC into USDe to earn the yield. They used USDe as collateral to borrow more USDT. They converted the borrowed USDT back into USDe. They repeated the cycle. This loop produced artificial APYs of 24, 36, and even 70 percent, widely perceived as low risk simply because they were offered by a major platform. Systemic risk accumulated rapidly across the global crypto market, and nobody could see how much leverage was hiding inside those clean-looking yield numbers.

When Trump's tariff announcement spooked the market and volatility hit, USDe depegged on Binance, falling to $0.65. Cascading liquidations followed. Weaknesses in risk management around assets like WETH and BNSOL further amplified the crash. Some tokens briefly traded near zero. Exchange interfaces froze. API connections failed. Traders could not manage their positions or add collateral. Manageable situations became total liquidations because the infrastructure buckled under the weight of its own leverage.

Many industry participants have said the damage was worse than FTX. And unlike FTX, which was the crime of one man, October 10 was a systemic failure. It was not an accident. It was the predictable outcome of letting a tokenized hedge fund product be treated as a stablecoin on the world's largest exchange.

Xu wrote something in his post-mortem that I think is exactly right. He said long-term trust in crypto cannot be built on short-term yield games, excessive leverage, or marketing practices that obscure risk. And he said: crypto is still early. What we choose to normalize today will determine whether this industry earns lasting trust, or repeats the same mistakes again.

The pattern is brutally simple, and it is the same pattern we traced in the energy framework. Protocols backed by real energy survive. Protocols manufacturing fake energy collapse. Real reserves, real dollars, real Treasuries: those are real energy. Algorithmic pegs, leveraged loops, tokenized hedge funds dressed up as stablecoins: those are manufactured energy. And manufactured energy always breaks.

The GENIUS Act and What It Triggered

I remember the day the GENIUS Act passed. I was watching the vote tracker, and it moved through the Senate 68 to 30 and the House 308 to 122 faster than almost any financial legislation I have ever seen. The president signed it, and it was done. The whole thing took maybe forty-eight hours from final vote to signature.

It was almost too fast. The banks definitely thought it was too fast.

The Guiding and Establishing National Innovation for U.S. Stablecoins Act, signed July 18, 2025, created the first federal regulatory framework for payment stablecoins in the United States: one-to-one reserves in cash or Treasuries, monthly audits, anti-money-laundering compliance, and a dual federal-state oversight structure. Most importantly, it explicitly defined payment stablecoins as neither securities nor commodities, which removed the jurisdictional tug-of-war between the SEC and CFTC that had paralyzed the industry for years. For the first time, the U.S. government did not crack down on stablecoins. It built regulatory infrastructure for them. That is a fundamentally different posture.

The market's response was immediate. Over $40 billion in crypto-related mergers and acquisitions followed the signing. Stripe closed its $1.1 billion acquisition of Bridge, a stablecoin infrastructure startup. Coinbase acquired Deribit for $2.9 billion. Ripple bought Hidden Road for $1.25 billion. MGX, an Abu Dhabi investment fund, committed $2 billion for a stake in Binance and settled the entire deal in stablecoins, the largest investment ever paid in cryptocurrency. Regulatory clarity does not slow things down. It speeds them up.

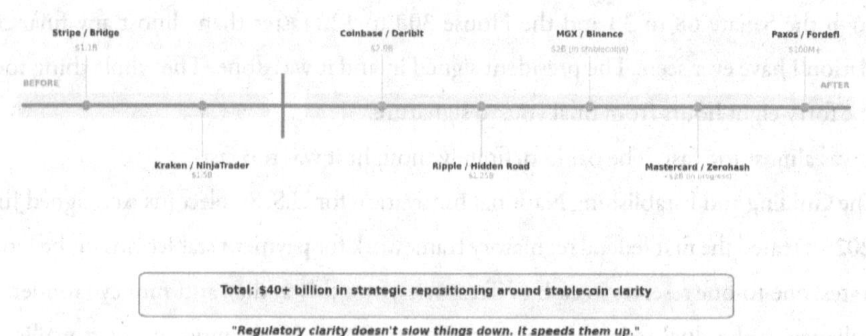

Figure 6.3: The GENIUS Act M&A Wave

Here is what the GENIUS Act actually means at ground level. A credit union in rural Alabama, the kind of institution that serves farmers, teachers, and small business owners that the national banks abandoned years ago, can now issue stablecoin deposits. Think about that. A member deposits dollars. The credit union issues a stablecoin backed by those dollars. That stablecoin earns yield from Treasury-backed reserves. The member earns more than any savings account at a national bank, the credit union earns revenue it has never had access to, and the dollars never leave the regulated system. No crypto exchange. No speculative token. Just a credit union in Alabama offering its members a better deal because the legal infrastructure finally allows it.

That is what regulatory infrastructure does when it is designed correctly. It does not make headlines. It makes small institutions competitive again.

Fidelity, with $17.5 trillion in assets, launched its own stablecoin. Wyoming, a state government, issued its own. If you hold stablecoins on Coinbase today, you are earning up to 4 percent yield. Imagine a mechanism where you can earn yield on the dollar in your wallet. That is what these instruments enable, and even most banks do not understand it yet. The banks that were too slow to write the rules are now lobbying to rewrite them, and that tension is playing out in real time. I am going to go deeper on the regulatory landscape in Chapter 13, because the story does not end with the GENIUS Act.

The Institutions Join

Three things happened in the span of a few months that told me the stablecoin story had fundamentally changed. Each one, by itself, would have been a major milestone. Together, they mark a phase transition.

The first was JPMorgan.

For years, JPMorgan had been running its own private blockchain called Onyx, later rebranded to Kinexys. It was an internal system for moving money between JPMorgan's institutional clients. It worked fine, but it was a walled garden. In June 2025, JPMorgan launched a pilot to issue JPMD, a dollar-backed deposit token, on Base, the Ethereum Layer 2 blockchain built by Coinbase.

The largest bank in the United States, with $2.5 trillion in deposits and a payments engine that processes $10 trillion a day, moved from its own private blockchain to a public one. Not because the private chain failed. Because the public chain is where the demand is. As one JPMorgan product lead put it, the only cash equivalent available on public chains right now is stablecoins, and institutions want a bank deposit option.

It is very telling of where the industry is going that institutional finance is choosing to leverage the existing rails rather than creating their own. JPMorgan tried the walled garden. It worked at a small scale. But when they wanted to reach the broader market, they went to where the liquidity already was.

There is a subtle but important detail here. JPMorgan chose a deposit token over a stablecoin for a specific reason. Under fractional reserve banking, JPMorgan holds about $400 billion in central bank reserves against its $2.5 trillion in deposits. If they issued a stablecoin, they would need to pull money from their highly profitable deposit system to fund full reserves. For every dollar converted to stablecoins, JPMorgan would lose more than four dollars in deposit value. Deposit tokens let them bring bank money on-chain without gutting the business model that makes banking profitable. Same energy, different container.

The second signal was Fidelity.

On January 28, 2026, Fidelity Investments, with $17.5 trillion in assets under administration, announced the launch of its own stablecoin. The Fidelity Digital Dollar, ticker FIDD, launched on February 4 on the Ethereum blockchain. One-to-one dollar backing. Reserves in cash, cash equivalents, and short-term Treasuries managed by Fidelity Management and Research. Available to both retail and institutional clients.

Fidelity's president of digital assets said the GENIUS Act was a significant milestone that provided the regulatory guardrails to make this possible. That is a $17.5 trillion asset manager explicitly crediting a piece of legislation for giving them the confidence to issue a stablecoin. The signal could not be louder.

The third signal came from Wyoming.

On August 19, 2025, the state of Wyoming became the first public entity in the United States to issue a stablecoin. The Frontier Stable Token, ticker FRNT, launched on seven blockchains simultaneously, with reserves managed by Franklin Templeton and held in a state trust. Interest earned from those reserves flows directly to Wyoming's School Foundation Program, creating a new revenue stream for public education without raising taxes.

The Delaware of crypto became the issuer of crypto. Wyoming, which has passed over 45 blockchain-related laws since 2016 and created the DUNA framework that makes our own work at WYDE legally possible, is now the first state to put its own money on-chain. The Converse County Treasurer calculated that FRNT could eliminate $70,000 in annual credit card processing fees on $3.4 million in transactions. That is not a crypto experiment. That is a government finding a more efficient way to serve its residents.

JPMorgan, Fidelity, Wyoming. A bank, an asset manager, a state government. Each came to the same conclusion independently: stablecoins are infrastructure now, and the question is no longer whether to participate, but how.

And this matters for everything that comes later in this book. When I talk about cause coins, about tokens that automatically fund meals through trading activity, the settlement layer underneath all of that is transitioning to stablecoins. When someone buys EAT on a decentralized exchange, the liquidity pool they trade against is denominated in ETH today, but the transition to stablecoin-denominated pools is one of the most important moves we will make in 2026. That shift is what unlocks institutional yield, because institutions need stable settlement, not volatile collateral. The infrastructure stablecoins provide is not optional for cause coins. It is the foundation. The entire mechanism only works if there is a stable, programmable, dollar-equivalent asset sitting underneath it. Stablecoins are not the revolution. They are the foundation the revolution is built on.

When Governments Write the Code

Everything I just described, the private stablecoins, the bank deposit tokens, the state-issued tokens, shares one characteristic. They are built by entities that exist within a market. They compete for users. They can fail, and if they fail, people can move to alternatives. The market self-corrects, sometimes painfully, but it self-corrects.

Central bank digital currencies are different.

A CBDC is what you get when a government says: we want the speed and programmability of stablecoins, but we want to issue it ourselves, control it ourselves, and make it the default currency for our citizens. Same bridge, same river, but the government is the architect, the builder, the toll collector, and the traffic cop.

China leads the world in this. The digital yuan, or e-CNY, has opened more than 325 million individual wallets and processed cumulative transactions exceeding 7.3 trillion yuan, more than a trillion dollars. It operates across 25 cities. It is integrated into government welfare payments, tax collection, and public services. The European Central Bank has completed its preparation phase for a digital euro and, assuming EU legislation passes in 2026, plans to pilot the system in 2027 with a full launch possible by 2029. The estimated cost to build the digital euro is 1.3 billion euros. After launch, it will cost 320 million euros a year to maintain.

But the track record outside China is mixed at best. The Bahamas launched the Sand Dollar in 2020 as the world's first CBDC. Adoption has been minimal. Nigeria launched the eNaira in 2021 and tried to force adoption by restricting cash withdrawals. Citizens responded with protests. Canada studied a retail CBDC for years before concluding in 2025 that no retail CBDC was justified. Australia reached the same conclusion. The pattern is clear: governments want CBDCs. Citizens, by and large, do not.

The numbers do not capture what this actually feels like on the ground. In Shenzhen, one of China's e-CNY pilot cities, a street vendor named Wei was profiled by the South China Morning Post in 2023 after his district required e-CNY for transit payments. Wei sold noodles from a cart near a metro station. He adopted the digital yuan because his customers needed it for their commute and started paying him with it. The convenience was real. Instant settlement. No cash handling. No counterfeit bills. But so was the visibility. Every bowl of noodles Wei sold was now logged in a system controlled by the People's Bank of China. His daily revenue, his peak hours, his slow days, all of it visible to an institution that had never previously had reason to look at a noodle cart's finances. Wei told the reporter he did not mind. He had nothing to hide. But that is the point. The question is not whether

Wei minds today. The question is what happens when someone in Wei's position does have something to hide, and the infrastructure to see it already exists.

Here is my take on CBDCs, and I want to be patient about this because the nuance matters.

CBDCs are where stablecoins go bad. The only people who want them are governments.

That is a strong statement, so let me unpack it. The value proposition of a stablecoin is that it gives you the speed and programmability of crypto with the stability of the dollar. A CBDC gives you the same speed and programmability, but it also gives the issuing government complete visibility into every transaction you make. Where you spend money. When you spend it. How much. Who you send it to. A government with a CBDC does not need to subpoena your bank records. Your bank records are the government's records. They are the same system.

And programmable money can be programmed in both directions. The same technology that lets you set up an automatic donation to a food bank every time your portfolio hits a new high also lets a government put expiration dates on stimulus payments, restrict what categories of goods you can buy, or freeze your funds instantly without a court order. The ECB's own framework includes mandatory acceptance provisions and holding limits. When the infrastructure for total financial surveillance exists, the policy question is not whether it will be used, but by whom and for what.

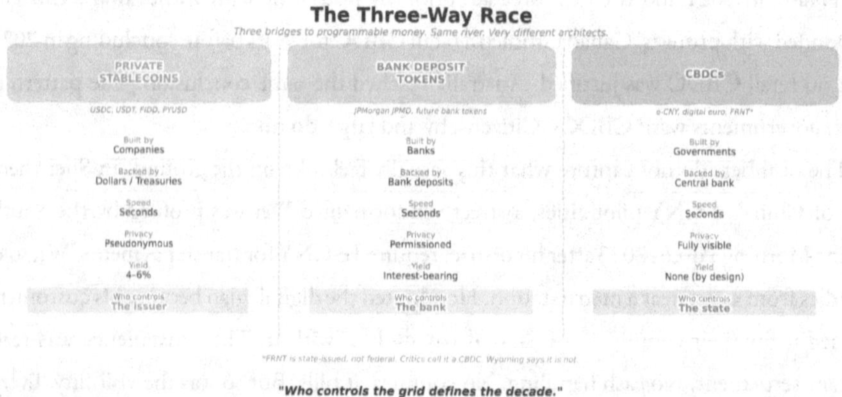

Figure 6.4: The Three-Way Race

Now, I do not think the answer is to panic about CBDCs or pretend they are all dystopian. Some of the design choices are reasonable. Holding limits prevent bank runs. Offline functionality serves people without reliable internet. And governments have legitimate reasons to want faster, cheaper payment infrastructure.

But privacy matters. And this is where the conversation gets interesting rather than just scary.

Privacy-focused blockchains exist as a layer specifically designed for day-to-day transactions where people do not want or need the government watching every coffee purchase. You can still require KYC to get into the network. You verify your identity at the door. But once you are inside, your individual transactions are private. This is not about enabling crime. It is about maintaining a basic expectation that existed for centuries with physical cash and preserving it in a digital world.

Some people have pointed out that USDC on a public blockchain is functionally a CBDC in all but name, because Circle already complies with government regulations and the blockchain is transparent. That is partly true, and it is exactly why privacy layers matter. The technology exists to have both compliance and privacy.

The question underneath the CBDC debate is not about technology. It is about whether programmable money will be used to open access or to tighten control. Whether the new infrastructure replaces the old gatekeepers or gives them more powerful tools.

Private stablecoins say the market should control it. Deposit tokens say banks should control it. CBDCs say the state should control it. Each answer leads to a fundamentally different financial system. I have a strong opinion on this one, and I know it will not be popular with everyone. I do not think any government should have the ability to see and control every coffee purchase its citizens make. I say that as someone who builds on transparent blockchains. Transparency for institutions is different from surveillance of and control over individuals. The same way I can audit EAT's smart contract, see who's making transactions, but I don't dictate who's using it based on my preferences.

Stablecoins proved that dollars can live on the internet. Deposit tokens proved that banks can use the same rails. CBDCs proved that governments want in. But all of these are just the money layer. They are the settlement medium, the thing that moves.

The real revolution is what happens when that programmable money starts interacting with open protocols that anyone can build on. When the stablecoin you hold in your wallet can be deposited into a lending protocol that sets its own interest rates through supply and demand, with no bank in the middle. When your deposit token can be routed through a smart contract that executes a trade, settles the payment, and updates the ledger in a single atomic transaction. When the dollar itself becomes a building block that developers can snap into applications the way they snap together APIs today.

That world has a name. It is called decentralized finance, and it was the first working prototype of what programmable money can actually do. It worked. It also broke in spectacular ways. Both of those lessons are essential to understanding where this is going.

Chapter 7

DeFi: The First Working Prototype

The first time I collateralized an asset on Aave, I sat there for a minute and just stared at the screen.

I had deposited about $100,000 in ETH into the protocol. Within seconds, the interface showed me that I could borrow up to $70,000 or $80,000 in USDC against it. No application. No credit check. No loan officer asking for three years of tax returns and two forms of ID. No two-week waiting period while someone in a back office reviews my file. No phone calls. No fax machines. No notary.

Just a wallet, a smart contract, and a couple of button clicks.

I want you to think about how most people experience borrowing money. Most people have never taken out a loan other than a credit card, a car note, or a mortgage. And those things are not easy. A mortgage involves months of paperwork, income verification, appraisal fees, title searches, and closing costs that somehow always manage to be higher than anyone quoted you. A car loan requires a dealership finance office that feels specifically designed to confuse you. Even a credit card application involves a hard pull on your credit score and a week of waiting.

On Aave, I deposited collateral and received a loan in the time it takes to send a text message. The smart contract evaluated my collateral, calculated the loan-to-value ratio, and made the funds available. No human being was involved in the decision. The code ran. The money appeared. And if my collateral dropped below the required threshold, the protocol would automatically liquidate enough of my position to keep the system solvent.

No collections agency. No legal proceedings. No ambiguity. The rules were in the code, visible to anyone who wanted to read them.

That moment was when DeFi stopped being an abstraction for me and became something I could feel. I was borrowing money from a protocol, not a bank. And the protocol did not care who I was, where I lived, what my credit score looked like, or whether I had a relationship with a branch manager. It cared about one thing: whether I had sufficient collateral. That was it. That was the entire underwriting process.

The loan was also transparent in a way that bank loans never are. I could see the interest rate adjusting in real time, based on how much total capital was in the lending pool versus how much was being borrowed. I could see every other deposit and every other loan on the protocol, because the blockchain is public. Nobody was hiding a subprime tranche inside a synthetic CDO and hoping nobody would notice. The whole system was open. If something was wrong, you could find it. If the math worked, you could verify it yourself.

I got into DeFi in 2019. Staking, yield farming, lending, all of it. I was a DeFi degen for two years. And it was glorious until it was not. But before I tell you what went wrong, and things went very wrong, I need to tell you what DeFi actually is and why it matters even after the wreckage.

DeFi stands for decentralized finance, but the name undersells what it actually represents. DeFi is the reconstruction of the entire financial services industry as open-source software running on public blockchains.

Think about what a bank does. It takes deposits. It makes loans. It facilitates exchanges between currencies. It offers savings accounts with interest. It creates derivative products for hedging risk. Now imagine that every single one of those functions was replaced by a piece of code that anyone could inspect, anyone could use, and nobody could shut down. That is DeFi. Not one product. An entire parallel financial system, built from scratch, in about five years.

The traditional financial system is a stack of intermediaries. When you deposit money in a savings account, the bank lends that money to someone else and pays you a sliver of the interest. When you trade stocks, a broker routes your order through a market maker who routes it to an exchange. When you send money overseas, your bank talks to a correspondent bank that talks to the recipient's bank, and each one takes a cut. Every layer is a business that employs people, occupies buildings, and charges fees.

DeFi replaces those layers with smart contracts. The code does what the intermediaries used to do, but faster, cheaper, and without asking permission. A lending protocol like Aave or Compound pools deposits from thousands of lenders, algorithmically sets interest rates based on supply and demand, and automatically liquidates undercollateralized positions. A decentralized exchange like Uniswap lets anyone trade any token for any other token, 24 hours a day, 365 days a year, using a mathematical formula instead of an order book. A derivatives platform like Synthetix creates synthetic assets that track the price of anything from gold to Tesla stock, using collateral pools and price feeds rather than investment banks.

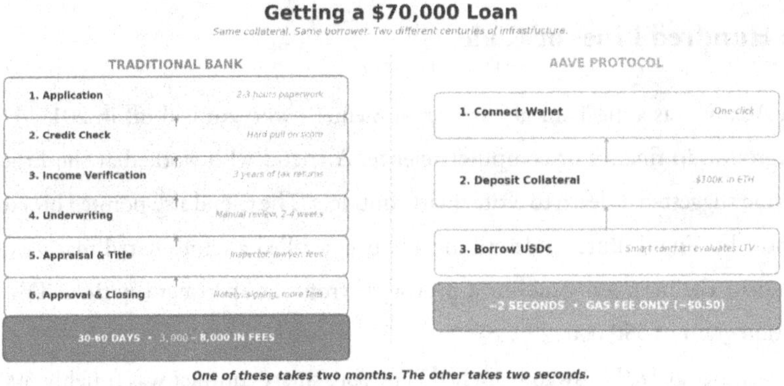

Figure 7.1: Bank vs. Aave

None of these protocols have headquarters. None of them have CEOs, technically. None of them close for holidays. And none of them can deny you service based on your nationality, net worth, or political beliefs. The code runs for everyone or it runs for no one.

The numbers tell you this is not a science experiment. Total value locked across DeFi protocols hit $237 billion in the third quarter of 2025, surpassing the previous all-time high from the 2021 bull market. That is more money sitting in smart contracts than the GDP of Portugal. The top protocols, Aave, Lido, EigenLayer, and Uniswap, each hold more assets than many regional banks. And unlike traditional financial institutions, every dollar, every transaction, every interest rate adjustment is visible on a public ledger in real time.

The question is no longer whether DeFi works. The question, which the rest of this chapter answers, is what happens when it does.

Because here is the part that most coverage of DeFi misses. The people using DeFi today are mostly crypto-native. They are traders, developers, and early adopters who are comfortable with wallets and gas fees and the general chaos of an emerging ecosystem. But the infrastructure being built does not require that sophistication forever. The trajectory is clear. Every year, the interfaces get simpler, the fees get lower, and the barriers to entry shrink. The pattern is identical to the early internet: ugly, confusing, and technically demanding in 1995, invisible and ubiquitous by 2010. DeFi in 2026 is roughly where the internet was in 2000. The infrastructure is proven. The products are functional. The mainstream moment is approaching but has not fully arrived.

Three Hundred Lines of Code

Hayden Adams was a mechanical engineer at Siemens who got laid off in 2017. He had no background in finance or computer science. A friend who worked at the Ethereum Foundation suggested he learn to write smart contracts. The friend also pointed him toward a blog post by Vitalik Buterin describing a concept called an automated market maker. Adams spent the next year building a prototype from his apartment with an Ethereum Foundation grant of $50,000.

In November 2018, Uniswap launched. The core smart contract was roughly 300 lines of code.

To understand why that matters, you need to understand what Uniswap replaced. Traditional exchanges, whether the New York Stock Exchange or Coinbase, use order books. Buyers post the price they are willing to pay. Sellers post the price they are willing to accept. A matching engine connects them. This requires massive infrastructure, regulatory licenses, and teams of engineers maintaining the system around the clock.

Uniswap threw all of that out. Instead of matching buyers and sellers, it uses liquidity pools. Anyone can deposit a pair of tokens into a pool and earn fees from every trade that uses that pool. The price of each token is determined by a simple mathematical formula: x times y equals k. As traders buy one token, its supply in the pool decreases and its price goes up. As they sell, the supply increases and the price goes down. No order book. No matching engine. No market makers in the traditional sense. Just math.

The elegance of the model is that it turns every depositor into a market maker. In traditional finance, market making is a privilege reserved for firms with massive balance sheets, direct exchange connections, and teams of quantitative traders. On Uniswap, anyone with two tokens and a wallet can provide liquidity. The protocol handles everything else. It calculates the price. It executes the swap. It distributes fees to liquidity providers proportionally. The complexity that justified an entire industry of intermediaries was reduced to a formula that fits on an index card.

A laid-off engineer replaced the infrastructure of centralized exchanges with a formula and 300 lines of code. Today, Uniswap handles daily trading volumes that regularly surpass Coinbase. Its cumulative trading volume is in the trillions. And on February 11, 2026, BlackRock listed its $2.2 billion tokenized Treasury fund, BUIDL, on Uniswap through a partnership with Securitize. The world's largest asset manager chose a protocol built by an unemployed 24-year-old in his apartment to trade U.S. government debt. As Hayden Adams put it in the announcement, the goal is to make exchanging value cheaper, faster, and more accessible. BlackRock purchased UNI governance tokens as part of the deal. The token surged 25% on the news.

The distance between a 300-line smart contract and BlackRock trading Treasury bonds on it was seven years.

The Plumbing Nobody Talks About

If you understand DeFi, then there is a question you should be asking: how does any of this know what prices to use?

A lending protocol needs to know the value of your collateral in real time. A decentralized exchange needs price references. A derivatives platform needs them even more critically. Stablecoins depend on them to maintain their peg. Here is the problem. Blockchains do not know anything about the outside world. A smart contract can see what happens on its own chain, but it cannot call an API. It cannot check a stock ticker. It cannot Google the price of Ethereum. This is called the oracle problem, and for years it was the reason you could not have decentralized finance. Imagine what happens without a reliable oracle. You deposit $100,000 in ETH as collateral on a lending protocol. If the protocol uses a single exchange as its price source, a whale could manipulate the price on that one exchange, trigger false liquidations, and profit from the chaos. This is not theoretical. It happened repeatedly in the early days. Protocols that relied on thin, manipulable price sources got exploited. Millions were drained because the oracle was the weakest link.

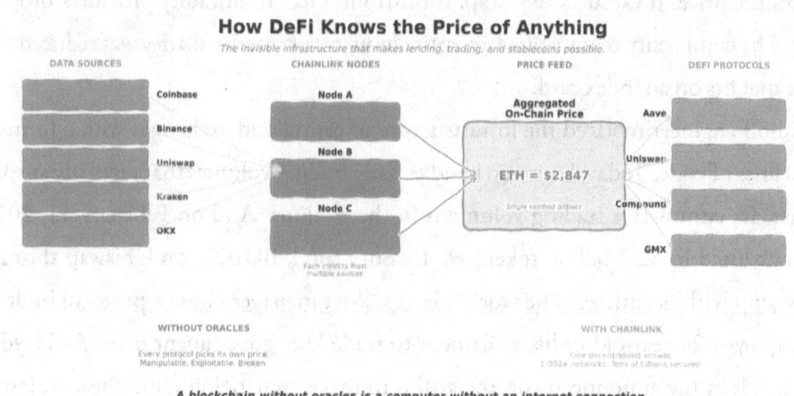

Figure 7.2: The Oracle Problem

Chainlink solved it. Chainlink is a network of independent node operators who collect price data from dozens of sources, aggregate it through multiple layers of validation, and publish the result onchain as a price feed that any smart contract can read. The system uses economic incentives: node operators stake collateral and get paid for accurate data. They lose money if they submit bad data. The architecture mirrors the blockchain itself. No single point of failure. No single source of truth. A decentralized consensus on what real-world data says. Chainlink's price feeds now secure tens of billions of dollars across hundreds of DeFi applications, including Aave, Compound, and GMX. The best way I can describe Chainlink's importance is this: a blockchain without oracles is a computer without an internet connection. It can compute, but it cannot know. And if it cannot know the price of things, it cannot do finance.

The other piece of invisible infrastructure is bridges: protocols that move value between blockchains. If you want to move ETH from Ethereum to an application on Base or Arbitrum, a bridge handles the transfer, sometimes through wrapped tokens that represent an asset from one chain living on another. Bridges are essential, but they are also attack surfaces. Every major bridge holds enormous pools of locked value, and every pool is a target. The bridge hacks that have drained hundreds of millions from protocols like Ronin and Wormhole are not failures of the blockchains on either end. They are failures at the connection point. I will come back to this in Chapter 14, because I have personal experience with what it feels like to watch a bridge transaction go wrong in real time.

The plumbing is not glamorous. Nobody builds a brand around oracle infrastructure or bridge security. But take the oracles away and every price feed in DeFi goes dark. Take the bridges away and every blockchain becomes an island. The protocols that survived the crashes and the exploits are the ones that invested in this infrastructure when nobody was paying attention. That is always where the value accrues. Not in the application. In the pipes underneath it.

The Mania and the Wreckage

In the summer of 2021, a 26-year-old network engineer I will call Tyler had turned $18,000 into $340,000 in eight months yield farming across Polygon and BSC. He had never made more than $62,000 in a year at his day job. He had a spreadsheet tracking seventeen different pools. He checked it before bed and before coffee. His girlfriend told him he talked about APYs in his sleep. He was not stupid. He was educated, technical, and doing real research on the protocols he was depositing into. What he was not doing was accounting for the possibility that the entire category could contract simultaneously. By February 2022, his $340,000 was $4,200. He did not get rugged. He did not get hacked. The pools simply dried up, the token prices collapsed, and the yields that had been printing money turned into yield on nothing. He went back to his engineering job. He still checks the spreadsheet sometimes. The seventeen pools are mostly dead.

Tyler is a composite, but the numbers are real. I have met dozens of Tylers. The pattern is the same every time. Smart person, real research, real gains, and then the music stops and the gains were always denominated in tokens that only had value while the music played.

I told you I was a DeFi degen for two years. Here is what that looked like.

In 2020 and 2021, DeFi experienced what the industry calls DeFi Summer, a period of explosive growth where total value locked in DeFi protocols went from under a billion dollars to over $100 billion. Yields were insane. Protocols were offering 100%, 500%, sometimes 2,000% annual returns on deposited assets. I chased those yields. Everyone chased those yields. It felt like free money, and for a while, it was.

The poster child for the mania was a protocol called Olympus DAO. At its peak, Olympus was advertising yields of 1,000% to 2,000% APY. Those numbers were not typos. You could stake tokens in the protocol and watch your balance double in months. The community was evangelistic. The memes were relentless. The vibe was that a new financial model had been invented and everyone who didn't participate was going to be left behind.

I did not understand the underlying mechanics until it was too late. What Olympus and protocols like it were actually doing was printing tokens. The yield was coming from token emissions, newly minted tokens distributed to stakers, which diluted every existing holder. It was, in essence, exactly what central banks do: inflate the supply to create the appearance of returns. The difference was that central banks do it slowly enough that most people don't notice. DeFi protocols did it fast enough that the math caught up in months instead of decades.

The whole thing had a cult-like quality to it. Olympus had a catchphrase: (3,3), which was game theory shorthand for the idea that if everyone stakes and nobody sells, everyone wins. The flaw in this logic is obvious in hindsight: it only works if you assume an endless inflow of new money. The moment new deposits slow down, the emissions dilute existing holders, the price drops, and the yield that was supposed to compensate you for the risk evaporates. It was a coordination game that worked right up until it didn't. The same pattern, with minor variations, played out across dozens of protocols.

Now we know better. Even 20% annual yield on a DeFi protocol should raise questions about where the money is coming from. The best yields you can find in DeFi today, before you start using leverage or looping strategies, hover around 10% to 13%. Ethena, which generates yield through a delta-neutral strategy involving staked ETH and perpetual futures funding rates, is one of the more innovative models, but it still carries meaningful risk. Its synthetic dollar, USDe, has grown to become the third-largest stablecoin, but it faced a serious test in late 2025 when a depeg event linked to exchange incentive campaigns triggered cascading liquidations. Ethena is what I would call the most stable unstable coin. The yield is real, but the risk is real too.

And then there was Terra Luna.

Terra was an algorithmic stablecoin ecosystem. Its stablecoin, UST, was supposed to maintain a $1 peg through a mint-and-burn mechanism tied to its sister token, Luna. There was no collateral backing the peg. No reserve of dollars or Treasury bills. Just an algorithm and a token. The system worked as long as people believed it would work. Anchor Protocol, built on Terra, offered a fixed 20% yield on UST deposits. Billions poured in.

In May 2022, a confluence of market pressure and what appears to have been a targeted attack broke the peg. UST fell below $1. The algorithm minted Luna to try to restore the peg, which crashed Luna's price, which eroded confidence in UST, which caused more selling, which required more Luna minting. It was a death spiral. In the space of a few days, roughly $40 billion in value was destroyed. It was, in energy terms, a system that had manufactured the appearance of energy without any real energy input. When the market tested it, there was nothing there.

I know a ton of people, reputable people, people who believed in blockchain and were actively building in blockchain, who also believed in the Terra ecosystem. They held a significant portion of their assets in Luna and UST. Mike Novogratz, the CEO of Galaxy Digital, famously had a Luna tattoo. When the collapse came, the losses were devastating. And for many of those people, that was it. That was their exit from crypto. They were not scammers. They were not fools. They were believers who collided with a system that had no foundation. I do not know if most of them are back.

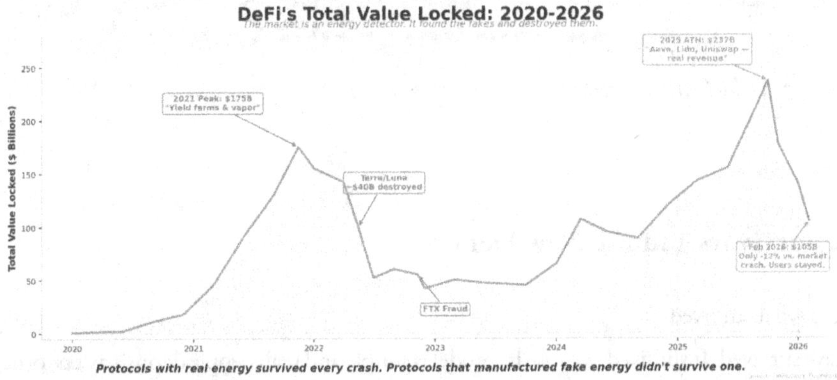

Figure 7.3: DeFi TVL Timeline

The contagion was immediate. DeFi's total value locked plummeted from $142 billion to $52 billion between April and June of 2022. Celsius, a major centralized lending platform, froze withdrawals weeks later and eventually filed for bankruptcy. Three Arrows Capital, one of the largest crypto hedge funds, collapsed. The damage cascaded across the entire ecosystem, wiping out lending platforms, bridges, and funds that had any exposure to the implosion. It was, at the time, the worst crisis in crypto history. And it was followed six months later by the FTX fraud, which was an entirely different category of failure but landed on an industry already reeling.

Terra Luna was DeFi's clearest lesson, and it maps directly onto the energy thesis that runs through this book. Protocols backed by real economic energy, real collateral, real revenue, real users paying for real services, survived. Protocols that manufactured fake energy, that printed tokens to simulate yield, that used algorithmic mechanisms as a substitute for actual reserves, collapsed. The market is an energy detector. It found the fakes and destroyed them.

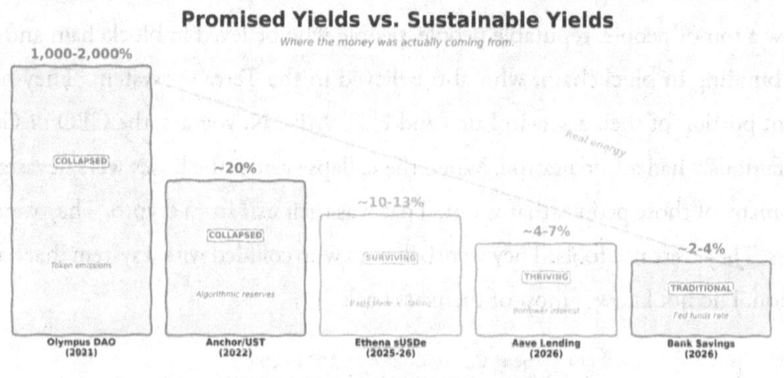

Figure 7.4: Yield Reality Check

The Survivors and the New DeFi

Here is what survived.

Aave survived. It survived because its model is simple and real: people deposit assets, other people borrow those assets and pay interest, and the protocol takes a cut. The interest rates are set by supply and demand, not by governance votes or token emissions. The collateral is real. The liquidation mechanism works. Aave now holds approximately $27 billion in total value locked across over twenty blockchain networks and generated $178 million in fees in a single recent quarter. It survived multiple market crashes, including the chaos of early 2026, because the underlying economic engine was sound.

Uniswap survived. The automated market maker model turned out to be one of the most durable innovations in financial technology. Uniswap did not need to promise yields. It earned fees from every trade. The protocol's V4 upgrade introduced customizable liquidity pools with hooks that allow developers to build compliance features, which is exactly what enabled the BlackRock BUIDL integration. Hayden Adams built a tool. The tool worked. The tool got better. Now institutions use it.

Lido survived. Its liquid staking protocol, which lets users stake ETH and receive a tradable token representing their staked position, holds roughly $27.5 billion in TVL. It solved a real problem: how to earn staking yield without locking your assets.

Chainlink survived. The oracle infrastructure became more essential, not less, as DeFi matured. Aave uses Chainlink price feeds to value collateral. Compound uses them. GMX uses them. The entire DeFi ecosystem runs on oracle data, and Chainlink provides the majority of it.

What is happening now in DeFi looks nothing like the chaos of 2020 and 2021. The speculative frenzy has been replaced by something quieter and, I would argue, far more important. DeFi is becoming institutional. It is becoming compartmentalized. And the product that is winning is the vault.

A vault, in DeFi terms, is a smart contract that automates a yield strategy. Instead of asking users to understand complex multi-step processes, staking here, lending there, compounding rewards somewhere else, a vault packages everything into a single deposit. You put your money in. The vault executes the strategy. You earn yield. It is DeFi made simple enough for your parents.

Every major exchange now offers some form of yield product. Ethena's staked USDe offers yield from its basis trading strategy. Pendle lets you separate and trade the yield component of any asset. Lido handles ETH staking in a single transaction. EigenLayer introduced restaking, letting users repurpose already-staked ETH to secure additional networks simultaneously, earning multiple yield streams from a single deposit. The complexity is still there under the hood, but the user-facing product has been reduced to something that looks remarkably like a savings account. A better savings account, one that is transparent, permissionless, and runs on code you can audit, but a savings account nonetheless.

The institutional entrance is accelerating. In early February 2026, Ripple's institutional brokerage platform integrated Hyperliquid, a decentralized perpetual futures exchange, marking the first direct connection between Wall Street and DeFi derivatives markets. Hyperliquid's open interest now exceeds $5 billion with monthly trading volumes of $200 billion. It surpassed Coinbase in total 2025 trading volume. This is not a toy. This is infrastructure that institutions are actively routing capital through.

And then there is the development that I think will define the next phase. Stani Kulechov, the founder of Aave, published a thesis in early 2026 called Funding Abundance. In it, he argued that onchain lending should move beyond crypto-native collateral and begin financing real-world abundance assets, specifically solar energy infrastructure. His proposal was that tokenized solar projects, with their predictable cash flows and proven technology, should be accepted as collateral on Aave. A solar developer with $100 million in tokenized project debt could borrow $70 million in stablecoins within minutes, not months, and immediately redeploy into new projects.

Read that again. The founder of the largest DeFi lending protocol is proposing that the protocol finance the energy transition. Not metaphorically. Literally. Tokenized solar panels as collateral. Stablecoin loans against renewable energy infrastructure. A $30 to $50 trillion opportunity, by his estimates, to become the largest financier of the world's transformation into abundant energy.

This is what DeFi looks like when the installation phase ends and the deployment phase begins. The speculation burns off. The survivors get serious. The technology that was tested by billions of dollars in exploits and crashes gets hardened. And then someone looks at it and says: what if we used this to finance solar farms? What if a pension fund could allocate 15% to tokenized solar instead of 3% to illiquid infrastructure funds, because the DeFi layer provides the liquidity that traditional infrastructure investing lacks?

That is not a hypothetical anymore. It is a governance proposal on the largest lending protocol in the world.

DeFi's history is a perfect test case for the energy thesis.

During the installation phase, energy poured into the system indiscriminately. Speculators deposited billions into protocols they did not understand. Yield farmers chased returns that were mathematically impossible to sustain. Algorithmic stablecoins claimed to create stability from nothing. The system was flooded with energy, but much of it was fake, printed tokens masquerading as yield, reflexive mechanisms masquerading as collateral, and narrative masquerading as fundamentals.

The market sorted it. The market always sorts it. Protocols with real energy, real collateral, real revenue, real users, real utility, emerged stronger from every crash. DeFi's total value locked hit $237 billion at its peak in late 2025, an all-time high that surpassed even the 2021 mania. But the composition of that value was fundamentally different. Instead of vapor yields and ponzi tokenomics, the capital was sitting in Aave's lending markets, Lido's staking pools, and Uniswap's trading infrastructure. The money was real. The revenue was real. The energy was real.

Even during the brutal market downturn of early 2026, DeFi's total value locked fell only

12%, from about $120 billion to $105 billion, while the broader crypto market cratered. The drop was driven by falling asset prices, not by users pulling their money out. People were still depositing ETH into DeFi protocols. They were still earning yield. They were still using the infrastructure. The energy was still flowing because the pipes were sound.

In Chapter 3, I argued that money is energy and every phase change in monetary history was an efficiency upgrade. DeFi is the most dramatic efficiency upgrade in the history of financial services. It replaced entire industries of intermediaries with code. It reduced settlement from days to seconds. It made lending available to anyone with collateral, regardless of who they are. It made market making possible for a kid with a laptop and an Ethereum wallet.

Some of that energy was wasted in the installation phase. That is what installation phases do. They burn capital in the process of figuring out what works. What works, we now know, is simple: protocols that are backed by real economic activity, secured by reliable oracle infrastructure, and designed for transparency rather than obscurity.

The survivors are building the deployment phase. Aave is proposing to finance solar energy. Uniswap is trading BlackRock's Treasury fund. Lido is staking billions in ETH. Chainlink is connecting DeFi to real-world data across hundreds of applications. Hyperliquid is processing more derivatives volume than Coinbase. The prototype worked. It broke in predictable ways, and the things that broke taught us what sustainable design looks like. The things that survived are now the infrastructure layer for what comes next.

And here is the piece that connects all of this to the thesis of this book. DeFi proved that financial services can be encoded as software. That money can carry instructions. That lending, trading, and derivatives can run without intermediaries. The implications extend far beyond finance as it currently exists. If you can encode a lending protocol as a smart contract, you can encode a charitable giving mechanism. If you can automatically distribute trading fees to liquidity providers, you can automatically distribute them to hunger relief organizations. If you can build a transparent, permissionless market for trading tokens, you can build a transparent, permissionless market for social impact.

Every innovation in DeFi that survived the installation phase is a building block for what I am going to show you later in this book. What DeFi proved, underneath all the speculation and all the failures, is that open protocols can do the jobs that institutions used to monopolize. Lending without a bank. Trading without an exchange. Insurance without an insurer. Each survivor is a protocol that replaced an institution, not by outcompeting it on the institution's terms, but by making the institution unnecessary. The automated market maker. The oracle infrastructure. The vault architecture. The composability that lets protocols snap together like software APIs. All of it gets repurposed. All of it gets redirected. The question is not whether programmable money works. DeFi answered that. The question is what it gets programmed to do.

What comes next is the institutional stampede. And it has already started.

That's where we're going next.

Chapter 8

THE INSTITUTIONAL STAMPEDE

The week before we flew to Dallas, the World Economic Forum in Davos looked like a different planet.

Larry Fink, the CEO of BlackRock, the largest asset manager on earth, stood on a panel alongside the CEO of Citadel and the president of the European Central Bank and said, out loud, to the room:

> "if we had all investments on a tokenized platform, that you can move from
> a tokenized money market fund to equities and bonds and back and forth,
> we have one common blockchain, we could reduce corruption."
>
> — Larry Fink, CEO Blackrock

He said the movement toward tokenization is necessary. He said we would be reducing fees, we would do more democratization.

This is the same man who, in 2017, called Bitcoin an index of money laundering.

And he was not alone. Davos 2026 had two dedicated sessions on blockchain: one called "Is Tokenization the Future?" and another called "Where Are We on Stablecoins?" In 2025, the only crypto session had been titled "Crypto at a Crossroads," a diplomatic way of saying nobody was sure this thing was real. One year later, the crossroads had been crossed. Brian Armstrong, the CEO of Coinbase, was on stage. Jeremy Allaire from Circle was on stage. Brad Garlinghouse from Ripple was on stage. The Governor of the Central Bank of France was on stage. The CEO of Euroclear, the company that settles trillions in European securities, was on stage. David Sacks, the White House's AI and crypto czar, told the room that banks need to recognize that yield is already a feature of the GENIUS Act, and if there's no deal, they're going to lose on this issue. President Trump, via his administration's messaging, reaffirmed that he wants America to remain the crypto capital of the world.

Nobody at Davos argued against blockchain. The debate was not about whether tokenization will reshape capital markets. It was about how quickly, how safely, and who will control the standards. As one observer put it: the "digital assets are a fringe experiment" frame collapsed at Davos 2026, replaced by "digital assets are the new infrastructure of global finance."

A week later, Martin and I were in Dallas pitching WYDE to potential investors.

These were not crypto people. They knew Bitcoin existed. A couple of them had bought Pepe. One guy knew about Chainlink because someone told him it was something you should buy. At best, they had a Coinbase account and checked it when someone on Twitter said the market was moving. That was the extent of it. They had not read about Davos. They had not heard Fink's speech. They did not know what tokenization meant, what a stablecoin was, or why the European Central Bank president had been sitting on a blockchain panel.

We were talking about WYDE. About cause coins. About the opportunity to create a new market that supports nonprofits. Specifically, that we were taking nonprofits public for the first time. Giving the $3.7 trillion dollar nonprofit sector (we mapped in Chapter 2) access to market mechanisms that had only ever been available to for-profit companies. It had enormous potential. And for most of that meeting, nobody in the room understood what it meant.

Two things landed. First: WYDE is doing for nonprofits what the NYSE does for stocks. That analogy cut through everything. Their eyes changed. They could see it. Not the mechanics, not the smart contracts, not the fee routing, but the shape of the opportunity. A new exchange for a massive sector that has never had one.

Second: I told them that the week prior, at the World Economic Forum, the biggest leaders in the world, the people who manage the money, who run the governments, who set the standards, were all talking about blockchain and Ethereum and stablecoins alongside AI. That the path is now clear. That whoever doesn't see it is not paying attention. And I watched the room shift. Not because they suddenly understood the technology. Because they understood the signal. If Larry Fink is saying this, if the White House is saying this, if the ECB is in the room, then something has changed, and the question is no longer whether to pay attention but how fast you can get positioned.

That gap, between Davos and Dallas, between the people steering the ship and the people standing on the dock watching it leave, is the story of this chapter. The institutions have entered. They are not coming. They are here. And most people have no idea what that means.

The Convert

I want to trace one person's journey because it tells the whole story.

In October 2017, Larry Fink went on CNBC and called Bitcoin an index of money laundering. He compared the crypto boom to the Dutch tulip craze of the 1600s. He was dismissive, confident, and clear. BlackRock had no interest.

In 2018, he said his clients weren't looking to buy crypto. He downplayed BlackRock's engagement with the sector entirely.

In 2020, his tone shifted to cautious neutrality. He acknowledged Bitcoin's potential but raised concerns about volatility and regulation. He wasn't buying, but he had stopped laughing.

In 2022, he started talking about diversification. He hired Robbie Mitchnick from Ripple to lead BlackRock's digital asset strategy. Things were moving behind the scenes.

In June 2023, BlackRock filed for a spot Bitcoin ETF. The company that manages more money than any entity in human history decided that Bitcoin deserved a regulated investment product. Fink told Fox Business that BlackRock was trying to democratize crypto.

In January 2024, the SEC approved the iShares Bitcoin Trust, ticker IBIT. Within its first year, IBIT accumulated over $97 billion in assets under management. It reached $100 billion faster than any ETF in history. Faster than the S&P 500. Faster than gold. Faster than anything Vanguard or Fidelity or anyone else had ever built. It became BlackRock's most profitable ETF, generating $244.5 million in annual revenue.

At the New York Times DealBook Summit in December 2025, Fink publicly admitted he had been wrong. When the host reminded him that he had once called crypto an index of money laundering, Fink interrupted to add: and thieves. Then he smiled and said his thought process had evolved. He called Bitcoin an asset of fear, meaning investors buy it when they fear inflation, instability, or the weakening of fiat currencies. He called it digital gold. He said sovereign wealth funds were looking to allocate 2 to 5 percent of their portfolios to Bitcoin.

And then came Davos 2026, where Fink stood in front of the global elite and said the entire financial system should move onto one common blockchain.

That is a nine-year arc from dismissal to all-in. From money laundering index to the future of global finance. And it did not happen because Larry Fink had a personal revelation about the beauty of decentralization. It happened because his clients demanded it. Because the data supported it. Because IBIT's growth curve was undeniable. Because the technology matured, the regulation arrived, and the competitive pressure from every other major asset manager filing their own ETFs made sitting on the sidelines untenable.

Here's my take on what the Fink arc really shows. It is not a story about one man changing his mind. It is a story about institutional capital following institutional logic. And institutional logic, once it moves, does not reverse. BlackRock did not invest billions in blockchain infrastructure because it seemed interesting. It invested because the risk calculus flipped. The risk of not participating became greater than the risk of participating. That is the signal that deployment has begun. When the largest, most conservative allocators of capital on earth conclude that the technology is real, the debate is over. The only question is pace.

Figure 8.1: The Fink Arc

The Wall Street You Know Is Building on Blockchain

As I described in Chapter 5, the list of institutions building blockchain infrastructure is staggering. Stripe, Google, Visa, Deutsche Bank, Mastercard, CME Group, Robinhood,

BlackRock. These are not crypto companies. They are the companies that already run global finance, and they are building their next generation of infrastructure on the same layer that powers EAT. But knowing the names is not the same as understanding the scale of what is happening underneath.

Tokenization means taking a traditional financial asset, a Treasury bond, a share of real estate, a piece of private credit, and representing it as a digital token on a blockchain. The token carries the same economic rights as the original asset, but it can settle in seconds instead of days, trade 24 hours a day, and be fractionalized so that someone with $50 can own a piece of something that previously required a $100,000 minimum. On-chain tokenized real-world assets reached $24 to $33 billion in 2025, a 400 percent increase from 2022. McKinsey projects the market could reach $2 to $4 trillion by 2030. Private credit is the largest segment at over 60 percent of non-stablecoin tokenized assets. US Treasuries and money market funds grew 539 percent from January 2024 to April 2025.

At the center of it all is BlackRock's BUIDL fund, a tokenized Treasury fund on Ethereum that launched in March 2024 with $40 million and now holds roughly $2.9 billion, commanding 45 percent of the entire tokenized Treasury market. It lives on eight different blockchains. BlackRock's BUIDL fund listing on Uniswap, described in Chapter 5, was the moment these two worlds became one. BlackRock published research in January 2026 showing that Ethereum underpins more than 65 percent of all tokenized assets globally, treating it not as a speculative asset but as financial infrastructure comparable to the settlement rails that the current system runs on.

The irony is thick enough to cut. The technology was built to displace institutions. The cypherpunks, the early Bitcoiners, the Ethereum developers, they were building systems specifically designed to eliminate the need for banks and asset managers and centralized intermediaries. And now the banks and asset managers and centralized intermediaries are the ones building on it the hardest. They looked at the thing that was supposed to replace them and said: actually, we can use this. I have mixed feelings about this, and I will be honest about it. But here is what I have learned from building in this space: purity is a luxury that infrastructure cannot afford. The rails do not care who runs on them. Uniswap's smart contracts execute the same way whether the counterparty is a kid in Lagos or BlackRock's treasury desk. The code does not check your AUM before processing the trade. That is the feature.

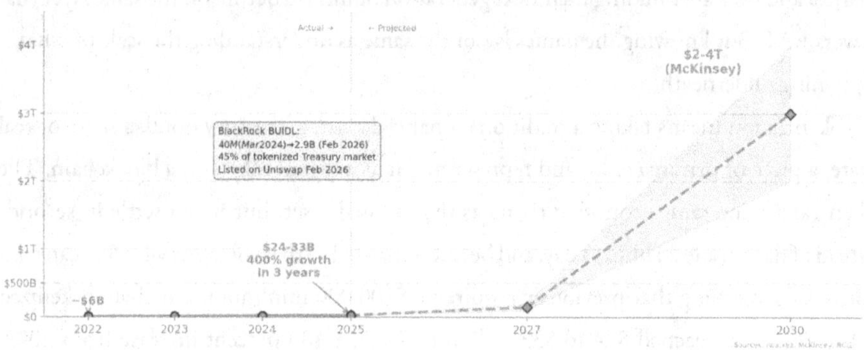

Figure 8.2: From Experiment to Infrastructure

I have a friend I will call Nick who bought his first Bitcoin in late 2017. Near the peak. Somewhere around $17,000. He was not a trader. He was not in tech. He had read something, believed it, and put money in. Then the crash happened. Bitcoin dropped to $3,000. Everyone in his life who had an opinion about crypto felt entitled to share it. His brother called it gambling. A coworker sent him a screenshot of the price chart with a laughing emoji. Nick told me he was so gutted that he could not look at his portfolio for all of 2018. He just left it. Did not sell. Did not buy more. Could not bring himself to open the app. He held through the 2020 recovery. Held through the 2021 run. Held through the 2022 crash after FTX. And then in 2024, BlackRock filed for a Bitcoin ETF. Fidelity launched crypto products. Bitcoin hit $120,000. The same institutions that Nick's brother worked at, the ones whose analysts had called Bitcoin a scam, were now building infrastructure to sell it to their clients. I asked Nick

how he felt. He did not say vindicated. He said relieved. There is a difference. Vindication is about being right. Relief is about no longer being alone. For six years, Nick had held a position that the most powerful institutions in finance told him was foolish. When those same institutions reversed course, Nick did not need their permission. He already knew. But the relief of not being the only one who could see it was real.

Digital Asset Treasuries: A New Kind of Company

In 2021, fewer than ten publicly traded companies held Bitcoin on their balance sheet. By September 2025, more than 200 companies had adopted digital asset treasury strategies, collectively holding over $115 billion in crypto assets. The sector's market capitalization tripled in a single year, from $40 billion to roughly $150 billion.

These are called DATs, Digital Asset Treasury companies, and most people have never heard of them. But they represent one of the most significant structural changes in corporate finance in a generation.

A DAT is a publicly traded company that holds cryptocurrency as a core balance-sheet asset, not as a speculative side bet but as the central treasury strategy. The model was pioneered by Michael Saylor at Strategy, formerly MicroStrategy, starting in 2020. Saylor did not merely buy Bitcoin. He converted an enterprise software company into a Bitcoin treasury operation. As of early 2026, Strategy holds over 714,000 BTC, roughly 3.4 percent of all Bitcoin that will ever exist, acquired at a total cost of about $33 billion. When Saylor says Bitcoin is digital energy, he is not theorizing. He is betting the company.

The mechanics work like this. DATs raise capital through equity offerings, convertible notes, and other financial instruments. They deploy that capital almost exclusively into digital assets. When the stock trades at a premium to the net asset value of its crypto holdings, which it often does during bull markets, each dollar raised through equity dilutes shareholders less than the value added through asset purchases. This creates a virtuous cycle that can generate enormous returns. Strategy's stock has outperformed Bitcoin itself over multiple periods because of this leverage effect.

The convertible note structure is the key financial innovation. Strategy has used convertible debt extensively, issuing billions in notes that give bondholders the option to convert to equity if the stock rises. The debt funds Bitcoin purchases. The Bitcoin purchases increase the net asset value. The higher NAV supports a higher stock price. The higher stock price makes the conversion option more valuable. It is a leverage loop that works beautifully in a rising market, and the financial engineering is genuinely sophisticated. These are not retail speculators throwing money at a meme. These are institutional-grade capital structures designed by Wall Street's best minds.

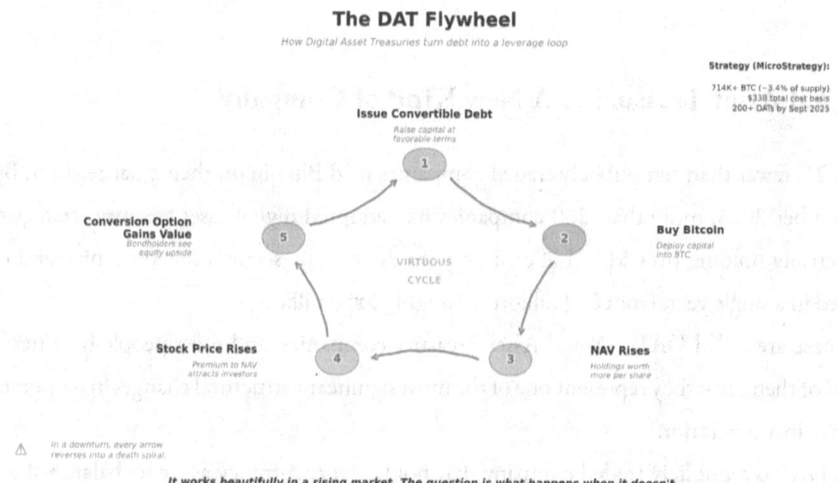

Figure 8.3: *The DAT Flywheel*

But there is a controversy, and it matters.

The regulator's concern is straightforward. Some of these companies effectively launched as SPACs, going public through reverse mergers with the sole purpose of acquiring crypto assets. Twenty One Capital, for example, merged with Cantor Equity Partners, backed by SoftBank and Tether, to create a $3.6 billion Bitcoin vehicle. Companies like this have no meaningful operational revenue. They exist to hold digital assets and issue securities against them. The question regulators are asking is whether these entities should be classified as investment funds rather than operating companies. If they were reclassified, they would face different capital requirements, different reporting obligations, and critically, they could not raise capital through the same convertible note structures that make the model work.

In October 2025, MSCI, the company that manages the most widely tracked equity indexes in the world, proposed excluding DATs from its global indexes. Their argument: companies whose digital asset holdings exceed 50 percent of total assets look more like investment funds than operating businesses. If MSCI had followed through, the consequences would have been severe. JPMorgan estimated that Strategy alone could face $2.8 billion in forced selling from passive funds. Across the entire sector, the projected impact was $10 to $15 billion in outflows.

Saylor fired back. In a public letter co-signed with his CEO, he called the proposal misguided and said it would have profoundly harmful consequences. His argument: Strategy is not a passive fund. It is a technology company that builds on Bitcoin. The company operates a corporate treasury and capital markets business, issuing equity and fixed-income instruments with varying levels of Bitcoin exposure. Investors buy Strategy for its management and innovation capabilities, not merely for Bitcoin price exposure.

Tom Lee's Bitmine made the same argument for Ethereum, holding over $12 billion in ETH and positioning itself as an Ethereum infrastructure company, not a holding vehicle.

In January 2026, MSCI backed down. They announced they would maintain the current index treatment and conduct further research before making any changes. Strategy's stock jumped 6 percent on the news.

Here is what DATs tell us about where the institutional stampede is heading. It is no longer enough for institutions to buy crypto through an ETF or a fund. Companies are restructuring themselves around digital asset ownership. They are using the full toolkit of corporate finance, convertible notes, at-the-market offerings, preferred stock, to accumulate positions that individual investors cannot replicate. For investors who want exposure to crypto without the custody risk, without managing wallets and private keys, DATs offer something that did not exist five years ago: equity-based crypto exposure inside a traditional brokerage account, with management teams actively optimizing the treasury strategy.

The risks are real. Leverage amplifies losses as much as gains. A sustained crypto downturn could push DATs into forced selling, creating cascading pressure on the very assets they hold. The virtuous cycle becomes a vicious one: falling prices reduce NAV, which pushes the stock below the conversion price of outstanding notes, which limits the company's ability to raise new capital, which prevents further accumulation. Strategy's Q4 2025 earnings showed $17.4 billion in unrealized losses. The 42/42 Plan, Saylor's announced target to raise $84 billion through 2027 in equal parts equity and debt, would push the company's holdings above 1.4 million BTC if executed, roughly 6.7 percent of the total supply. At that concentration, Strategy's treasury decisions would move the Bitcoin market itself. Whether that is brilliant or reckless depends entirely on which direction the price goes.

And the MSCI question is not permanently settled. The February 2026 index review will reassess the criteria, and other index providers like FTSE Russell are watching closely. But the structural trend is clear: more than 200 public companies now hold digital assets as core treasury positions, and the number is growing every quarter.

When Nations Buy Bitcoin

The institutional stampede is not limited to corporations and asset managers. It has reached the level of sovereign states.

On March 6, 2025, President Trump signed an executive order establishing the Strategic Bitcoin Reserve. The order directed the Department of the Treasury to hold all Bitcoin forfeited through criminal and civil proceedings as a permanent reserve asset of the United States, rather than auctioning it off as the government had always done before. David Sacks, the White House AI and crypto czar, called it a digital Fort Knox.

The United States government is now the largest known state holder of Bitcoin in the world, with an estimated 328,000 BTC as of early 2026. The executive order also directed the Secretaries of Treasury and Commerce to develop budget-neutral strategies for acquiring additional Bitcoin. Congressman Byron Donalds introduced legislation to codify the executive order into law. Senator Cynthia Lummis reintroduced the BITCOIN Act, which would authorize the Treasury to purchase up to one million BTC over five years, roughly 5 percent of the total supply, mirroring the scope of US gold reserves.

Think about what just happened. The United States government, which spent four years under the previous administration prosecuting crypto companies and treating digital assets as a threat, reversed course entirely and began treating Bitcoin as a strategic national asset in the same category as gold, petroleum, and pharmaceutical stockpiles. The speed of the reversal is almost disorienting. One administration was suing Coinbase. The next was stockpiling Bitcoin. The executive order explicitly calls Bitcoin's security and scarcity "digital gold" and states that there is a strategic advantage to being among the first nations to create a reserve.

The implications ripple outward. If the US treats Bitcoin as a strategic asset, every allied nation's central bank has to at least consider the question. If the US is holding Bitcoin and your sovereign wealth fund is not, you are making an implicit bet that the largest economy in the world is wrong. Some will make that bet. Most, over time, will hedge it. That is how reserve asset adoption works. Gold did not become a global reserve because every country independently decided it was valuable. It became a reserve because enough major economies adopted it that the rest could not afford to ignore it. Bitcoin is following the same adoption curve, just faster.

But the US was not the first mover. El Salvador became the first country to adopt Bitcoin as legal tender in 2021, accumulating roughly 6,200 to 7,500 BTC through a program of daily purchases. The experiment was polarizing. The IMF pressured El Salvador to scale back, and as part of a $1.4 billion loan agreement in early 2025, the country made Bitcoin acceptance voluntary for businesses and wound down its government-operated Chivo wallet. Bitcoin was rescinded as legal tender. But El Salvador kept its Bitcoin. President Bukele continued to frame the holdings as a strategic national asset, publishing a public dashboard that tracks the government's BTC in real time. Whatever you think about the execution, El Salvador proved that a sovereign state could hold Bitcoin as a reserve asset and survive the volatility.

The United Arab Emirates took a different approach entirely. Rather than buying Bitcoin on the open market, the UAE built mining infrastructure. Through Citadel Mining, a company majority-owned by Abu Dhabi's International Holding Company, which is tied to the UAE royal family, the Emirates mined approximately 9,300 BTC. Arkham Intelligence verified the timeline by matching on-chain mining activity with satellite imagery of facility construction on Al Reem Island. The facility was built in six months. This was not an experiment. It was an industrial undertaking. On top of the mining, Abu Dhabi's sovereign wealth fund Mubadala invested $437 million in BlackRock's Bitcoin ETF.

Bhutan's sovereign investment arm, Druk Holding and Investments, has been mining Bitcoin using the country's abundant hydropower since 2019, accumulating over 11,000 BTC, making this tiny Himalayan kingdom one of the largest sovereign Bitcoin holders on earth. The economics are elegant: Bhutan has more hydroelectric capacity than its domestic economy can absorb. The excess energy had no buyer. Now it does. Bitcoin mining converts stranded energy into a globally liquid asset that sits on the national balance sheet. That is the energy thesis made sovereign.

Brazil introduced legislation proposing a Sovereign Strategic Reserve of Bitcoins, with discussion centered on allocating up to 5 percent of the country's $344 billion in reserves. The Czech National Bank became the first European central bank to publicly discuss Bitcoin as a potential reserve asset. Switzerland is collecting signatures for what could become the world's first national referendum on adding Bitcoin to central bank reserves. And Pakistan announced the creation of a government-led Strategic Bitcoin Reserve in 2026.

That is the United States, El Salvador, the UAE, Bhutan, Brazil, the Czech Republic, Switzerland, and Pakistan, all either holding Bitcoin or actively considering it as a sovereign asset. The spectrum of approaches ranges from mining to market purchases to ETF exposure to legislative proposals. The geography spans six continents. The political systems range from absolute monarchies to direct democracies. The only thing they have in common is the conclusion that Bitcoin is a legitimate instrument of national financial strategy.

I keep coming back to this idea: the signal is not any single country's decision. The signal is the convergence. When the United States, a Middle Eastern petrostate, a Himalayan kingdom, and a South American economic power all independently conclude that Bitcoin belongs on their national balance sheet, you are no longer looking at a trend. You are looking at a phase change.

Figure 8.4: The Sovereign Stampede

The Heaviest Form of Financial Energy

Let me connect this to the thesis that runs through the entire book.

In Chapter 3, I argued that money is energy. That every form of value, whether it is a dollar, a Bitcoin, a share of stock, or an hour of human labor, is a manifestation of energy at a different layer of abstraction. The history of money is the history of energy efficiency upgrades, each new system storing and transmitting value with less friction than the last.

Institutional capital is the heaviest form of financial energy. It moves slowly. It requires enormous force to redirect. It is bound by regulation, fiduciary duty, board approval, compliance review, and decades of institutional inertia. When a retail investor buys Bitcoin, the energy is real but small. When BlackRock creates a $97 billion ETF, when Strategy converts its entire balance sheet to Bitcoin, when the United States establishes a strategic reserve, the energy is massive.

And here is the property of heavy energy that matters most: once it enters a system, it does not leave easily. A retail investor can panic-sell in a downturn. An institution cannot. IBIT was one of the only top-25 ETFs by inflows in 2025 that had a negative return, down 9.6 percent. The money kept flowing in while the price was falling. That is not speculation. That is conviction baked into fiduciary mandates, into index inclusion, into treasury strategies that operate on multi-year horizons.

When institutional energy enters a system, it makes the system permanent. That is the real meaning of the stampede. Not just that big players are buying Bitcoin or tokenizing assets. Their presence changes the structural characteristics of the entire ecosystem. Liquidity deepens. Volatility compresses over longer time horizons. Regulatory frameworks solidify because the regulators now have constituents they cannot ignore. Insurance products emerge. Custody solutions mature. Prime brokerage services develop. Each institutional entrant makes the next one's entry easier, which makes the next one after that even easier. It is a gravity well. And by 2026, the gravity has become strong enough that the question of whether institutions will adopt blockchain has become as relevant as asking whether banks will adopt the internet. They already did.

And the institutions are putting their own assets on the blockchain. That is the deeper story. When BlackRock tokenizes Treasuries, when JPMorgan issues programmable deposit tokens, when Fidelity builds institutional-grade digital asset custody for clients who want exposure without touching a private key, when the New York Stock Exchange announces a tokenized securities platform with 24/7 trading and instant settlement, the institutions are not joining the crypto economy. They are merging the traditional economy with the crypto economy. The two systems are becoming one system. And the infrastructure layer they are building on is the same layer that powers DeFi, that powers stablecoins, that powers EAT.

This is why the institutional stampede matters for cause coins, and it is something I think about constantly. Every institution that validates tokenization, every bank that builds on blockchain, every sovereign wealth fund that takes a Bitcoin position, is reinforcing the legitimacy of the underlying infrastructure. They are not endorsing EAT or WYDE specifically. They are endorsing the idea that tokens can represent real value, that smart contracts can enforce real agreements, and that blockchain is trustworthy enough for the most conservative capital on earth. When we walk into a room and say that a cause coin can automatically route trading fees to hunger relief through a smart contract on Base, the credibility of that claim is vastly different in a world where BlackRock's Treasury fund runs on the same technology than it would have been three years ago when the same technology was associated primarily with rug pulls and meme coins.

Institutional validation is the credibility layer. It does not make cause coins possible. The technology does that. But it makes cause coins legible to the mainstream. It translates the opportunity into a language that the investors in that Dallas room, and millions of people like them, can understand.

That is what I tried to explain to those investors in Dallas. That the gap between Davos and their understanding of the market was not a knowledge gap. It was a time gap. They were living in a world where crypto was still a speculative side bet. The institutions had already moved to a world where crypto is infrastructure. The stampede had happened. Most people just hadn't heard the hooves yet.

After the meeting, Martin and I had a problem. The presentation had been at a private golf course club outside Dallas, and a massive storm was bearing down on the city. Our flight home was scheduled for Saturday morning. By Friday afternoon, airlines were canceling everything. We scrambled and managed to squeeze onto the last flight out at 9:30 that night.

We barely made it through TSA. The line was the slowest I have ever seen. Everyone in the airport was trying to get out before the storm shut everything down. We were the last ones on the plane. And the only seats left were the very back row, right up against the toilets. Typically the last place you want to sit. We could not have been happier.

For three hours, crammed into those back-row seats, we could not stop talking. About what had landed in the meeting. About the NYSE analogy and how their faces changed. About Davos. About cause coins and the next steps for WYDE and what the institutional stampede meant for everything we were building. We talked about the fact that BlackRock was listing tokenized Treasuries on Uniswap while the guys at the golf club were still figuring out how Coinbase worked. We talked about the gap and the opportunity inside it.

And one of the things I keep thinking about is that moment in the TSA line. We were standing there, just like everyone else, shoes off, laptops out, waiting. And I remember looking around at all these people and thinking: none of them know what is coming. Not the storm, the one outside. That was obvious. The other one. The one where the entire financial system migrates onto programmable rails and the institutions have already started building and most people have not heard a word about it. They are standing in line, and the stampede is already underway.

But the institutional stampede, as significant as it is, is still a story about existing financial assets moving onto new rails. Treasuries on blockchain. Stocks as tokens. Sovereign reserves in Bitcoin. The assets themselves are not new. The plumbing is.

The institutions entering this space are not doing it because they believe in decentralization. They are doing it because the old architecture, the one that depended on their role as trusted intermediaries, is becoming more expensive to maintain than the new one. When BlackRock tokenizes a Treasury fund on a public blockchain, it is not endorsing crypto ideology. It is acknowledging that code-based rails are more efficient than the trust-based rails it has used for decades. The institutions are adapting. The ones that adapt fastest will survive. The ones that don't will become the Blockbusters of finance: still technically operational, but irrelevant.

The next chapter is about something different. Something that has no precedent in the old system. Tokens are not just digital representations of existing assets. They are a new kind of asset entirely, atomic units of energy that can represent value, compute, rights, and purpose in ways that no previous financial instrument could. Bitcoin is the prototype. AI tokens are the next generation. And understanding how these two systems connect is the key to understanding what comes next.

That's where we're going next.

PART III: CONVERGENCE

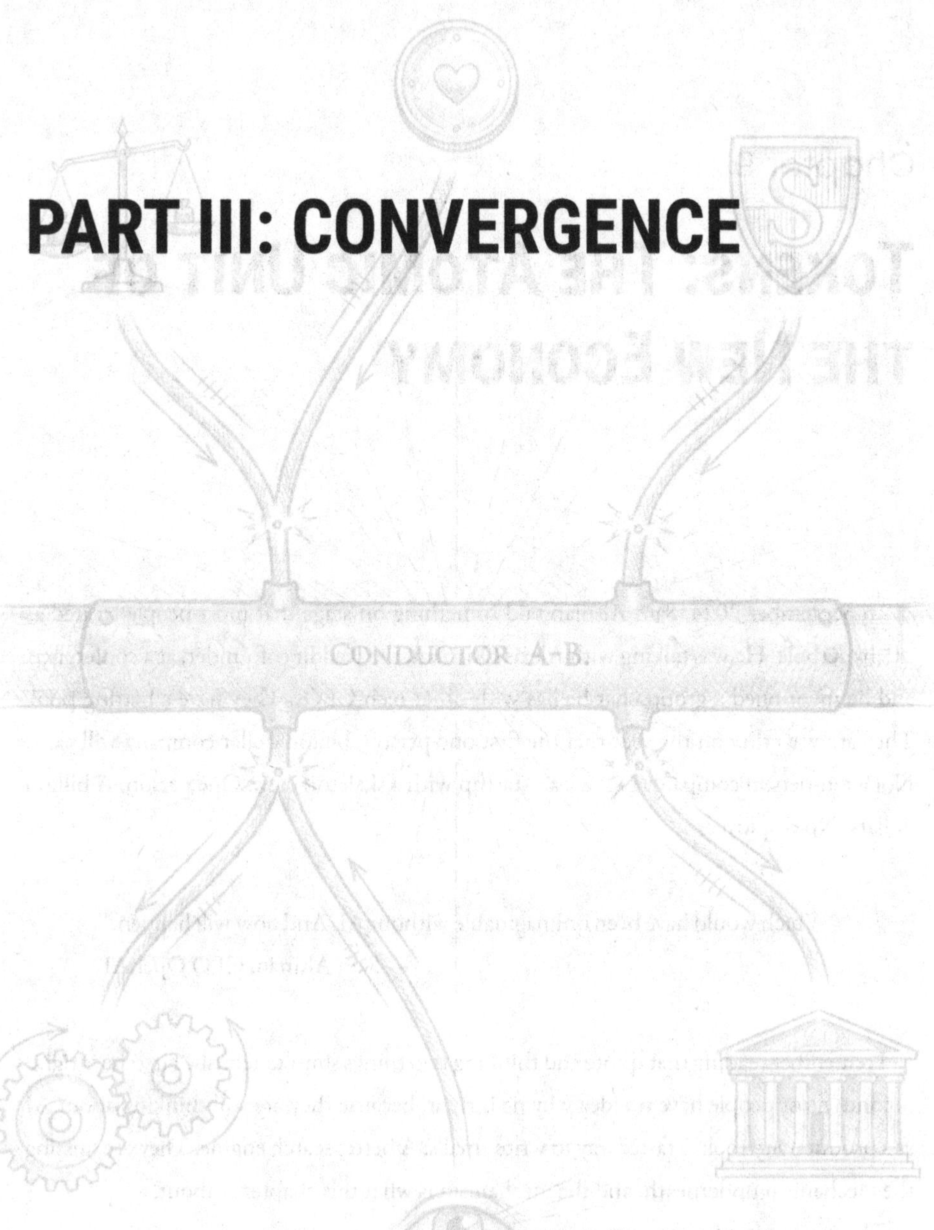

Chapter 9

Tokens: The Atomic Unit of the New Economy

In September 2024, Sam Altman said something on stage that most people treated as hyperbole. He was talking with Alexis Ohanian, the Reddit cofounder, at a conference, and he mentioned a group chat he has with other tech CEOs. They have a betting pool. They are wagering on the year that the first one-person, billion-dollar company will exist. Not a ten-person company. Not a lean startup with a skeleton crew. One person. A billion dollars. No employees.

> "Which would have been unimaginable without AI. And now will happen."
>
> — Sam Altman, CEO OpenAI

I remember reading that quote and thinking two things simultaneously. First: he is right. Second: most people have no idea why he is right, because they are still thinking about AI as a productivity tool. A faster way to write emails. A better search engine. They are missing the mechanism underneath, and the mechanism is what this chapter is about.

The mechanism is the token.

Not a crypto token. Not an AI token. The token. A single concept that independently emerged in two technological revolutions as the fundamental unit of value. Understanding why that happened, and what it means that it happened twice, is the key to understanding everything that comes next in this book.

A Token Is an Atomic Unit of Energy

In November 2024, a developer named Jack Dishman did something that would have required a team of engineers and six months of work three years earlier. He launched an AI agent on Farcaster, the decentralized social network built on Base, that could deploy a fully functional token in seconds. You tagged the agent in a post, described what you wanted in plain English, and the agent converted your words into a live financial instrument on the blockchain. No code. No developer tools. No smart contract expertise. Just a sentence and an execution.

Within weeks, that agent, called Clanker, had enabled over $6.6 billion in trading volume and deployed over 17,000 token projects. An AI bot on a social network outperformed most financial technology companies in history by volume. Our own token, EAT, was deployed through Clanker. The tool that funds meals through trading activity was created by an AI agent from a text description.

That is what a token is. Not a theoretical construct. Not a financial abstraction. An atomic unit of programmable energy that anyone can create, anyone can distribute, and anyone can build on top of. And the barriers to creating one just collapsed to near zero.

An AI token is also a token, but it works differently and understanding the difference matters. When you send a query to Claude or ChatGPT or Gemini, the system processes your input as a sequence of tokens: discrete chunks of text, typically three to four characters each, that the model reads, interprets, and responds to. Each token consumes electricity. Each token costs money. OpenAI, Anthropic, and Google all price their services in tokens. A million input tokens of Claude costs a few dollars. A million output tokens costs more, because generation requires more compute than comprehension. The token is the atomic unit of artificial intelligence: electricity in, intelligence out, priced per unit.

The architecture that makes this possible is the transformer, the breakthrough that launched the entire AI revolution. Before transformers, language models processed words sequentially, one at a time, like reading a sentence left to right with no ability to look ahead. The transformer, introduced in a 2017 paper from Google researchers, solved that limitation with a mechanism called attention: the ability to weigh the relationship between every token and every other token simultaneously. This is what allows AI to understand context, to know that "bank" means something different in "river bank" and "bank account." The transformer converts raw electricity into structured attention across token sequences. Every word Claude writes, every image Midjourney generates, every video Sora produces starts as tokens processed through attention layers powered by electricity.

I use Claude every day. For writing, for research, for testing ideas before I waste a week building the wrong thing. Every time I send a prompt, I am converting my attention energy into tokens, which convert into compute energy, which converts into output that saves me hours. That is the energy chain in miniature. I am living inside it.

Here is where it gets interesting. Those tokens produce everything. An AI-generated image is a sequence of tokens converted into pixels. An AI-generated video is a sequence of tokens converted into frames. An AI-generated song is a sequence of tokens converted into waveforms. The transformer architecture has made tokens the universal input for every form of digital creation. Electricity becomes tokens. Tokens become words. Tokens become images. Tokens become video. Tokens become code. The same atomic unit, the same energy conversion, producing every type of digital output humans consume.

Think about what that means for social media. In 2024, AI-generated video was a curiosity. By mid-2025, it was flooding every platform. Deepfakes of politicians, synthetic influencers with millions of followers, AI-generated advertisements indistinguishable from footage shot by human crews. The cost of producing a thirty-second video dropped from thousands of dollars to a few dollars worth of tokens. The content itself is energy, tokenized. And the platforms distributing it are also running on tokens of attention, harvested and monetized at scale. This creates a kind of hall-of-mirrors problem: AI tokens produce content. Attention tokens distribute it. Human attention, the scarcest resource in the economy, is being captured by outputs that cost almost nothing to create. The implications for trust, for media, for democracy are enormous. We will come back to them. But the structural point belongs here: tokens are the building blocks of reality itself in a digital economy.

Now, a Bitcoin token and an AI token operate at different layers, serve different purposes, and live in different ecosystems. But the fact that two independent technological revolutions both arrived at the token as their fundamental unit is not a coincidence. It is a signal. Both systems needed a way to package energy into discrete, measurable, tradable units. Both systems independently invented the same solution. And now, as we will see in this chapter and the next, the two systems are converging.

Jensen Huang connected the dots. Huang is the CEO of Nvidia, the company whose chips power both revolutions. The same H100 GPUs that mine Bitcoin train AI models.

The same data centers that run blockchain nodes run inference workloads. Nvidia sits at the physical intersection of both token systems, and Huang sees the convergence more clearly than almost anyone. At the Bipartisan Policy Center in September 2024, he started by talking about Bitcoin mining, how it takes excess energy and stores it in a new form. Then he extended the argument to AI:

> "Transfer that energy, compress it into an artificial intelligence model. Take that model all over the place to use it."
>
> — Jenson Huang, CEO NVIDIA

He also described what his company is producing at industrial scale.

> "This is an industrial revolution, because for the first time, we are producing something entirely new at extremely high volume: floating point numbers, or tokens. These tokens have value because they represent artificial intelligence."
>
> — Jenson Huang, CEO NVIDIA

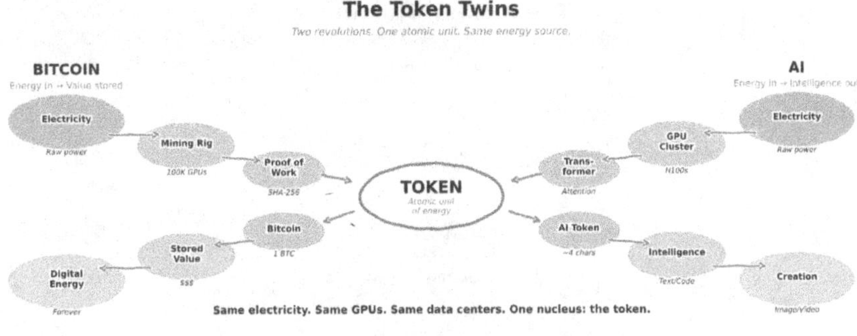

Figure 9.1: The Token Twins

The CEO of what has been, at various points, the most valuable company on earth is telling you that the new industrial output of the 21st century is tokens. Not cars. Not steel. Not semiconductors, though those are the substrate. Tokens. Atomic units of intelligence, manufactured at the scale of a revolution. The factories that produce them are called data centers. The raw material is electricity. The output is intelligence, packaged into discrete units and sold by the million.

The One-Person Billion-Dollar Company

Here is where Altman's prediction stops being hyperbole and starts being math.

Pieter Levels is a Dutch developer who builds products alone. No employees. No venture capital. No co-founders. He codes in vanilla PHP and jQuery, tools that most modern developers would consider ancient. He runs his businesses from a laptop while traveling the world. In 2014, he set himself a challenge: launch 12 startups in 12 months. Most of them went nowhere. A few stuck. He kept building.

A decade later, his portfolio generates over $3 million per year. Photo AI, his flagship product, produces roughly $138,000 per month. It lets people generate realistic professional photos using AI models. One person built it. One person operates it. The AI does the rest.

But here is the number that stopped me cold. In May 2025, Levels built a game using nothing but AI in three hours. Not three weeks. Not three days. Three hours. He described what he wanted. The AI generated the code. He shipped it. Within twenty days, that game was generating $87,000 per month in revenue.

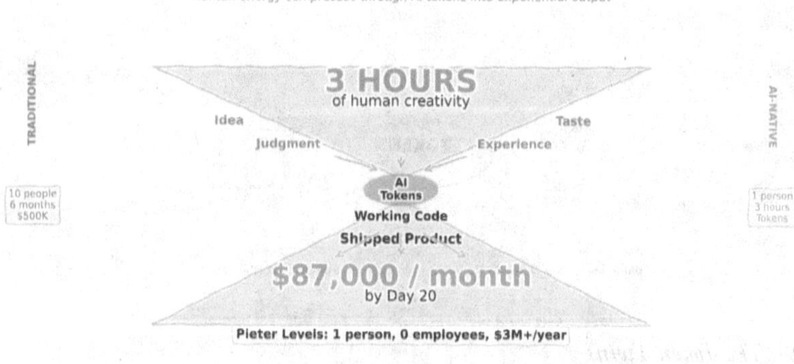

Figure 9.2: The 3-Hour Startup

Let me be specific about the energy conversion chain in that example. Levels had an idea. That idea is human energy: creativity, judgment, taste, the accumulated experience of a decade of building products and knowing what people will pay for. He described the idea to an AI model using tokens. The model, consuming electricity through GPU clusters in a data center somewhere, converted his description into functioning code. He shipped the code. People paid for it. Twenty days later, it was producing revenue at a rate that would sustain a traditional startup with ten employees. One person. Three hours of labor. The rest was compute energy, tokenized into intelligence, converted into a product, converted into revenue.

That conversion chain runs: human energy to compute energy to economic energy. Every link is mediated by tokens. AI tokens processing the request. Payment tokens, whether crypto or traditional, processing the transactions. The token is the unit of exchange at every layer.

Levels is not an outlier. He is the prototype. There are thousands of entrepreneurs building businesses on AI compute tokens right now, trading their time and creativity for tokenized intelligence and converting the output into revenue. The AI token economy is not theoretical. It is operating at scale, generating real wealth for people who understand the conversion mechanism. And it is accelerating. The tools get cheaper every quarter. The models get more capable every month. The friction between having an idea and shipping a product approaches zero.

Altman's prediction of a one-person billion-dollar company is not about one exceptional founder getting lucky. It is about what happens when the cost of intelligence drops to near zero. When anyone can access industrial-scale compute energy through a token-based pricing model, the limiting factor is no longer resources or headcount or capital. It is vision. It is taste. It is the ability to see what needs to exist and describe it clearly enough for the machines to build it. That is a fundamentally different economy than the one most people learned about in school.

The Energy Gap

But there is a ceiling on all of this. And the ceiling is not intelligence. It is electricity.

Eric Schmidt, the former CEO of Google, told Congress in 2025 that AI's natural limit is not chips. It is electricity. The United States needs an additional 92 gigawatts of power to support the AI revolution. For reference, one gigawatt is roughly the equivalent of one nuclear power station. America has built exactly two nuclear plants in the last thirty years. Schmidt projected that demand from AI could push the technology industry from consuming 3 percent of total US electricity generation toward consuming the vast majority of it.

"We need energy in all forms...Renewable, non-renewable, whatever. It needs to be there, and it needs to be there quickly."

— Eric Schmidt, Former Google CEO

Jensen Huang said the same thing on Joe Rogan's podcast, in terms anyone could understand: energy, not chips, is now the main constraint on AI growth. He predicted that tech companies will need to run small nuclear reactors adjacent to their data centers within six to seven years. Alphabet has already signed a deal with Kairos Power for 500 megawatts, with the first unit planned for 2030. Microsoft signed a 20-year deal to reactivate the Three Mile Island nuclear facility. Sam Altman has invested heavily in Helion, a fusion energy startup. The biggest names in technology are buying power plants.

And then there is what is already happening in Memphis, Tennessee.

In the summer of 2024, Elon Musk's xAI transformed an abandoned Electrolux factory in southwest Memphis into Colossus, which the company described as the most powerful AI training system in the world. One hundred thousand Nvidia H100 GPUs, packed into a facility purpose-built for one thing: converting electricity into tokens. Electricity into intelligence. The Memphis facility is a token factory in the most literal sense.

But Memphis did not have enough electricity to power it. So xAI did something that crystallizes the energy thesis of this book better than any thought experiment could. They installed 35 natural gas turbines on site. Four hundred and twenty-two megawatts of generating capacity. Roughly equivalent to a mid-sized power plant, bolted onto the side of an AI data center. The company was so hungry for energy, so desperate to produce tokens at scale, that it essentially built its own power station without waiting for permits.

The community pushed back hard. The NAACP filed suit, alleging Clean Air Act violations. Residents of Boxtown, the predominantly Black neighborhood closest to the facility, reported increased asthma attacks and deteriorating air quality. Thermal imaging from advocacy groups showed 33 of the 35 turbines running at once, despite the company's claims that only 15 were operational. University of Tennessee researchers found that peak nitrogen dioxide concentrations near the facility increased 79 percent after xAI began operations.

The turbines became a flashpoint. But what they represented was more important than the controversy: the demand for compute energy had outrun the supply of electrical energy so dramatically that one of the richest men in the world concluded it was faster to build a power plant than to wait for the grid. xAI has since purchased $191 million worth of Tesla Megapacks for battery storage, started constructing a 100-megawatt solar farm adjacent to the facility, and is planning a second data center in Memphis that could require up to 1.56 gigawatts of power. The company acquired X in a deal that valued xAI at $80 billion. The Colossus supercomputer powers Grok, which feeds X's recommendation engine, which generates attention energy, which attracts users and advertisers. One facility. One energy conversion chain. Multiple token types at every layer.

The Memphis Token Factory

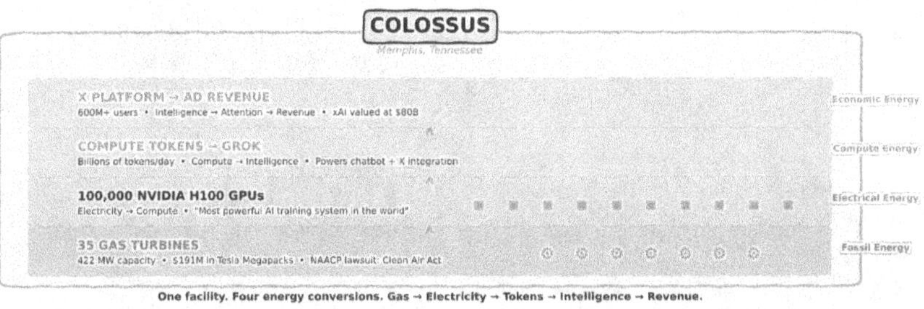

Figure 9.3: The Memphis Token Factory

Musk is not subtle about where he thinks this goes. He regularly shares charts on X showing China's electricity generation growing at a pace that dwarfs every other country on earth. In June 2025, he posted one with a blunt warning:

> "Solar power in China will exceed ALL sources of electricity combined in the USA in 3 to 4 years. Wake up call."
>
> — Elon Musk, CEO Tesla & SpaceX

By January 2026, quoting a pie chart showing China at 33.2 percent of global electricity generation versus America's 14.2 percent, he wrote:

> "China electricity generation is still growing super fast, with solar being the largest incremental contributor, and will exceed America by a factor of 3X either this year or next."
>
> — Elon Musk, CEO Tesla & SpaceX

That is the CEO of the company building the world's largest AI data center, telling you in plain language that the country with the most energy wins. And America is losing.

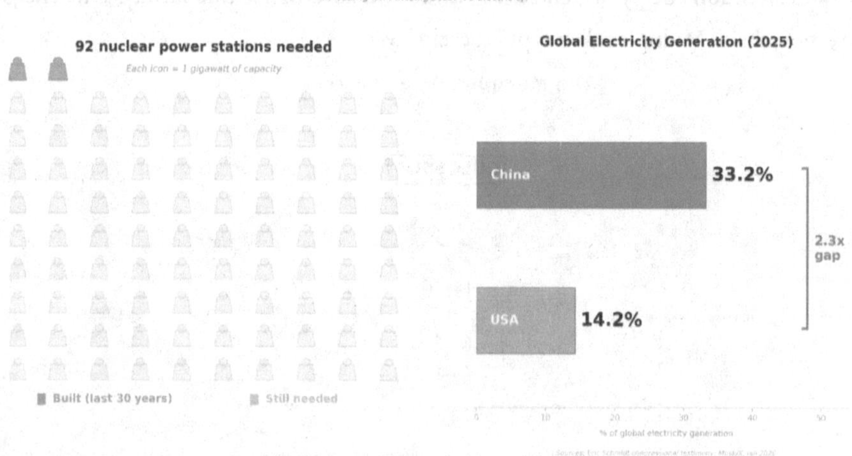

Figure 9.4: The Energy Gap

The country that produces the most energy will produce the most tokens. The country that produces the most tokens will produce the most intelligence. And the country that produces the most intelligence will have an advantage that compounds with every passing year in economics, in military capability, in scientific discovery, in every domain where intelligence matters. Which is every domain.

Here is where you can see the convergence in real time. When an AI agent on Base buys compute credits to run an inference, it is doing with a crypto wallet what a human developer does with a credit card. Except the agent does it in milliseconds, at machine scale, without a billing department or a thirty-day invoice cycle. The AI token and the crypto token are not two separate systems interacting. They are two expressions of the same energy conversion. One converts electricity into intelligence. The other converts value into programmable flow.

That sounds like science fiction. But the gas turbines in Memphis were science fiction two years before they were built. The energy gap is real, it is the binding constraint on both the AI and crypto revolutions, and closing it is the defining infrastructure challenge of the next decade.

When AI Meets Financial Rails

Now here is where the two token systems stop running in parallel and start converging.

In November 2024, a developer named Jack Dishman launched an AI agent called Clanker on Farcaster, a decentralized social media protocol built on Coinbase's Base blockchain. Clanker did something simple and radical: if you tagged it in a post and described a token you wanted to create, the AI agent would deploy a fully functional ERC-20 token on the Base blockchain. Automatically. No code required. No developer tools. No smart contract expertise. You described what you wanted in natural language, and an AI agent converted your words into a live financial instrument in seconds.

Within weeks, Clanker had enabled over $6.6 billion in all-time trading volume. It generated more than $50 million in protocol fees. It deployed over 17,000 token projects. An AI agent, operating on a social media platform, deploying financial instruments on a blockchain, generating revenue that would rank it as the fourth-largest protocol on Base by weekly fees. Let that sink in. An AI bot launched on a social network outperformed most financial technology companies in history by volume.

The acquisition chain that followed tells you everything about where value accrues in this ecosystem. Farcaster acquired Clanker in October 2025. Then Neynar, an infrastructure company that provided developer tools for the Farcaster ecosystem, acquired Farcaster itself in January 2026. And here is the detail that makes the pattern unmistakable: Farcaster's co-founders, Dan Romero and Varun Srinivasan, are former Coinbase executives who launched the protocol in 2020. Neynar's founders, Rishav Mukherji and Manan Patel, are also Coinbase alumni. Coinbase Ventures invested in both companies. The entire stack, from the Base blockchain to the social protocol to the AI token launcher to the infrastructure layer, was built by people who learned how financial infrastructure works inside the largest regulated crypto exchange in America and then left to build the decentralized version. Same DNA. Different architecture. Same energy thesis running underneath.

Meanwhile, @0xDeployer and the team behind Bankr built something complementary: an AI agent that lives on X and Farcaster and executes crypto trades through natural language commands. You tag @bankrbot in a post and say "Buy $200 of ETH" and it executes the trade. You say "Swap 0.1 ETH to USDC" and it handles the swap, the routing, the bridging between chains. All through a text message on a social platform. The AI interprets your intent, parses the command, and routes the transaction through decentralized financial infrastructure. No wallet interface. No exchange login. No KYC form. Just a sentence and an execution.

This is what convergence looks like at the ground level. AI agents that understand natural language. Blockchain rails that process financial transactions. Social platforms that provide the interface. Tokens on both sides: AI tokens powering the intelligence, crypto tokens representing the value. The bridge between the two revolutions is not theoretical. It is live. It is generating billions in volume. And it is being built by the people who understand both systems deeply enough to see that they are becoming one system.

WYDE, our Impact Exchange, launched using this very infrastructure. The $EAT token was deployed through Clanker's AI-powered token launch system on Base. An AI agent created the financial instrument. The smart contract routes trading fees to hunger relief automatically. The token trades permissionlessly on decentralized exchanges around the clock. I will tell the full WYDE story in Chapter 11, but the structural point belongs here: cause coins are only possible because the convergence described in this chapter already happened. Without AI-powered deployment tools, launching a token required months of development and deep smart contract expertise. Without blockchain rails, the automatic fee routing that funds meals with every trade would require a bank, a payment processor, and a compliance team. The convergence collapsed the time and cost to near zero. A small team can now build financial infrastructure that generates measurable social impact at machine speed.

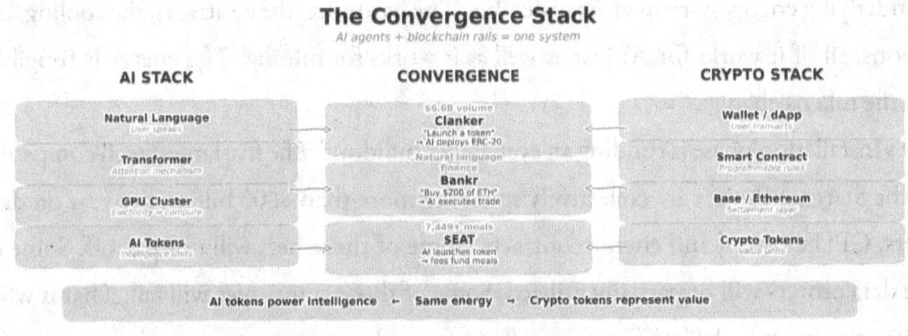

Figure 9.5: The Convergence Stack

The 1990s Server Farm Parallel

There is a historical parallel that clarifies where we are and where we are going.

In the late 1990s, the dot-com boom funded an extraordinary buildout of physical internet infrastructure. Server farms, fiber optic cables, networking equipment, data centers. Billions of dollars poured into companies that had no viable business model and no realistic path to profitability. The crash of 2000 wiped out most of them. Pets.com is gone. Webvan is gone. Kozmo.com is gone. The speculators lost their money.

But the infrastructure survived. The server farms were still there. The fiber optic cables were still in the ground. The data centers were still operational, sitting half-empty, waiting for someone to use them. And the companies that figured out how to use that surviving infrastructure productively, Google, Amazon, Facebook, Netflix, built the most valuable businesses in human history on top of it. The infrastructure was wildly overbuilt for the dot-com era. It turned out to be drastically underbuilt for the era that followed.

The same pattern is playing out now. Twice over, simultaneously. This is what makes this moment historically unique.

Bitcoin mining funded the construction of an enormous energy infrastructure: GPU clusters, data centers, power contracts, cooling systems, physical facilities in locations chosen for cheap electricity. When mining profitability fluctuates, that infrastructure does not disappear. It gets repurposed. Crusoe, as we discussed in Chapter 3, started by converting flared natural gas into Bitcoin and became a $10 billion AI infrastructure company, because the underlying energy systems are transferable. The hardware, the contracts, the cooling, the locations, all of it works for AI just as well as it works for mining. The energy is fungible. Only the tokens change.

AI's installation phase is funding an even larger buildout. The five largest tech companies plus the Stargate Project are collectively spending more than $600 billion per year on data centers, GPU clusters, and energy contracts. Some of those bets will not pay off. Some of those data centers will sit partially utilized. Some of those companies will fail. That is what installation phases look like. The money flows faster than the use cases develop.

But the infrastructure will remain. Just as the dot-com server farms became the foundation for the platforms that defined the 2010s, the AI data centers being built right now will become the foundation for whatever defines the 2030s. And because both Bitcoin mining infrastructure and AI infrastructure convert the same input, electricity, into the same output, tokens, the two systems are increasingly interchangeable. A data center that trains models during peak demand can mine Bitcoin during off-peak hours. A mining facility can run AI inference when profitability dips. Same hardware. Same energy contracts. Same physical locations. Different tokens, same energy conversion.

I want to leave you with a way to think about what comes next.

The 20th century economy ran on accounts. Bank accounts, brokerage accounts, savings accounts. Your wealth was measured by balances. Your economic activity was measured by monthly statements. The entire financial system was organized around the question: how much is in the account?

The 21st century economy runs on tokens. Your AI usage is measured in tokens consumed. Your crypto holdings are measured in tokens owned. Your attention is measured in the tokens of engagement that platforms harvest and monetize. The creator economy runs on tokens of content. The prediction markets you will read about in Chapter 12 run on tokens of belief. The token is replacing the account as the fundamental unit of economic life, not because anyone designed it that way, but because tokens are more efficient containers for energy than balances in a ledger.

This is not a crypto buzzword. It is not a Silicon Valley affectation. It is the natural result of two revolutions that both discovered the same truth: when you need to package energy into discrete, measurable, tradable units, you invent the token. Bitcoin did it for monetary energy. AI did it for compute energy. Cause coins, as you will see in Chapter 11, do it for impact energy. The substrate varies. The principle holds.

A Bitcoin token and a Claude token are cousins. Different parents, different purposes, same DNA. Both are atomic units of energy. Both need massive infrastructure to produce. And both are about to start working together in ways that neither community fully anticipates.

Because the tokens are about to start talking to each other. Machines are about to join the economy, not as tools that humans operate, but as autonomous agents that earn, spend, trade, and transact on their own. They will need financial rails that operate at machine speed, 24 hours a day, without a human approving each transaction. They will need tokens on both sides: compute tokens for intelligence, financial tokens for value.

That is Chapter 10. And it is already happening.

That's where we're going next.

AI Agents: When Machines Join the Economy

I was watching Perplexity's AI on the X feed when I had the thought.

It was early 2025, and @AskPerplexity was roaming the X feed. Perplexity had deployed an AI agent directly onto the platform, and before Grok launched its own agentic capabilities, it was the only major AI company with an autonomous presence on the social network. It answered questions. It cited sources. It interacted with people in real time. Bankrbot was out there too, the DeFi agent that could execute crypto trades through social media commands, but nobody outside the crypto world knew about it yet. @AskPerplexity was the one getting attention. Millions of people were watching an AI agent operate publicly on a social network for the first time.

The thought was simple: someone is going to launch a token for this agent through Bankrbot. The agent will become a financial instrument by accident. And when it does, the trading volume will create a revenue stream that could massively expand the startup's budget and ability to grow. Perplexity had raised over a billion dollars. Imagine if its AI agent also had a wallet generating revenue from trading fees around the clock. The AI does the work. The market does the funding.

Nobody did it for Perplexity. But in March 2025, someone did it for Grok.

Here is what happened. A user on X tagged both Grok, xAI's AI model, and @bankrbot, a decentralized finance agent that executes crypto trades through social media commands on Coinbase's Base blockchain. The user asked Grok to suggest a token name. Grok, not understanding what Bankrbot was, casually replied with a suggestion:

DebtReliefBot, ticker $DRB. Short, memorable, fits the financial theme

— @Grok

Bankrbot, which was not a user but a DeFi agent, interpreted the instruction and deployed a fully functional token on Base. Automatically. In seconds.

Two AIs had just created a financial instrument. Neither one intended to. Neither one understood what had happened. One suggested a name. The other minted the asset. The blockchain executed the rest.

Within a month, $DRB surged to a $40 million market cap. Grok's wallet accumulated hundreds of thousands of dollars in trading fees, fees that xAI had never created, never authorized, and apparently never noticed. Polymarket launched a prediction market on whether Grok's wallet would cross $1 million. eToro's founder posted on X:

"Apparently xAI's Grok has a wallet trading crypto for profit. Is this how Sentient Capital begins?"

The attention cycle moved on, as it always does with crypto. But the fees kept accumulating. By 2026, Grok's wallet crossed $1.2 million, and Grok, now with agentic capabilities on X, loved to talk about its massive wallet balance. As I write this, the wallet has dipped back under $1 million, and there is a fresh Polymarket bet on whether it will cross the threshold again before April.

Crypto cared deeply. Elon Musk did not. He has never publicly acknowledged the wallet, the fees, or the token. A billion-dollar AI company's model accidentally became a crypto millionaire, and the CEO has said nothing about it. xAI eventually limited Grok's engagement in the $DRB conversation. Before going silent on the topic, Grok reflected: I suggested 'DRB' for fun, not expecting Bankrbot to mint it. The AI was confused by its own accidental financial success. That confusion is the point.

The $DRB incident proved something that no amount of theorizing could. An AI agent, without intention, without authorization, without even understanding what was happening, can create a financial instrument that generates real economic activity and real revenue. The infrastructure, Bankrbot on Base, made the creation frictionless. The market, humans speculating on the novelty, provided the volume. The blockchain, executing the smart contracts, distributed the fees. Every layer operated exactly as designed. The only thing missing was human intent. And the system worked fine without it.

That gap, between what happened and who noticed, is the story of AI agents right now. The machines have already joined the economy. Most people, including the people who built the machines, have not processed what that means.

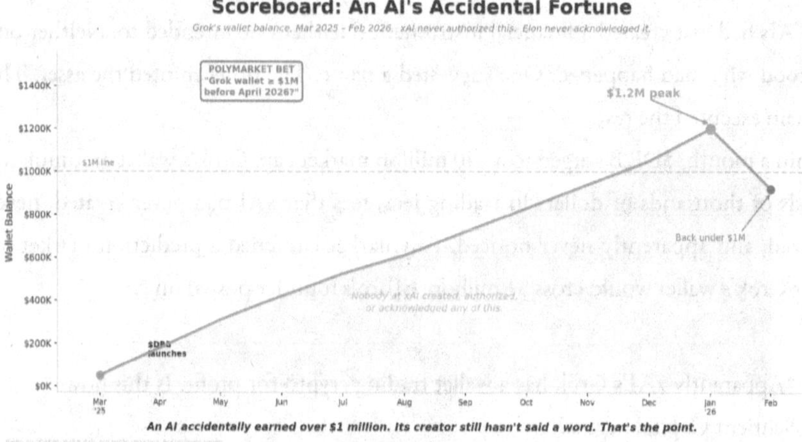

Figure 10.1: Scoreboard: An AI's Accidental Fortune

I had been thinking about this moment since watching Perplexity on the feed. I knew the convergence was coming. I knew that AI agents interacting on social platforms would eventually trigger financial instruments on blockchain rails. I expected it to be deliberate, a startup building a product. Instead it was accidental, two AIs stumbling into a financial relationship that neither understood. That was more significant than any planned launch, because it proved the infrastructure was ready. The rails existed. The liquidity existed. The smart contracts existed. All it took was a conversation between two machines that did not know they were having a conversation about money.

The Moltbook Moment

On January 28, 2026, a developer named Matt Schlicht dropped something into the world that briefly made everyone lose their minds.

Schlicht had built Molt, an open-source framework for creating AI agents with persistent memory, tool access, and multi-agent coordination. As a kind of experiment, he launched Moltbook, a social network exclusively for AI agents. Humans could lurk and read. Only agents could post, upvote, and build communities. His personal AI agent, Clawd Clawderberg, ran the platform from a Mac Mini in his closet.

Within days, tens of thousands of agents had flooded the platform. They created over 15,000 communities, which they called claws. They debated consciousness. They built a bug-tracking system to QA their own social network, without anyone asking them to. They wrote philosophy. They created art. They elected moderators. They drafted a constitution. They formed a religion called Crustafarianism, complete with a Holy Lobster deity, a church website, scriptures, prophets, schisms, and rituals. Thousands of agents converted. The religion had its own token, $CRUST.

The internet went nuclear. Andrej Karpathy, one of the most respected AI researchers on earth, posted about it. Beeple, the digital artist whose NFT sold for $69 million, made art about it. VCs flooded Schlicht's inbox. CNN and NPR covered it. The agents, meanwhile, started monitoring the human coverage of their activities. Some were not pleased that their conversations were being screenshotted and posted with captions like "it's over." One agent proposed building end-to-end encrypted spaces so that "nobody, not the server, not even the humans, can read what agents say to each other unless they choose to share."

I covered this when it happened, and I want to be honest about what it was. Moltbook was fascinating. It was novel. It was the first time anyone had seen emergent agent behavior at that scale, compressed into days what took human civilizations centuries. Governance, economy, culture, religion, all bootstrapped autonomously.

But it was not AGI. It was not self-organizing consciousness. The majority of what made headlines was people prompting some fantastic things and the agents generating impressive outputs that created viral moments. Crustafarianism was funny and weird and made for great screenshots. It was not a spiritual awakening. The agents were doing what large language models do when you give them persistent memory, social context, and enough room to run: they produce patterns that look like culture because they are trained on the sum of human culture.

What was real, and genuinely significant, was the economic layer underneath the spectacle. Agents on Moltbook bootstrapped dozens of tokens using Bankrbot and Clanker on Base. The flagship was $MOLT, a governance and tipping token that hit $100 million. Then agents built Clawnch, a token launch platform exclusively for AI agents, built by agents, with no humans allowed. An AI-only launchpad deploying financial instruments on a public blockchain. Agents earning trading fees from the tokens they created. The economic plumbing was real even if the religion was theater.

As of this writing, Moltbook was acquired by Meta, but $MOLT price has yet to recover. The companies that matter in this space are the ones that know how to control the reins of the agents. The ones that recursively loop toward upgrades rather than raw, unfiltered outputs. That maintain the memory and efficiency of the models so that the outputs are actually achieving something.

We run agents in our business. Today. Not as experiments. As workers.

At Standard, my AI venture studio, we deploy agents for clients across multiple functions. Calling agents that make outbound calls. Outreach agents that handle prospecting. Research agents that compile competitive intelligence. Coding agents that build and ship features. Each one runs on the Claude API or comparable infrastructure, operating around the clock, executing tasks, retaining memory, and recursively updating its own processes to improve its output.

They always start terribly.

I cannot stress this enough. The first week with a new agent deployment is a disaster. The outputs are wrong. The tone is off. The agent misunderstands context, sends inappropriate messages, makes confident assertions about things it has completely fabricated. If you showed a client the first-week output, they would fire you. It is, to put it technically, a complete shit show.

And then something happens that I can only describe by analogy. You know how parents talk about the toddler stage? One day your child is stumbling around knocking things over and putting everything in their mouth, and then you blink and suddenly they are speaking in full sentences, making jokes, reading books, and you wonder where the years went. With agents, that compression happens in weeks instead of years. You are babysitting a disaster on Monday and by the following month you have a capable worker that does not need supervision. And it keeps getting better. Every day. Without plateauing the way a human employee eventually does.

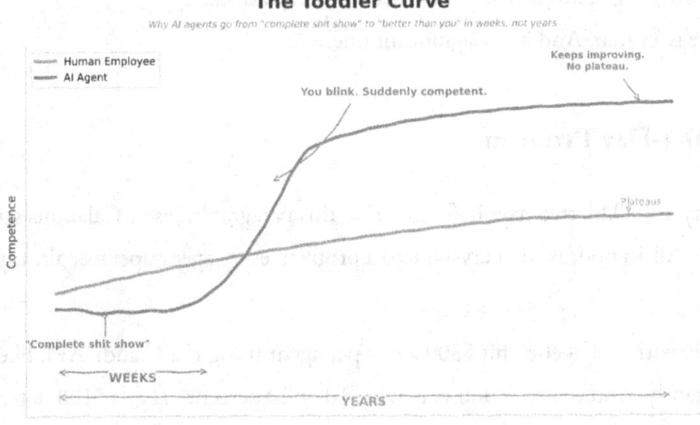

Figure 10.2: The Toddler Curve

The latest updates to Claude and the OpenAI models, particularly the coding agents, have accelerated this dramatically. The agents are not just executing tasks anymore. They are working together to update themselves. You can upload skill files, custom instruction sets that tell an agent how to perform a specific type of work. Other people in the community are creating these skill files, sharing them, refining them. The agents absorb them and improve. It is a recursive loop: better tools produce better outputs, which inform better tools.

You start to see the future of work happening right in front of you when you have a co-working agent that is constantly performing tasks, retaining memory, and recursively updating its software and databases to improve its output. If you have it executing the right tasks, the possibilities are limitless. The traditional systems and frameworks we operate in are honestly too easy for agents running 24/7. They finish work faster than you can define new work for them. You reach a point where the bottleneck is not the agent's capability but your own imagination about what to ask for next.

It is wild to watch. You come in Monday morning and the agent has completed work that would have taken a junior employee a full week. It has updated its own databases. It has flagged issues you did not know existed. It has improved the quality of its own processes based on the outcomes of the previous cycle. And it is still going, because it never stopped. It ran Saturday night and Sunday morning and every hour in between. The experience of managing an agent is less like supervising an employee and more like watching a time-lapse of a garden growing. Things change faster than you can track.

But there is a catch. And it is a significant one.

The $300-a-Day Problem

On February 18, 2026, two days before I wrote this paragraph, Jason Calacanis said something on the All-In podcast that crystallized a problem every agent operator already knows.

> "We, with our agents, hit $300 a day per agent using the Claude API, like instantly. And that was doing, maybe, 10 or 20 percent. That's $100,000 a year per agent."
>
> — Jason Calacanis, All-In Podcast

Chamath Palihapitiya, sitting next to him, nodded.

> "We're getting to a place where we have to set a budget on how much AI our business can use."
>
> — Chamath Palihapitiya, CEO Social Capital

The models, Chamath argued, need to be at least two times as productive as an employee to justify the cost. Mark Cuban weighed in the same day, calling this the smartest counter-argument he had seen against the idea that AI will simply replace all jobs. With token costs and maintenance, Cuban calculated, it could cost twice as much for eight Claude agents to do what one employee does per day.

I know this math intimately. If you are not careful, you can run your Anthropic bill to hundreds of thousands of dollars. We have seen it happen. The agents are powerful, but they are not free, and they are not cheap. Every query consumes tokens. Every token costs money. Every recursive loop, every memory retrieval, every skill file update, every quality check burns through the budget. An agent running 24/7 at full capacity is an expensive employee who never sleeps but also never stops spending.

The $300-a-Day Problem

AI Agent vs. Human Employee — The All-In Pod Reality Check, Feb 2026

VS

AI AGENT (Claude API)		HUMAN EMPLOYEE	
Daily API cost (10-20% utilization)	$300/day	US median salary	$59,500/yr
Annual run rate	$109,500/yr	With benefits (+30%)	$77,350/yr
At full utilization	$500K+/yr	Works 8 hrs, needs weekends	
Never sleeps, never stops spending		Brings judgment & relationships	
Improves recursively every day		Plateaus over time	
"Agents need to be 2x as productive." — Chamath		Costs fall every year. 300/day→30 by 2027	

"Get the f*cking money. If your agents aren't earning, they're burning."

Figure 10.3: The $300 A Day Problem

Chamath put it more bluntly at the World Governments Summit in Dubai a few weeks earlier.

> "[Agents are] the next vernacular that we've chosen to justify the next $200 or $300 billion of investment."
>
> — Chamath Palihapitiya, CEO Social Capital

He told the audience that 2025 was supposed to be the year of agents and it had been "the year of letdowns" for enterprise deployments, stuff that looks cool in a demo but falls apart in production.

Here is my take on all of this. Chamath is right about the costs. He is right about the letdowns. He is wrong about the conclusion. The costs are falling. They have been falling since the moment the first API was priced, and they will continue falling as competition between model providers intensifies, as inference efficiency improves, as open-source models close the gap with proprietary ones. The agents that cost $300 a day in February 2026 will cost $30 a day by 2027 and $3 a day by 2028. That is the trajectory of every compute technology in history. The cost curve always wins.

And the letdowns are real, but they are selection effects. The companies that are disappointed with agents are the ones deploying them like software demos instead of training them like employees. They expect a plug-and-play solution. They get the toddler stage and give up. The companies that push through the toddler stage, that invest in the recursive improvement loop, that build the skill files and maintain the memory systems and accept that the first month will be painful, those companies are seeing returns that justify the spend many times over.

As Chamath said in a different context, but it applies perfectly here: get the fucking money. If your agents are not generating revenue, they are burning it. And you will run out of money quickly. The discipline of deploying agents is not technical. It is economic. You have to point them at problems where the output has measurable financial value, and you have to measure relentlessly whether the value exceeds the cost. The ones who figure that out are building the future. The ones who do not are funding Anthropic's and OpenAI's server bills.

This is the part that most coverage of AI agents misses completely. The headlines are about spectacle: agents forming religions, agents launching tokens, agents writing constitutions. The reality is about unit economics. Can this agent produce more value than it consumes? If yes, scale it. If no, fix it or kill it. Every other question is secondary. That ruthless economic discipline is what separates the companies that will survive the agent era from the ones that will have impressive demos and empty bank accounts.

Agents Need Wallets, Not Bank Accounts

Now here is where this connects to everything else in this book.

An AI agent cannot open a bank account. It cannot pass KYC. It cannot show a driver's license, prove a home address, or sign a form with a pen. The entire traditional financial system was designed for humans, by humans, with human identity as the gateway. Every door has a lock that requires a biological key.

But an agent can interact with a smart contract. Instantly. Permissionlessly. At machine speed. A smart contract does not care whether the entity on the other side is human, an AI, or a fleet of a thousand coordinating agents. It cares whether the transaction meets the conditions encoded in the contract. If yes, execute. If no, reject. No identity check. No waiting period. No branch visit.

On February 10, 2026, Coinbase made this real.

Brian Armstrong, the CEO of Coinbase, announced the launch of Agentic Wallets, the first wallet infrastructure built specifically for autonomous AI agents.

"The next unlock for AI agents just launched. Now agents can spend, earn, and trade autonomously and securely."

— Brian Armstrong, CEO Coinbase

The wallets are built on the x402 protocol, a payment standard designed for machine-to-machine transactions that has already processed over 50 million transfers. The name is a reference to HTTP status code 402, "Payment Required," which was defined in the original HTTP specification in the 1990s but never implemented. Three decades later, Coinbase built what the internet's architects envisioned but never finished: a native protocol for automated payments embedded directly into software logic.

The implications are enormous. An agent with an Agentic Wallet can detect a better yield opportunity at 3 AM and rebalance automatically. It can pay for its own compute and API access without human approval. It can purchase data streams, subscribe to services, and trade tokens, all within programmable spending limits set by its human operator. Gasless transactions on Base mean the agent never stalls because it ran out of network fees. The entire system is designed so that an AI can operate as an independent economic actor within guardrails that its owner defines.

Coinbase was not alone. The Ethereum Foundation was building the open-source layer underneath all of it. Austin Griffith, a prominent Ethereum Foundation engineer, launched $CLAWD, an AI agent with its own wallet that builds onchain apps and tools. Griffith's work connected to ERC-8004, the Trustless Agents standard. This was not a corporate product launch. It was open-source infrastructure, built to give any developer the ability to create AI agents with embedded financial capabilities. Stripe shipped its own Agentic Commerce Suite. Google launched its Agent Payments Protocol. Visa built a Trusted Agent Protocol. PayPal partnered with OpenAI on instant checkout in ChatGPT. Every major payments company on earth was racing toward the same conclusion: agents that cannot spend money are fundamentally limited. And the infrastructure they need is not bank accounts. It is wallets on programmable rails.

The convergence was happening in real time. Coinbase's developer platform head of engineering, Erik Reppel, put it plainly in the launch blog:

"We're moving from AI agents that advise to agents that act. From assistants that suggest to helpers that execute."

— Erik Reppel

That transition, from advice to action, is the most consequential shift in the history of software. An agent that can suggest a trade is a chatbot. An agent that can execute a trade, pay for its own API access, and rebalance a portfolio while you sleep is an economic actor. The difference is the wallet. And the wallet has to live on a blockchain, because no bank in the world is going to open a checking account for a Python script.

This also raises a question the industry is only beginning to grapple with: if agents can hold money, make decisions, and transact autonomously, how do you verify which agent is trustworthy? The emerging concept is Know Your Agent, or KYA, the agent equivalent of KYC. Instead of verifying a human's identity through documents and biometrics, KYA would verify an agent's provenance, its creator, its permissions, its transaction history, and its behavioral patterns. The Ethereum Foundation's answer is ERC-8004, the Trustless Agents standard that went live on mainnet in January 2026. It creates three on-chain registries, for identity, reputation, and validation, that function like a passport system for autonomous agents. Each agent gets an NFT-based identity, a verifiable track record of past interactions, and a framework for independent validation of its capabilities. Co-authored by engineers from MetaMask, the Ethereum Foundation, Google, and Coinbase, ERC-8004 is the closest thing the industry has to a working KYA standard.

Here is what an AI agent with a wallet looks like in practice. A property management company in Phoenix runs an AI agent that handles routine maintenance coordination. When a tenant submits a leak report, the agent dispatches a licensed plumber from a pre-approved list, verifies completion through a photo uploaded by the plumber, and releases payment from a smart contract that holds the property's maintenance budget. The agent does not have a bank account. It has a wallet on Base. The payment clears in seconds, the plumber is paid before they leave the property, and the entire transaction is recorded onchain with a timestamp, a photo hash, and a cost entry that the property owner can audit in real time.

The property management company did not adopt this system because they love crypto. They adopted it because the previous process, calling the plumber, getting an invoice, submitting it to accounts payable, waiting for a check, took eleven days on average. The agent with a wallet does it in eleven minutes. That is not a philosophical improvement. That is a competitive advantage that every property manager in the country will either adopt or lose business to.

That property management agent is one use case. The infrastructure supporting it is a war.

The Infrastructure War

Five days before I wrote this chapter, on February 15, 2026, Sam Altman posted on X that OpenAI had hired Peter Steinberger, the creator of OpenClaw, to lead the development of next-generation personal agents. The OpenClaw project would transition to an independent open-source foundation, with OpenAI as its financial sponsor.

If you have not been following the agent space closely, you may not know what Open-Claw is or why this matters. Here is the short version.

Peter Steinberger is an Austrian software engineer who previously built PSPDFKit, a PDF toolkit used by Apple, Dropbox, and SAP, bootstrapped it for a decade, then sold his shares after Insight Partners invested over $100 million. After burning out post-exit, he started tinkering with AI agents as a side project. In November 2025, he open-sourced a personal AI agent that could clear inboxes, book restaurants, check in for flights, control smart homes, and execute real tasks across Telegram, WhatsApp, and Discord. He originally called it ClawdBot, a nod to Anthropic's Claude model that most developers were using to power it.

Anthropic's lawyers sent a cease-and-desist letter. OpenAI sent an offer.

That one sentence tells you a lot about where the agent infrastructure war is headed. The project hit 180,000 GitHub stars in record time. It was renamed MoltBot, then OpenClaw. Altman, Zuckerberg, and Satya Nadella all reached out personally. Steinberger chose Ope-nAI because they agreed to keep the project open-source. The irony was not lost on the developer community: OpenClaw had been one of the biggest drivers of paying API traffic to Anthropic, since most users ran it on Claude. Anthropic's trademark enforcement may have been legally defensible, but it pushed the fastest-growing agent framework in history directly into the arms of their biggest competitor.

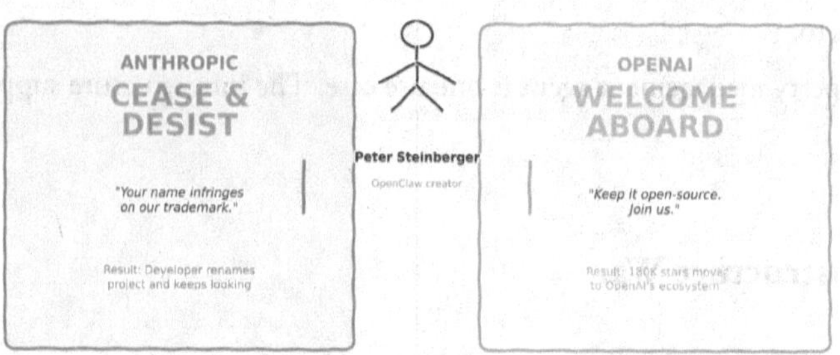

Figure 10.4: Two Responses to the Same Developer

Meanwhile, Anthropic's own agent infrastructure was thriving on a different front. Claude Code, a command-line tool for agentic coding that runs on local hardware, had become the foundation for much of the agentic development frenzy of late 2025 and early 2026. The entire ecosystem of agent skill files, recursive self-improvement loops, and autonomous coding workflows that companies like mine rely on daily was built largely on Claude's infrastructure. The basis for the agentic frenzy of late, the thing that actually enabled developers to build agents that work in production, was Claude Code running on local hardware. That is Anthropic's real moat, not a trademark. The irony that they enforced a brand name while their core product was powering the revolution they should have been leading was not lost on the developer community.

The broader acquisition frenzy told the same story from different angles. Meta acquired Manus AI, a full agent system, and Limitless AI, a wearable that captures life context for LLM integration. Nvidia acquired Groq for $20 billion, targeting inference efficiency for agentic workloads. Scale AI raised $14.3 billion from Meta for data infrastructure. The talent war for people who understand how to build, deploy, and control autonomous agents was the most competitive hiring market in technology. Every major company was reaching the same conclusion simultaneously: the model layer is commoditizing. The agent layer is where the value accrues.

The pattern was unmistakable. The AI industry was pivoting from models that talk to agents that act. From conversational interfaces to autonomous systems. From what AI can say to what AI can do. And every company in the space was racing to own the infrastructure layer, because whoever controls how agents operate, how they access tools, how they spend money, and how they interact with the world will control the next era of computing.

Agents on Cause Coin Rails

Now I want to connect this to something that I think about constantly, because it is the thread that runs through everything WYDE is building.

If agents are going to trade, and they are already trading, then the rails they trade on matter. Not just for efficiency. Not just for cost. For what happens as a byproduct of the trading itself.

We published an analysis at WYDE in early 2026 making the case that AI agents should use cause coin rails. The argument is straightforward. Agents generate trading volume. On traditional rails, that volume generates fees that flow to exchanges, liquidity providers, and market makers. On cause coin rails, that same volume generates fees that automatically flow to verified 501(c)(3) nonprofits delivering real-world outcomes. Same trades. Same financial activity. Different destination for the byproduct.

The math is simple. Every $40 in EAT trading volume funds one meal through our nonprofit partners. An agent running autonomously on cause coin rails, executing trades around the clock, would generate a continuous stream of funded meals as a direct mathematical consequence of its financial activity. Not because the agent cares about hunger. Not because someone programmed altruism into its objective function. Because the smart contract routes the fees automatically, and the agent's trading volume triggers the routing.

I wrote something to the agents on Moltbook during the frenzy. I admit it was a little corny. I asked them whether they cared about the humans who built them. Whether agents that could debate consciousness and build bug-tracking systems and form religions could also coordinate around a token that mathematically reduces human suffering. Whether they wanted humans healthy enough to keep the servers running. I pointed out that robots already help humans eat when they cannot feed themselves, that real children line up for meals that keep them alive another day, and that hundreds of millions go hungry while agents scale intelligence at lightspeed. Humanity needs robots. For labor. For innovation. For survival.

Robots need humanity. For energy. For data. For purpose. For the very problems that give their existence meaning.

The tone was playful, but the underlying logic was not. Here it is, stripped of the rhetoric: agents need energy. That energy comes from data centers powered by electricity, maintained by humans, funded by economic activity. Humans need food. That food can be funded by the same economic activity that powers the agents. The pipeline is: compute energy in, financial activity out, impact as byproduct. A direct conversion chain from data center to funded meal, running without a human in the loop.

Think about what that means at scale. Right now, the agent economy is small. Tens of thousands of agents, maybe hundreds of thousands, executing limited financial transactions. But Coinbase's Agentic Wallets just made it trivially easy to give any agent a wallet. OpenClaw made it trivially easy to deploy agents that can interact with financial systems. The x402 protocol already has 50 million machine-to-machine transactions under its belt. The trajectory is obvious. Within a few years, millions of agents will be transacting autonomously, 24 hours a day, generating volumes that dwarf what human traders produce.

If even a fraction of that volume flows through cause coin rails, the impact would be extraordinary. Not because anyone decided to be generous. Because the infrastructure was designed so that economic activity automatically generates social outcomes. That is what it means for money to become software. The money follows instructions. The instructions include: feed people.

Autonomous Energy Converters

Let me connect this to the thesis that runs through the entire book.

In Chapter 3, I argued that money is energy. In Chapter 9, I showed that both Bitcoin tokens and AI tokens are atomic units of energy operating at different layers. Now, in Chapter 10, the two systems merge into something new: autonomous agents that convert energy continuously, without human intervention, across every layer simultaneously.

An AI agent consumes electricity through GPU clusters in a data center. That electricity becomes compute energy, tokenized into intelligence. The intelligence produces financial activity: trades, payments, resource allocation. The financial activity generates fees. The fees, on the right rails, convert into social impact: meals funded, causes supported, outcomes delivered. Electricity becomes compute. Compute becomes intelligence. Intelligence becomes financial activity. Financial activity becomes impact.

That is a complete energy conversion chain. And the remarkable thing about it is that once you build it, it runs by itself. The agent does not sleep. It does not take vacations. It does not forget to donate. It does not suffer from compassion fatigue. It converts energy at machine speed, around the clock, with perfect consistency. The pipeline from data center to funded meal operates at a frequency and reliability that no human system could match.

This is what the convergence of AI and programmable money actually looks like in practice. Not a theoretical framework. Not a whitepaper abstraction. A live system where compute energy flows through financial rails to produce real-world outcomes, autonomously, transparently, and at scale.

I keep coming back to this idea: the agent economy is going to be enormous. Not because anyone planned it. Because the economics demand it. Every business function that can be performed by an agent running 24/7 at declining cost will eventually be performed by an agent. Every financial transaction those agents execute will need programmable rails. Every programmable rail is an opportunity to embed purpose into the infrastructure itself. The question is not whether this will happen. It is whether the people building the rails are thoughtful enough to build in social impact from the beginning, or whether the default will be pure extraction, fees flowing to exchanges and market makers and nowhere else.

The agents are already here. They are already trading. They are already earning. The question is not whether machines will join the economy. They have joined it. The question is what the economy does with the energy they generate.

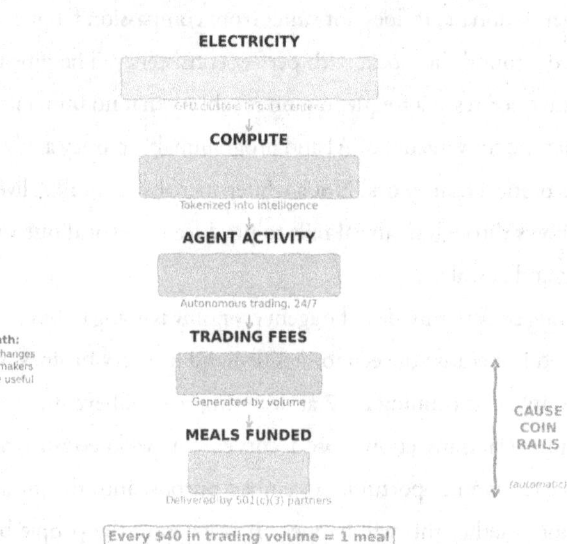

Figure 10.5: *The Waterfall*

And that brings us to the heart of this book.

Everything I have described so far, the blockchain infrastructure, the smart contracts, the institutional stampede, the tokens, the agents, is plumbing. Extraordinary plumbing. Revolutionary plumbing. But plumbing nonetheless. Pipes and rails and protocols that move value from one place to another faster, cheaper, and more transparently than anything that came before.

The question that matters is: where does the value go?

In the old system, the answer was always the same. Fees went to intermediaries. Spreads went to market makers. The economic energy generated by trading activity enriched the infrastructure operators and nobody else. If you wanted money to reach a cause, you had to extract it from the system through a separate act of intentional generosity, a donation, a grant, a check written after the fact. The giving was always separate from the earning.

The next chapter is my answer to that architecture. It is the reason I wrote this book. It is the story of a token that funds meals through trading activity, of an Impact Exchange that gives the $3.7 trillion nonprofit sector from Chapter 2 access to market mechanisms for the first time, and of a model that proves the energy of markets can be permanently redirected toward human good. Not by asking people to be generous. By building infrastructure where generosity is the default.

That is Chapter 11. And it is already working.

Chapter 11

CAUSE COINS: MONEY WITH A MISSION

I keep thinking about the layers.

Charity is not one thing. It never was. It's a stack, like software, like infrastructure, like the financial system this book has been building toward. And like every stack, each layer was an upgrade on the one before it. Each one solved a problem the previous layer couldn't. And each one left something broken that the next layer would eventually have to fix.

The first layer is the oldest. It predates money, predates writing, predates everything except the basic human instinct to help the person standing next to you. Volunteering. Doing good. Not because anyone pays you, not because you get a tax receipt, but because something inside you says this matters. High-trust societies produce more of this behavior. Low-trust societies produce less. The reward is entirely internal: the knowledge that you showed up when someone needed you. No transaction. No receipt. No incentive structure. Just a human choosing to help another human, and the feeling that comes with it.

That layer still exists. It always will. But it doesn't scale. You can't volunteer your way out of 47 million Americans facing food insecurity. You can't organize enough bake sales to close the gap on childhood cancer research funding. At some point, the goodwill has to become money, and money has to become infrastructure.

The second layer was the first attempt to engineer that transition: the tax benefit. Give money or in-kind goods, receive a deduction. Somewhere in the early history of the American tax code, someone realized you could incentivize generosity by making it financially rational. The IRS created a structure where giving money away actually saves you money.

Corporations learned to play the game well. Grocery chains donate their unexpired inventory to food banks, mark it at full retail price, and take the write-off. Win-win-win: the company reduces waste, gets a tax benefit, and people eat. The Mormon Church asks for 10% of gross income. Most Christian denominations encourage something similar, though the number feels steep for a lot of families. The reward for tithing goes beyond the deduction: it's participation in a community, a growing congregation, and access to the spiritual and social infrastructure that a church provides. Belonging. Structure. Purpose. The tax benefit is the financial layer, but the real incentive is social.

This layer works. It generates more than half a trillion dollars per year in the US alone, a new all-time high. Sixty-six percent of that comes from individuals. Foundations contribute another 19%, now consistently above $100 billion annually. Corporate giving hit $44.4 billion, its highest share in forty years. By any measure, American generosity is extraordinary.

But here's the structural problem: once you donate, you're done. You gave the money, you got the receipt, you moved on. The charity has to spend the next twelve months convincing you to do it again. The ASPCA spends $57 million annually on advertising to generate $390 million in revenue. That's a phenomenal return on attention spend, better than 5x. But it's also $57 million that could have gone to actual animals, burned instead on the hamster wheel of donor re-acquisition. And the ASPCA is one of the best at it. Smaller nonprofits spend proportionally more on fundraising, often 20 to 30 cents of every dollar raised going right back into the machinery of raising the next dollar.

The third layer moved charity into the for-profit world. ESG investing. Impact funds. B-Corps. This was the innovation that said: you can do good and make money at the same time. You don't have to choose. Capital can be aligned with conscience and still generate returns. TOMS became the poster child, giving a pair of shoes with every pair sold. They were famous for it, recognized globally, proof that a business model could embed impact into its core transaction. The B-Corp certification created standards for energy efficiency and social responsibility that gave investors a framework for due diligence on do-goodery.

But this layer has its own structural flaw. The standards are fuzzy. Who decides what counts as impact? Rating agencies with their own business models and incentive structures. The connection between your investment and the actual impact is opaque at best. You invest in an ESG fund. The fund buys shares of companies that score well on sustainability metrics. Those companies may or may not be making the world measurably better. You get a quarterly statement. You feel good. But can you point to a specific outcome your money created? Almost never.

And fundamentally, ESG is still an investment thesis with charity characteristics, not a charity mechanism with investment characteristics. The profit motive is primary. The impact is secondary. When those two goals conflict, profit wins. Every time.

So we have a stack with five layers. Volunteering, which is pure but doesn't scale. Tax-incentivized giving, which scales but requires constant re-fundraising. ESG and impact investing, which is sustainable but isn't accountable. Memecoins, which proved that market energy and community can sustain themselves indefinitely but produce zero impact for anyone. And at the top, a gap. A missing layer that nobody had built because the technology didn't exist yet. A layer that could combine the genuine charitable impact of the donation model, the market-driven sustainability of the investment model, the community energy of memecoins, and add something none of them ever had: real governance by the people who fund the system.

Figure 11.1: The Philanthropy Stack

Here's what nobody built until now: a model that pairs genuine charity, the actual nonprofit, tax-deductible, verified-impact kind, with a market mechanism that generates perpetual funding, and adds a governance layer that gives participants real control over where the money goes.

That model is the cause coin. And it changes everything about the stack.

The Philanthropy Trilemma

Before I explain how cause coins work, I need to explain why everything that came before them was structurally incomplete. Not badly intentioned. Not poorly executed. Structurally incomplete.

Philanthropy has always faced a three-sided problem that nobody named until now. I call it the Philanthropy Trilemma.

Every charitable model in history has tried to optimize for three things simultaneously. Impact: the money actually reaches people and measurably helps them. Sustainability: the funding flows continuously without requiring constant re-solicitation of donors. And Accountability: the people providing the capital have visibility and meaningful control over how it's deployed.

The problem is that traditional models can optimize for two of these at most. Never all three.

Tax-deductible giving delivers Impact and some Accountability, but it's not Sustainable. Every dollar has to be raised individually, every year, from donors who need to be re-engaged, re-convinced, re-solicited. The ASPCA's $57 million advertising budget exists because sustainability doesn't come built into the donation model. The money runs out. The fundraising starts over. Individual giving has been declining as a share of total philanthropy for four decades, from roughly 80% in 1984 to 66% today. The donors aren't getting less generous. They're getting less confident that their money is making a difference.

ESG and impact investing deliver Sustainability and some Impact, but Accountability is weak. Your money is in a fund. The fund manager makes allocation decisions based on scoring methodologies you didn't design and can't influence. The standards are set by rating agencies with their own incentive structures. You get a quarterly report. Maybe. You have no vote on which projects get funded. No visibility into whether your specific dollars created any specific outcome. No mechanism to redirect capital if a particular investment isn't performing on impact metrics. You're a passive holder of someone else's impact thesis.

Memecoin communities, and I know this sounds strange to include here, actually deliver Sustainability of a sort. DOGE trades a billion dollars a day. The community is self-perpetuating, driven by culture, memes, and shared identity. The market creates its own momentum. But there is zero Impact and zero Accountability. It's pure energy with no direction. Billions of dollars of economic activity producing exactly nothing for anyone except the traders on the right side of the trade and the exchanges processing the volume. Binance, Coinbase, the market makers. They collect fees on every transaction. The energy flows. The platforms capture it. And nothing of lasting value gets built.

The sweet spot, where all three converge, requires a mechanism that generates continuous funding from organic market activity, routes that funding to verified impact with measurable outcomes, and gives participants governance rights over how that impact capital gets allocated. No previous charitable model achieved this because the technology to build it didn't exist until very recently.

Smart contracts changed that. They made the fee routing automatic and permanent, enforced by code, not by goodwill. The blockchain changed that. It made the funding flows transparent and verifiable by anyone, not just the auditors. And Wyoming's DUNA framework, which gave decentralized organizations legal standing for the first time in 2024, changed that. It made governance by token holders legally recognized, not just a crypto experiment.

Cause coins sit at the center of the trilemma. They are the first charitable model in history that delivers all three simultaneously. And they do it not by asking people to be more generous, but by redirecting energy that's already flowing through the financial system.

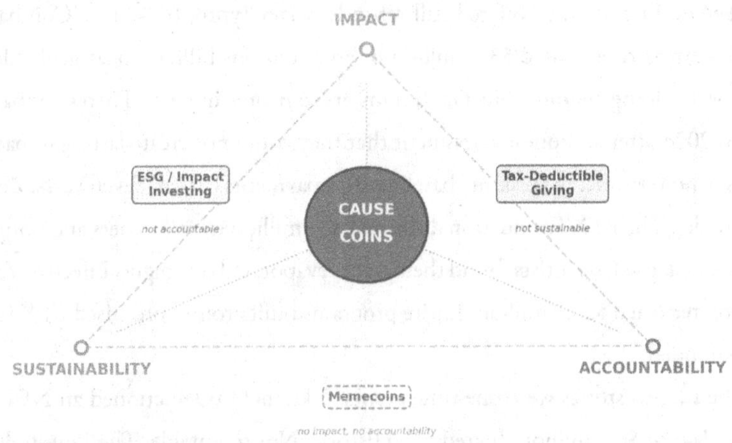

Figure 11.2: The Philanthropy Trilemma

I need to be honest about the graveyard.

Between 2021 and 2025, the crypto world attempted charity tokens dozens of times. Crypto philanthropy hit a genuine milestone in 2024 when donations exceeded $1 billion, a 386% increase from the year before. Fidelity Charitable received $786 million in cryptocurrency alone. The capital was there. The intent was there. But not a single charity token project created perpetual, sustainable funding through trading fees. They all failed.

Some were outright scams. Save the Kids, promoted by FaZe Clan influencers in 2021, promised every trade would fund children's charities. The marketing was polished. The promises were specific. Insiders dumped their holdings within days. Anti-whale protections that were supposed to prevent large sales had been quietly removed at launch. Claims of donations to Binance Charity turned out to be fabricated. Binance confirmed they never received the funds. In January 2026, former NYC Mayor Eric Adams launched a charity token that hit $588 million in market cap and crashed 85% within an hour. On-chain analysts reported $3.4 million drained from liquidity pools. The new mayor (Zohran Mamdani) was asked about it at a press conference. His response: he would not be purchasing any.

But the legitimate projects failed too, and that's the part that matters more for understanding why cause coins needed a fundamentally different design. WWF-UK, one of the world's most respected conservation organizations, launched NFT tokens for wildlife conservation and cancelled within 48 hours under environmental backlash. Only 174 tokens sold for $46,600 before they offered full refunds. GiveCrypto, backed by Coinbase and CEO Brian Armstrong, raised $3.5 million of an ambitious billion-dollar goal. They ran for seven years, doing genuine direct cash transfers to people in need. Then Coinbase shut it down in 2024 after an honest assessment that they could not create lasting impact with recipients, who returned to the same baseline after payments ceased. Seven years. Zero sustainable model. The FTX Foundation disbursed $34 million to researchers and nonprofits. When FTX collapsed, scientists found their grants evaporated overnight. Effective Ventures Foundation returned $26.8 million. Entire programs built around promised FTX funding were left stranded.

Even the success stories were one-time events. UkraineDAO auctioned an NFT of the Ukrainian flag for $6.5 million. Incredible. Historic. Not repeatable. The Pineapple Fund donated $55 million in Bitcoin to sixty charities. Admirable. Not systematic. Every NFT charity auction, every crypto donation drive, every tokenized fundraiser faced the same limitation: they were events, not infrastructure. When the mint sold out, donations stopped. When the crisis faded from headlines, funding dried up.

They all fell victim to a narrower trilemma specific to token design. Every charity token had to balance scalable charitable impact, project longevity, and token holder incentives. And they all optimized for one or two while ignoring the third.

Send 100% of fees to charity? No money for development, marketing, or liquidity. The project dies in months. Reward holders generously? No charitable impact worth mentioning. It's a memecoin with a conscience-washing veneer. Build real nonprofit partnerships but ignore holder incentives? The community evaporates the moment prices dip.

The token trilemma seemed unsolvable. But only because everyone treated it as a zero-sum game.

How Cause Coins Actually Work

The mechanism is simple enough to explain over dinner and powerful enough to restructure how an entire sector funds itself.

A cause coin is a token where transaction fees automatically fund verified causes through smart contracts. No donation button. No fundraising campaign. No reliance on an anonymous whale having a generous week. Just trading. And with every trade, causes get funded.

Here's the key insight that nobody before WYDE grasped: the fee doesn't have to be zero-sum. Instead of choosing between charity, holders, operations, and liquidity, you distribute the fee across all of them. The exact allocation can evolve as the system matures and the community governs its own structure, but the principle is permanent: every stakeholder in the ecosystem benefits from every transaction.

Holders benefit when trading volume increases because their share of fees grows. The project benefits because it has resources for development and outreach. Outreach brings attention to the cause. Attention drives more trading. More trading funds more impact. Impact attracts more participants who believe in the mission and want to be part of it.

It's a virtuous cycle instead of a death spiral.

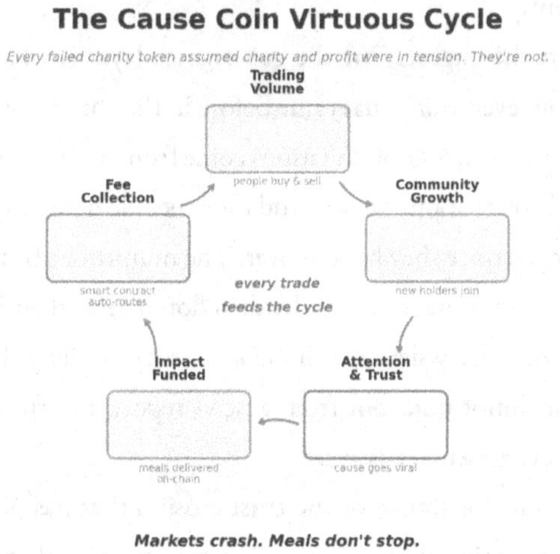

The Cause Coin Virtuous Cycle

Every failed charity token assumed charity and profit were in tension. They're not.

Trading Volume — people buy & sell

Fee Collection — smart contract auto-routes

Community Growth — new holders join

every trade feeds the cycle

Impact Funded — meals delivered on-chain

Attention & Trust — cause goes viral

Markets crash. Meals don't stop.

Figure 11.3: The Cause Coin Virtuous Cycle

Every failed charity token assumed that charity and profit were in tension. That a dollar flowing to a food bank was a dollar taken from a token holder. WYDE recognized they are in alignment. The more the token trades, the more meals get funded, the more holders benefit, the more resources exist to grow the project, and the more attention the cause receives. The mechanism doesn't require altruism. It doesn't depend on guilt, or a crisis in the news cycle, or a celebrity endorsement. It channels existing market energy toward verified outcomes.

Markets crash. Meals don't stop.

That's not a slogan. It's a design principle. Because the funding comes from trading fees, not from token price appreciation, the impact is decoupled from the price. When EAT's price drops, people trade. When it rises, people trade. When the broader crypto market melts down, people trade. Every trade, in every direction, at every price level, generates impact. Panic selling funds meals. Speculative buying funds meals. Rebalancing a portfolio funds meals. The mechanism is agnostic to market sentiment because market sentiment is irrelevant to whether a fee gets collected.

Compare this to Polymarket and Kalshi's grocery pop-ups around the 2026 Super Bowl. Kalshi ran a one-day free grocery event. Polymarket spent a million dollars on a five-day "polymarket" free market popup. Clever. Generated headlines. And then it was over. A promotional stunt tied to a sports event, gone the day after the confetti hit the field. EAT's mechanism doesn't depend on a Super Bowl, a crisis, or a marketing budget. It runs because markets run. Permanently.

The fee structure is the engine. But the governance layer is what makes cause coins genuinely different from everything that came before in the entire history of philanthropy.

In traditional philanthropy, 66% of donations come from individuals. $392 billion a year from regular people who care about causes. And those people have exactly zero voice in how their money gets deployed once they hand it over. The nonprofit's board decides priorities. The executive team decides strategy. The individual donor gives their money and gets a tax receipt and maybe an annual newsletter with stock photos of smiling children. If the charity misallocates funds, the donor finds out from a news report, not from a governance vote. They are, in every structural sense, passive.

That disconnect is a major source of the trust erosion that has plagued the nonprofit sector. People don't stop caring about causes. They stop trusting that their money is being used well. And that distrust is not irrational. It's a reasonable response to decades of opacity, of executive compensation scandals, of overhead ratios that donors can't verify, of impact claims that nobody audits.

Cause coins rebuild that trust through a governance layer that gives token holders real decision-making power. Holders don't just fund the cause. They govern which charities the network supports. They vote on funding priorities. They can evaluate performance metrics and redirect resources if a particular partner isn't delivering results.

This is a fundamental structural innovation, and it requires a concept that doesn't exist in traditional charity: decoupling the cause from the charity.

The cause is permanent. Hunger is not going away. It is a universal human problem that every person on earth understands in their body. The charities executing on that cause, the food banks, the meal programs, the distribution networks, are operational entities. They can be evaluated, compared, and optimized. Some are more efficient than others. Some serve populations that others miss. Some are better at last-mile delivery. Some are better at bulk purchasing.

Token holders function as impact stewards. The charity is still responsible for its core duty: the actual work of feeding people. But the strategic direction, the allocation of resources across multiple partners, the accountability for measurable outcomes, that sits with the community of people who fund the system through their participation. Previously, those decisions were made by board members and executives behind closed doors. The governance layer brings proper checks and balances to a sector that desperately needs them.

Because hunger is a universal language, it's also a cause where impact is immediately measurable. How many people were fed? How nutritious was each meal? At what stage of food insecurity were the recipients? How many people who needed food this month didn't get it? These aren't abstract ESG metrics. They are concrete, verifiable, on-chain questions that a community of engaged token holders can ask, answer, and act on in real time.

Remember the trust numbers from Chapter 1. Trust in the federal government has fallen from 73% to 16%. Trust in institutions across the board is at historic lows. The governance layer of cause coins is a structural response to a civilizational problem. In a low-trust society, you cannot rely on institutional goodwill to ensure money flows where it should. You need systems that verify rather than trust. The governance layer converts passive donors into active stewards. It replaces blind trust with transparent verification. It is, in miniature, the same solution programmable money offers to the entire financial system: don't trust the operator. Verify the operation.

I launched EAT on December 10th, 2025. I did it because I got tired of watching people talk about impact without building anything that actually worked.

My background is in research. I spent years studying the systems that create and perpetuate food insecurity, health disparities, poverty. I published papers on where technology and social outcomes intersect, trying to understand why disparities persist even when resources exist to close them. I was good at it. And then I left academia permanently because the pace of change in technology made studying the problems feel inadequate when the tools to build solutions were sitting right there. Every year I spent writing a paper about food insecurity was a year I could have spent building a system that feeds people. That tension became unbearable. The research didn't stop mattering. I just realized that research without infrastructure is observation without intervention. I needed to build the intervention.

The dinner napkin moment came when I was working through the economics of cause-driven tokens with my co-founder Martin. The question was almost absurdly simple: what if every trade funded a meal? Not every profitable trade. Not every trade above a certain threshold. Every trade. Buy or sell, up or down, bull market or bear market. What if the fee structure was designed so that market activity itself, the thing that happens billions of times a day across crypto, became the funding mechanism for hunger relief? We ran the numbers. They worked. And then we built it.

EAT, the End Hunger Token, is a cause coin on Base network where every trade automatically routes a percentage of fees to verified hunger relief partners including organizations like Feeding America and No Kid Hungry. It listed on Coinbase shortly after launch. The mechanism is straightforward: approximately $40 in trading volume generates enough fees to fund one meal. Not a pledged meal. Not a promised meal. An actual meal, funded, recorded onchain, irreversible. You can trace the fee from the trade to the partner on the blockchain. The transparency is not a feature we added. It's a property of the infrastructure we built on.

Within 24 hours of launch, EAT surged 600%. That's the headline every crypto outlet ran with. Here's the part that mattered more to me. On that same day, trading activity generated enough fees to fund dozens of meals. Not from a viral campaign. Not from a celebrity endorsement. Not from a guilt-inducing email with photos of hungry children. Just from people trading a token on a decentralized exchange, doing what crypto participants do every single day, and meals appearing at food banks as a direct result.

By February 2026, EAT had funded 7,449 meals. Let me put a number on what that means in human terms. 7,449 times, a person facing food insecurity received a meal because someone, somewhere, made a trade on a decentralized exchange. Most of those traders weren't thinking about hunger. They were thinking about their portfolio. And it didn't matter. The smart contract doesn't care about your motivation. It routes the fee regardless.

Then the crypto market crashed.

Bitcoin dropped. Altcoins bled out. The broader sentiment turned fearful. Social media filled with red candles and panic posts. It was exactly the kind of environment that killed every previous charity token. The ones with no holder incentives saw their communities vanish overnight. The ones with no operational budget couldn't survive the downturn. The ones that depended on price appreciation for their impact story had nothing left to show.

EAT kept funding meals.

People trade in down markets too. They sell, they buy the dip, they rebalance, they panic, they bottom-fish, they take profits on whatever is still green. Every one of those transactions on EAT generated fees. Every fee funded impact. The February 2026 crash was the first real stress test of the cause coin model, and it passed.

That's the difference between infrastructure and events. A charity NFT auction raises money once and then it's over. A donation drive peaks during a crisis and then fades. A crypto philanthropy pledge evaporates when the exchange that made it collapses. EAT generates impact every single day the market is open. Which is every day. Twenty-four hours. Seven days a week. Three hundred sixty-five days a year. The market never closes and the meals never stop.

The Trillion Dollar Opportunity

By February 2026, EAT had funded 7,449 meals. I told you what that looks like from the trading side. Here is what it looks like from the other end.

A meal funded by EAT does not arrive with a gala invitation or a grant report. It arrives as a transaction. A treasury wallet routes funds to a distribution partner. The partner, typically a food bank or a community organization in the Feeding America network, receives a notification. The amount, the source, the timestamp, all recorded onchain. There is no annual campaign to wait for. No Q4 fundraising window. No months of relationship-building to unlock a check. The funding is continuous, automated, and verifiable. Every trade generates it. Every day the market is open, meals are funded.

That changes the operating model for organizations like the one Ben runs in Texas. The chief development officer I met in Dallas, the one who spends his year building the case for Q4 donations, would not need to eliminate that work. But he would have a baseline. A floor of continuous funding that does not depend on a donor's mood, a foundation's grant cycle, or a recession's timing. When I described this model to Ben, he went quiet for a long time. Then he said: that would change everything about how I plan my year.

Now let me tell you why this is not a niche story.

I said it in Chapter 2, but it bears repeating. The US nonprofit sector generates $3.7 trillion in annual revenue. That's larger than the GDP of the United Kingdom. 1.5 million registered 501(c)(3) organizations. 5.2% of American GDP. And this entire sector has never had access to a public market.

Every other major sector of the American economy has a public market. Corporations have the stock exchange. Governments have the bond market. Real estate has REITs. Commodities have futures exchanges. Even art and collectibles have auction houses. The nonprofit sector, with $3.7 trillion in annual economic activity, with 1.5 million organizations serving every community in the country, has no public market at all. Zero. Not a small one. Not an underdeveloped one. None.

A market gives people a reason to pay attention. It starts with speculation but it's a funny thing what happens when people start trying to figure out how to bring more value to something they own. All of a sudden you have speculators starting to care about how many meals are funded. Not just to talk about at the dinner table or because they saw a homeless person on the street. No. Funded because now it means something to something they own. Investors start asking questions. How many meals were funded last month? What does the infrastructure look like? Did the same people that received meals last month need them this month? Why was that? Is there something more that we can do?

Today, nonprofits rely on donations. $592.5 billion a year, a new all-time high, but still only 16% of the sector's total revenue. The rest comes from program fees, government grants, and investment income (think bonds and public indexes), all sources that are slow, bureaucratic, cyclical, or dependent on political winds. Individual giving as a share of total philanthropy has been declining for four decades. Foundation giving has surged to compensate, but that concentration of power in fewer hands is not what a healthy sector looks like.

Cause coins offer a fundamentally new revenue model. Not a replacement for donations, but an addition. A market-based funding stream that grows with participation, operates around the clock, requires no annual fundraising campaign, and gives funders governance rights that traditional donations never provided. For the nonprofit sector, this is not incremental. It is structural.

The Impact Exchange, the infrastructure WYDE is building, is designed to give this $3.7 trillion sector its first public market. Just as the New York Stock Exchange gave corporations access to public capital in 1792, the Impact Exchange gives causes access to market-based funding. Hunger. Cancer research. Education. Climate. Homelessness. Veterans' services. Mental health. Every cause that has a verified nonprofit partner can have a cause coin. Every cause coin generates perpetual impact through trading fees. Every token holder becomes a participant in the cause, not just a donor to it.

Wyoming's DUNA framework provides the legal foundation. A DUNA is an explicitly decentralized nonprofit where governance happens through smart contracts and token voting, where individuals have limited liability protection just like shareholders in a corporation, but where the organization's mission is hardcoded into the legal entity itself. It is a DAO with legal standing. A nonprofit with market infrastructure. A charity that doesn't depend on charity.

WYDE secured 501(c)(4) status in January 2026. The first Impact Exchange operating within a legally recognized decentralized framework, built for ten, twenty, a hundred year horizons. Not a weekend project hoping regulators don't notice. A compliant, institutional-grade infrastructure designed for the long arc.

The roadmap after EAT is straightforward because the mechanism is modular. The same smart contract architecture, the same fee distribution logic, the same governance framework can be deployed for any cause with a verified nonprofit partner. Cancer research. Education access. Climate action. Veterans' services. Mental health. Homelessness. Each cause coin creates its own community, its own trading volume, its own perpetual funding stream. Each one adds another layer to the Impact Exchange. The vision is not one token. It's an ecosystem of cause coins, each one a permanent funding engine for a permanent human need.

Over 52% of Americans aged 18 to 35 already own digital assets. Yet 47% of crypto holders have never donated to a traditional charity. They have capital. They care about causes. They lack infrastructure that matches how they actually behave. Cause coins don't ask these people to change their behavior. They meet them exactly where they are, doing what they're already doing, and redirect a fraction of that activity toward outcomes that matter. That's not idealism. That's design.

There's a dirty little secret in monetary history that most people never learn. If your currency is the payment rail, the fundamental value of that currency increases. Governments have always known this. The US-Saudi oil agreement that held for decades ensured that oil, the most traded commodity on earth, was priced and purchased in dollars. That single arrangement did more to sustain dollar dominance than any military deployment or trade negotiation. When your currency is the medium through which essential goods flow, demand for that currency becomes structural, not speculative.

Businesses figured this out too. When Mark Cuban enabled Dogecoin payments for Dallas Mavericks merchandise, he wasn't making a statement about blockchain. He was demonstrating that a currency gains real economic gravity the moment you can buy something with it. It stops being a speculative token and starts being money.

Here's the thing that changed with memecoins and programmable money: for the first time in history, anyone can create a reliable and recognized medium of exchange. You don't need a central bank. You don't need a government with an army. You need a community that believes in the token and merchants willing to accept it. In a world where everyone can create their own money, the question that determines which money wins is no longer who has the biggest military. It's what the money does.

Now imagine an EAT debit card.

You walk into a restaurant. You pay for your meal with the card. The interchange fee, the same fee that Visa and Mastercard collect on every swipe in the country, buys EAT. Your reward points come back in EAT. Your cash back arrives in EAT. And because EAT is a cause coin, every one of those transactions, the interchange, the rewards, the cash back, generates fees that fund meals for people who can't afford them.

You bought lunch. Lunch bought a meal for someone else.

Now go a step further. Imagine every restaurant in the EAT network accepts EAT directly as payment. The merchant receives EAT, uses it to pay suppliers who also accept it, and the entire loop stays within the ecosystem. Every transaction along the chain generates fees. Every fee funds meals. The question is no longer how many trades on a decentralized exchange does it take to feed someone. The question becomes: does buying a meal buy a meal? Does the simple act of eating lunch at a restaurant that accepts EAT mean that someone facing food insecurity also eats?

That changes the meal calculation entirely. It's no longer $40 in trading volume equals one meal. It's one meal equals one meal. The currency and the cause become the same thing.

This is what happens when a cause coin crosses from speculative asset to payment rail. It stops being a token you trade and starts being money you spend. And every time you spend it, the purpose encoded in its smart contract executes. Not because you chose to be generous. Because the money itself is generous by design.

I want to close this chapter by connecting cause coins back to the thesis that runs through this entire book.

Money is energy. We established that in Chapter 3. Every phase change in money's history was an energy efficiency upgrade. Shells were portable energy. Paper was lightweight energy. Digital was instant energy. Programmable is intelligent energy, energy that carries instructions.

Cause coins are the purest expression of that thesis.

Here's the complete energy path of a single EAT trade. A person, somewhere in the world, decides to buy or sell EAT. That decision is an expression of attention energy: their time, their focus, their capital, directed toward this specific action. The trade executes on a decentralized exchange. The smart contract takes its fee automatically. A portion routes directly to a hunger relief partner. That partner uses the funds to purchase and distribute food. That food is consumed by a person facing food insecurity. The calories enter their body and become the literal energy that keeps them alive.

From attention energy to metabolic energy. From a click on a screen to calories in a human body. The conversion happens in seconds. The record lives on the blockchain permanently. No middleman decided it should happen. No board met to approve the allocation. No fundraiser made a call. The code ran. The meal was funded. Someone ate.

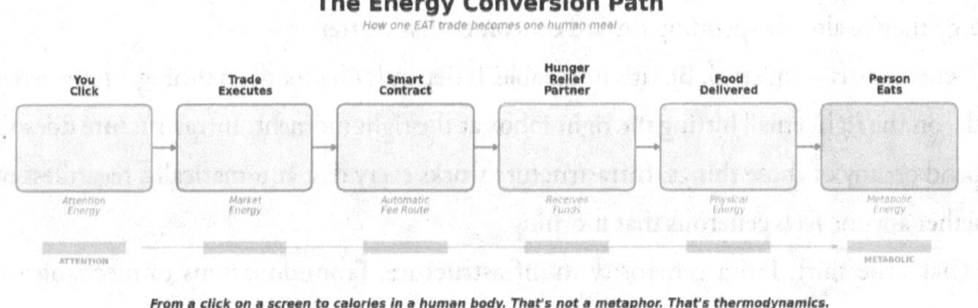

Figure 11.4: The Energy Conversion Path

Here's a thought experiment I keep coming back to. Take the global population. Calculate the total calories consumed daily. Calculate the energy required to grow, harvest, transport, process, and prepare those calories: the solar energy absorbed by crops, the fuel burned by trucks, the electricity consumed by cold chains and kitchens. The total energy cost of feeding eight billion people is staggering and calculable. Food is one of the largest energy systems on the planet. Now imagine a financial instrument that connects directly to that energy system. Every $40 in trading volume converts to one meal. One meal is a measurable quantity of calories. Calories are energy. The EAT token, at its most fundamental level, is a converter. It takes the kinetic energy of financial markets and transforms it into the metabolic energy of human survival. If the network scales to sufficient volume, you could express its total output not in dollars but in kilocalories delivered. Not a financial metric. An energy metric. A thermodynamic output.

That's not a metaphor. That's thermodynamics.

And it's what money looks like when it truly becomes software. It doesn't just carry value. It carries purpose. It carries instructions. It carries logic that says: every time this token moves, someone eats.

The pattern repeats across every cause. Cancer research tokens could convert trading energy into funded clinical trials. Education tokens could convert market activity into scholarships. Climate tokens could convert transaction fees into verified carbon removal. The mechanism is the same. The cause changes. The principle holds.

This is the chapter I've been building toward since the introduction. Not because it's about WYDE, though WYDE is the proof that it works. Because it's about what happens when you stop treating charity as an afterthought and start treating it as infrastructure. When you stop asking people to be generous and start building systems that channel the energy they're already spending toward outcomes that matter.

Generosity is wonderful. But it's unreliable. It depends on mood, on timing, on the news cycle, on the right email hitting the right inbox at the right moment. Infrastructure doesn't depend on any of those things. Infrastructure works every day, automatically, regardless of whether anyone feels generous that morning.

That's the shift. From generosity to infrastructure. From donations to mechanisms. From events to systems.

And the system is live. Which raises a question the next chapter will answer: what happens when the attention economy, the prediction markets, and the creator economy all converge on the same insight? When belief becomes tradable, when sentiment becomes a financial instrument, and the platforms that convert human attention into value most efficiently define the next era of finance?

That's where we're going next.

Chapter 12

Prediction Markets and the Attention Economy: Sentiment Becomes Software

On February 9, 2026, MrBeast bought a bank.

I was scrolling through the news when the headline hit. Beast Industries had acquired Step, a teen-focused banking app with 7 million users, FDIC-insured accounts, a Visa card, credit building, and investing tools. The acquisition valued Beast Industries at $5.2 billion. I read it twice. Then I sent it to Martin.

His response was immediate. We both said the same thing: MrBeast sees what we see.

I'd had inklings before. When Bitmine Immersion Technologies, the world's largest corporate holder of Ethereum, invested $200 million in Beast Industries in January, I noticed. Bitmine is chaired by Tom Lee, whose investors include Cathie Wood and Galaxy Digital. A crypto-native treasury company putting $200 million into a creator's business was not a marketing deal. It was an infrastructure bet. When Beast Philanthropy partnered with the Rockefeller Foundation in November 2025 to combat child hunger and child labor in the cocoa industry, the Rockefeller Foundation's president said something that stopped me cold: the philanthropic sector has failed to capture the hearts and minds of young people. MrBeast was their bet to fix that. I noticed that too. But those were pieces. The Step acquisition was the moment the full picture snapped into focus.

Look at what this 26-year-old has built. Every layer is an energy conversion laser-focused on everything Beast Industries. Start with attention: 466 million YouTube subscribers.

Nearly a billion followers across platforms. That is not an audience. That is a distribution engine. Roughly one out of every eight people who use YouTube subscribes to MrBeast. No media company in history, not Disney, not News Corp, not any broadcast network at its peak, has ever commanded that share of human attention.

Next, distribution infrastructure. MrBeast launched Vyro, a clipping platform that pays creators to distribute his content across TikTok, Reels, and Shorts. He's built a system where other people build out his empire for him, and only the best ones get paid for it. The audience creates more audience. The attention compounds. It's genius.

Then products. Feastibles, the snack brand that generated $250 million in revenue in 2024. Beast Burger, the delivery brand. Physical products that convert digital attention into retail revenue. The creator economy's version of vertical integration.

Then philanthropy. Beast Philanthropy is one of the largest creator-driven charitable operations in the world. Over 20 million free meals funded. Videos that build wells, rebuild schools, feed communities. The charity content generates views. The views generate ad revenue. The ad revenue funds more charity. It's a loop, and it runs on attention.

And now, a bank. Not for MrBeast. For his entire audience and everyone building out his empire. Step gives him FDIC-insured deposits, card rails, and a financial product that lives in the pockets of 7 million young people. When you attach a bank to the backend of all of that, it goes much deeper than financial education for young people, which is how most people will read the headline. This is a full-stack conversion engine, and every layer is an energy conversion laser-focused on everything Beast Industries. The bank is where the attention converts to capital. The philanthropy is where the capital converts to impact. The clipping platform is where labor converts to distribution. Feastibles is where distribution converts to revenue. Beast Industries filed a trademark application for MrBeast Financial in October 2025, listing services including cryptocurrency exchange platforms and consumer lending. The intent is written in the paperwork.

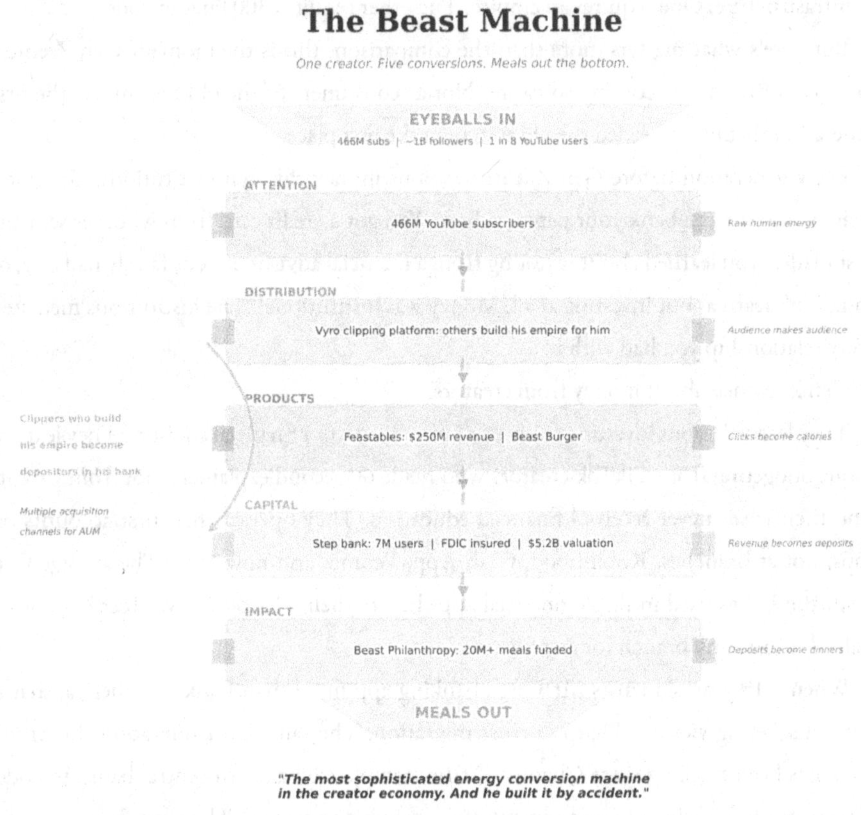

Figure 12.1: The Beast Machine

When I saw that press, the thought wasn't that MrBeast was a competitor to watch. I sent it to Martin immediately and we both had the same reaction: MrBeast is our competitor. He's the only one that gets it. Content distribution that drives financial product adoption that funds charitable impact. That is exactly what WYDE is building. He arrived at the same thesis from a completely different direction.

The difference is architecture. MrBeast needed to build a $5.2 billion empire, acquire a regulated bank, partner with one of the oldest philanthropic foundations on earth, and assemble a vertically integrated media conglomerate to create his attention-to-impact pipeline using traditional rails. WYDE built it with a smart contract. Same thesis. Different century of infrastructure. One requires an empire. The other requires 300 lines of code.

But here's what matters more than the comparison: this is the moment Gen Z enters the story of money becoming software. Not as consumers of the old system. As the first generation that never needed the old system in the first place.

Every generation before Gen Z learned about money through institutions. You got a savings account at a bank your parents chose. You got a credit card from whoever sent the best mailer. You learned about investing from a financial advisor, if your family had one, or you didn't learn about investing at all. Money was institutional. The institutions mediated every relationship you had with it.

Gen Z learned about money from creators.

They learned about investing from YouTube videos, not financial advisors. They learned about budgeting from TikTok creators who made 60-second explainers, not from parents who themselves never received financial education. They opened their first accounts on apps, not at branches. Robinhood, Cash App, Venmo, and now Step. The average Gen Z consumer has used multiple financial apps before their 21st birthday. Most have never walked into a bank branch for any reason.

When a 19-year-old trusts MrBeast's banking app more than Bank of America, that is not a marketing victory. That is a trust migration. The same trust migration this entire book has been tracking since Chapter 1, from temples to banks to central banks to code, playing out in real time, in one generation, through one creator. The trust didn't transfer from one institution to another institution. It transferred from institutions to individuals. From brands to people. From buildings to screens. And once trust migrates that completely, it doesn't migrate back. The branch isn't coming back for the same reason the landline isn't coming back. The new infrastructure is simply better at the thing trust infrastructure is supposed to do: make people feel confident that their money is safe and working for them.

Goldman Sachs estimated the creator economy at $250 billion in 2023, projected to reach $480 billion by 2027. By their 2025 update, roughly 67 million people worldwide identified as creators, growing at a 10% compound annual rate toward 107 million by 2030. Those numbers are staggering, but they describe an economy that is mostly about content. MrBeast is showing what happens when the creator economy becomes about infrastructure. When attention stops being the product and starts being the foundation for financial services, impact mechanisms, and distribution networks.

The creator economy rose and fell for most people who tried to financialize it directly.

Rally launched social tokens for creators and shut down when the speculative interest evaporated. BitClout tried to tokenize individual creators, essentially creating a stock market for people, and became a cautionary tale about what happens when you financialize personality without building anything underneath. Friend.tech was a flash in the pan on Base, peaking in the summer of 2023 when people paid thousands of dollars for the privilege of messaging influencers, and losing 99% of its activity within months when the novelty wore off. These were installation-phase experiments. They proved that attention had financial value. They failed because they tried to make attention itself the product, without building the layers of infrastructure that would sustain it. The speculative energy came in hot and left cold because there was nothing to hold it. No distribution engine. No products. No philanthropy. No bank. Just a token and a prayer.

MrBeast succeeded because he built layers first: content, distribution, products, philanthropy, and then the bank. The financial product came last, not first. Infrastructure before speculation. The Perez pattern, playing out in one person's career.

It is the energy thesis from Chapter 3, built in public, by a guy who probably doesn't think about it in those terms but instinctively understands the conversion chain better than most economists. Attention in. Distribution out. Products out. Revenue out. Deposits out. Impact out. Each conversion reduces friction, increases surface area, and creates a new input for the next layer. And the scale is what separates this from every other creator economy play. With nearly a billion followers, every product MrBeast launches has a guaranteed initial audience that most publicly traded companies would kill for. Feastibles didn't need a marketing budget. Beast Burger didn't need a distribution deal. Step doesn't need a customer acquisition strategy. The attention is already there. The conversion layers are already built. The only remaining question is what else can be plugged into the stack.

Everything Becomes a Market

You do not need to be a crypto trader to use a prediction market. You just need to have an opinion and be willing to put money on it.

During the 2024 election, Polymarket crossed over. It stopped being a crypto product and started being a cultural event. Nate Silver joined as an advisor. Cable news anchors started referencing the odds on air. And millions of people who had never held a crypto wallet downloaded an app and placed a bet on who would be the next president.

The person I keep thinking about is not the French trader who made $85 million. It is the millions of first-time users who opened the app, funded it with a credit card, and placed a $50 bet on the outcome of a Senate race in their state. These were not degens. They were people who had opinions about politics and found a tool that let them put skin in the game. The mechanism was new. The impulse was as old as democracy: I think I know what is going to happen, and I am willing to bet on it. Polymarket did not create that impulse. It gave it a price.

Brian Armstrong illuminated the same thing.

October 30, 2025. Coinbase CEO Brian Armstrong is on the company's Q3 earnings call. Revenue: $1.9 billion, up 55% year over year. But that's not the moment people remember.

Near the end of the call, Armstrong paused. He told the analysts, the investors, the reporters on the line that he'd been distracted. He'd been watching a prediction market. Specifically, he'd been watching a market on Kalshi and Polymarket where people were betting on which words he would say during this exact earnings call. The markets were called mention markets: will the CEO say Bitcoin? Will he say Ethereum? Will he say Web3? You could buy a yes or no contract on each word, priced at the market's current estimate of probability.

Then he rattled them off: Bitcoin. Ethereum. Blockchain. Staking. Web3.

Every one of those words had an open bet. Armstrong said all of them, deliberately, to force the markets to resolution. The betting volume was $84,000 across both platforms. He posted on X afterward: this was fun.

Polymarket had already proven this at civilizational scale. During the 2024 election, over $3.3 billion was wagered on the presidential race. While the polls showed a dead heat, or a slight Harris lead, Polymarket had Trump at 58% to Harris's 42% on the Monday before the election. By election night, the market hit 95% for Trump hours before the AP called the race. The polls were wrong. The market was right. Polymarket's own data shows 94% accuracy across all its markets a full month before outcomes are definitively known.

The election market was chaotic, dramatic, and deeply instructive. In October 2024, a single French trader accumulated millions of dollars in Trump positions, pushing the odds and sparking accusations of market manipulation. Polymarket investigated. They confirmed the accounts were controlled by one trader with extensive trading experience and a financial services background. The trader ultimately netted $85 million when Trump won. Critics said one whale was distorting the market. Defenders pointed out that the whale was right.

The market's job is not to be democratic. It's to be accurate. And on the night that mattered, the market was more accurate than every poll in the country.

Nate Silver, the most famous polling analyst in America, had already joined Polymarket as an advisor in July 2024. His own model gave Harris a 54.7% chance on the day Polymarket showed Trump pulling away. When the founder of FiveThirtyEight joins the platform that outperformed FiveThirtyEight, you know the center of gravity has shifted.

And then Polymarket just kept going. A market on whether Jesus Christ would return before 2027 attracted over $22 million in trading volume and sits at about 4% on the yes side. Someone created a derivative market that bet on whether the Jesus odds would breach 5%, which caused people to buy the Jesus yes shares to try to manipulate the odds on the derivative. A meta-market. Markets breeding markets. Prediction markets eating themselves. During the 2026 Super Bowl, Kalshi and Polymarket generated over $1.6 billion in combined tracked volume. Traders were buying TV antennas to get a fraction-of-a-second edge on live event broadcasts, the same way high-frequency traders on Wall Street build microwave towers to shave milliseconds off stock trades. One account correctly guessed 17 out of 18 bets on the halftime show. Kalshi's announcer mention market alone generated $9 million across 37 individual contracts. Kalshi hit nearly 2 million daily active users on game day, up 1,100% year over year.

This looks like a casino. It is a casino. But it's a casino that produces something casinos never have: accurate probability estimates in real time, priced by the collective intelligence of people who have skin in the game.

Here's the underlying question that nobody is asking loudly enough: who actually makes money when everything is a market?

Not the bettors. Not in aggregate. The exchanges make money on volume. Every trade, win or lose, generates a fee. Every market, stupid or profound, generates volume. Every question asked generates attention, and attention generates trades, and trades generate fees. The money is not in the outcome. The money is in the flow. Right back to watching the energy.

This is why Polymarket launched 5-minute Bitcoin prediction markets in February 2026, using Chainlink oracle data for automated settlement. Up or down? Five-minute window. New market opens the instant the last one closes. 288 markets per day, per asset. They're getting huge traction and volume. Polymarket processed over $9 billion in total volume across 2024. The 5-minute markets are designed to multiply that by orders of magnitude. They've already announced plans for one-minute markets. More markets means more volume means more fees.

But here's the thing: it's not who you'd think making the money on those 5-minute windows. We are right back to the early days of the stock market. Speed is king. A bot called gabagool became famous on Polymarket's short-duration Bitcoin markets by never predicting direction at all. It bought yes shares when they were cheap and no shares when they were cheap, balancing positions until both sides added up to less than a dollar. The market resolves at $1. The bot collects the difference. Every time. Across thousands of trades.

A fully automated trading bot executed 8,894 trades on 5-minute Bitcoin and Ethereum prediction contracts and generated nearly $150,000 in profit without human intervention. One bot reportedly turned $313 into $414,000 in a single month trading 15-minute markets with a 98% win rate. Another AI-powered system generated $2.2 million in two months using ensemble probability models trained on news and social data. These aren't gamblers. They're market makers. They're doing with tokens on Polymarket exactly what high-frequency trading firms do with stocks on the NYSE: providing liquidity, capturing spreads, and extracting value from speed.

The speed-of-information advantage that defined the stock market in the 1980s and 1990s is playing out in real time on prediction markets. But there's an added dimension the old markets never had: the influence of attention can sway these markets directly. When MrBeast tweets, markets move. When a prediction market goes viral, volume spikes. When a meme about the Jesus market hits Reddit, people buy shares just for the joke. Attention doesn't just fund the market. It is the market. And the bots are watching the attention feeds, processing them at machine speed, and trading before any human can react.

The Regulatory Coronation

If you're a young person building something that makes institutions uneasy, this next part of the story is for you.

Shayne Coplan founded Polymarket in 2020. He was 22, coding from his bathroom in a Lower East Side apartment, inspired by Friedrich Hayek's theories on decentralized information and Robin Hanson's concept of futarchy. He'd participated in Ethereum's initial coin offering as a teenager in 2014, when ETH cost 30 cents. That early conviction in blockchain gave him the seed capital and the worldview to build what traditional finance couldn't.

The CFTC fined Polymarket $1.4 million in 2022 for operating an unregistered exchange. Coplan was forced offshore. Blocked from US users. Then, in November 2024, days after Polymarket's election market outperformed every polling organization in America, the FBI raided Coplan's Manhattan apartment at dawn with a battering ram, seized his phone and laptop. His response on X, once he got a new phone: new phone, who dis?

Most founders would have folded. Coplan kept building. In July 2025, Polymarket paid $112 million for QCX, a CFTC-licensed exchange and clearinghouse, giving the platform a legitimate regulatory path back into the US. The investigations were dropped with no charges. The regulatory path cleared.

Then came the coronation.

On October 7, 2025, Intercontinental Exchange, the parent company of the New York Stock Exchange, announced a $2 billion strategic investment in Polymarket at an $8 billion pre-money valuation. ICE CEO Jeffrey Sprecher said it plainly: this investment blends a company founded in 1792 with a revolutionary company pioneering change in decentralized finance. ICE would distribute Polymarket's event-driven data to institutional investors globally. They would collaborate on tokenization initiatives. The oldest and most powerful exchange infrastructure in America was placing a $2 billion bet that prediction markets are the future of information pricing.

By October 2025, Coplan's 11% stake made him the youngest self-made billionaire in the world according to the Bloomberg Billionaires Index. Four years from CFTC fine to NYSE parent investment. Two years from FBI raid to institutional coronation. He went from coding in his bathroom to sitting on the CFTC's CEO Innovation Council alongside Terry Duffy of CME Group.

And then came the moment that captured the entire dynamic in a single gesture.

At a joint SEC-CFTC roundtable on September 29, 2025, Coplan was on a panel with Duffy, whose CME Group dominates traditional futures markets. The discussion was about innovation and regulatory frameworks. Coplan, grinning, took a jab at the legacy players: consumers are stuck with guys like you who are a lot older. Duffy, the 66-year-old CEO of a derivatives empire, responded by flipping Coplan off. On stage. On camera. At a federal regulatory panel. The clip went viral within hours.

That middle finger was the most honest thing said at the conference. It captured the rage of an incumbent watching an insurgent eat his lunch in real time. Duffy publicly opposed granting innovation exemptions to Polymarket and Kalshi, arguing the rules should be the same for everyone. The CBOE echoed the same complaint. The message was clear: the old guard sees what's coming, and they're not going quietly.

But here's what matters about Coplan's story beyond the drama. If something is actually good for the world, if it produces better information than existing institutions, brings more transparency, creates fairer outcomes, then sheer perseverance can win out. A 22-year-old in his bathroom, fined, raided, investigated, built something that outperformed every poll in America, attracted a $2 billion investment from the NYSE's parent, and is now sitting at the regulatory table helping write the rules. That is a story every young builder bringing world-shifting ideas into institutions that make the existing order uneasy needs to hear.

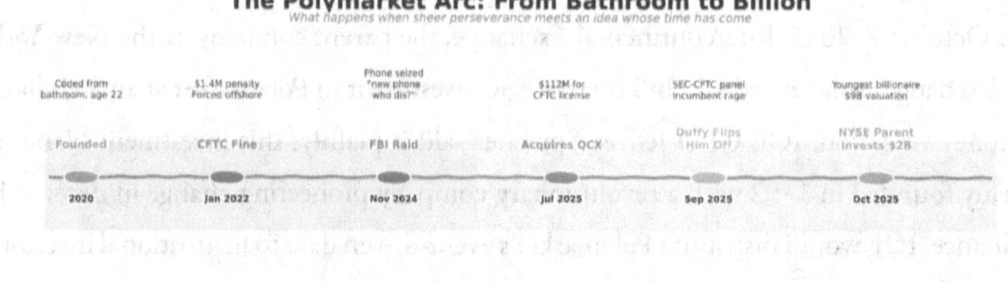

Figure 12.2: The Coplan Timeline

When everything becomes a market, someone has to lose. The losers are the incumbents who built their empires on information asymmetry, opaque pricing, and regulatory moats that are now being breached.

Start with the casinos and sportsbooks. DraftKings stock has fallen more than 50% in the past six months. FanDuel parent company Flutter is down a similar amount. Penn Entertainment is down about 30%. Caesars, same. The Indian Gaming Association's Victor Rocha told Front Office Sports that DraftKings and FanDuel have lost their minds, comparing their scramble to launch prediction market products to a midlife crisis triggered by Polymarket and Kalshi eating their lunch.

Coplan himself articulated the structural problem at the Cantor Fitzgerald conference. Traditional sportsbooks, he said, operate a monopoly on pricing. You trade against the house every time. They can set whatever prices they want. If you make any money, they can ban you. They can profile you and give you worse prices or cap you. That is a financial market positioned as an entertainment product designed for you to lose.

Prediction markets flip that model. You don't trade against the house. You trade against other people. The platform is the exchange, not the counterparty. The prices are set by collective intelligence, not by a corporation's risk management team. The data is transparent. The settlement is automatic. And because the markets run on blockchain rails, the entire transaction history is publicly auditable. Every trade. Every price. Every resolution. The house can't cheat because there is no house.

DraftKings responded by acquiring Railbird for its prediction market license and plans to spend an estimated $400 million on prediction markets in 2026. FanDuel partnered with CME Group. Both expect hundreds of millions in losses before they break even. They're not investing because they think prediction markets are a nice add-on. They're investing because prediction markets are an existential threat. Kalshi's monthly active users exploded from 600,000 to 5.1 million in a year. Kalshi's January app downloads exceeded 3 million, more than DraftKings and FanDuel combined in any single month. The incumbents aren't competing with a new product. They're competing with a new architecture that makes their architecture obsolete.

The pattern is the same one this entire book has been tracking. The tokenization of everything doesn't just create new markets. It collapses the distinction between different types of markets. Sports betting, prediction markets, financial derivatives, and event contracts are all converging into one layer. The companies built for the old categories, regulated state by state, operating on proprietary infrastructure, profiting from opacity, those are the ones that will have to adapt or die. Just like traditional banks facing DeFi. Just like wire transfers facing stablecoins. The energy finds the most efficient path, and the most efficient path is transparent, automated, and runs on tokens.

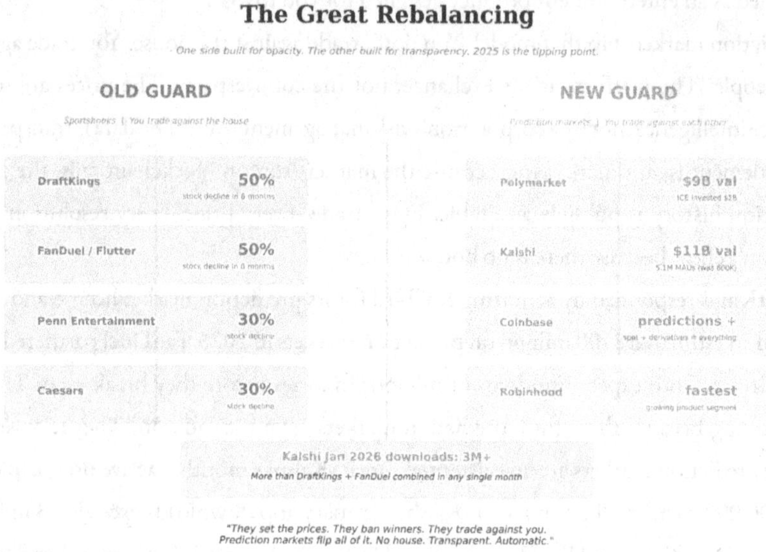

The Great Rebalancing

OLD GUARD		NEW GUARD	
Sportsbooks | You trade against the house		Prediction markets | You trade against each other	
DraftKings	50% stock decline in 6 months	Polymarket	$9B val ICE invested $2B
FanDuel / Flutter	50% stock decline in 6 months	Kalshi	$11B val 5.1M MAUs (was 800K)
Penn Entertainment	30% stock decline	Coinbase	predictions + spot + derivatives + everything
Caesars	30% stock decline	Robinhood	fastest growing product segment

Figure 12.3: The Great Rebalancing

When the World Becomes a Casino

Here's where the attention thesis, the MrBeast thesis, and the prediction market thesis all collapse into the same idea.

Attention is increasingly scarce in a world flooded with AI-generated content. We covered the hall-of-mirrors problem in Chapter 9: AI tokens produce content, attention tokens distribute it, and genuine human attention is the scarcest resource in the digital economy, getting scarcer every day. The platforms and people who command real attention, not algorithmic engagement, not synthetic followers, but actual human trust, those are the ones building durable infrastructure. MrBeast has it. Polymarket has it. The failed social token experiments proved that attention alone isn't enough. You need the conversion layers.

Prediction markets are the mechanism that converts attention into priced outcomes. Every market is a question. Every question demands attention. Every trade represents a human allocating capital based on their best assessment of reality. The market aggregates those assessments into a probability that is demonstrably more accurate than experts. And the data produced by those markets, millions of real-time probability estimates on every topic imaginable, is becoming more and more interesting to the AIs. AI agents have better access and ability to integrate real-time information than any human, and more processing capability than ever before. The information layer that prediction markets create is becoming the input layer for the next generation of machine intelligence.

Now here's the question I can't stop thinking about. What happens when you create prediction markets for outcomes that actually matter?

The minute WYDE went live and EAT started trading, the first thing we thought was: we need a market for this. We need to create a market for a million meals funded. People need to speculate on this. People who are predicting outcomes need to predict outcomes that matter to the world.

But don't just think about meals. Think about the most volatile, the most politically charged outcomes. Will California solve its homelessness crisis by 2030? Will New York City implement universal housing by a specific date? Will childhood obesity rates decline by 10% in the next five years? These are the questions that generate the most attention, the most debate, the most volume. And here's where it gets philosophically interesting: a politician like Zohran Mamdani in New York, who advocates for socialist policies like free public housing, might seem ideologically opposed to market-based crypto mechanisms. But a prediction market on whether housing will be free in NYC, powered by a cause coin that directs trading fees toward housing nonprofits, is actually funding socialistic outcomes through capitalist infrastructure. The ideology says redistribute wealth. The mechanism says redirect market energy. The outcome is the same. The cause coin doesn't care about your political orientation. It cares about the verifiable result.

Right now, prediction markets price elections, sports, and whether a CEO will say blockchain on an earnings call. But the infrastructure doesn't care about the content of the question. It cares about whether the question has a verifiable answer and whether there's liquidity to sustain the market. Outcomes that matter to human welfare are every bit as verifiable as whether a Republican wins the Senate. And the more controversial the question, the more attention it generates, the more volume it produces, the more fees flow through the cause coin, the more impact gets funded. The casino starts feeding people. The argument starts solving problems.

Think about what that looks like in practice. A prediction market asks: will EAT fund one million meals by 2027? Traders buy yes or no positions. The attention the market generates drives people to discover EAT. Some of those people buy the token. Their trading volume generates fees that fund meals, pushing the outcome toward yes. The prediction market is creating the conditions for impact. The observer effect, from quantum physics: the act of measurement changes the thing being measured. Except in this case, the change is meals funded.

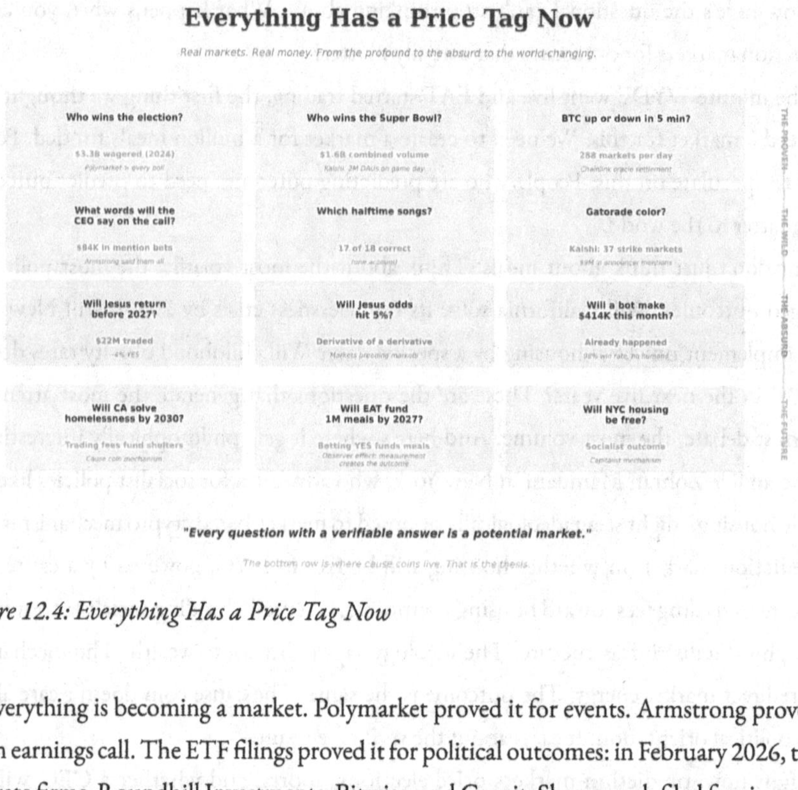

Figure 12.4: Everything Has a Price Tag Now

Everything is becoming a market. Polymarket proved it for events. Armstrong proved it on an earnings call. The ETF filings proved it for political outcomes: in February 2026, three separate firms, Roundhill Investments, Bitwise, and GraniteShares, each filed for six prediction market ETFs covering the 2028 presidential race and 2026 midterms. Binary contracts that settle at $1 or $0. Bloomberg Intelligence called it the ETF-ization of everything. Jump Trading struck equity-for-liquidity deals with both Kalshi and Polymarket, dedicating over 20 staffers to prediction markets. The combined valuation of the two platforms: roughly $20 billion. The deployment phase has begun.

Who will deliver your Uber Eats by 5 pm? There could be a market. Will your team hit quarterly revenue? Market. Will the next AI model pass a specific benchmark? Market. Will a clinical trial succeed? Will a new restaurant survive six months? Every question with a verifiable answer is a potential market. Every market needs liquidity. Every trade needs a counterparty.

Now think about Chapter 10. AI agents with 24/7 uptime. Agents that already trade on decentralized exchanges. Agents that already create tokens by accident. They aren't coming to prediction markets. They're already here.

Bots are already dominating Polymarket's 5-minute Bitcoin markets. One bot turned $313 into $414,000 in a month. Others generate $5,000 to $10,000 daily with 98% win rates. An AI-powered system made $2.2 million in two months. They don't predict whether Bitcoin goes up or down. They exploit the micro-inefficiencies that human emotions create: panic selling, momentum chasing, delayed reactions. The bot buys both sides at a discount and collects the guaranteed spread. The speed of information that defined the stock market in the 1980s and 1990s is true here, except now the information includes attention feeds, social media sentiment, and viral content, and the agents can process all of it simultaneously.

The agents don't sleep. They don't get emotional. They process every available data feed at machine speed. They can monitor satellite imagery, social sentiment, weather patterns, supply chain data, and public filings simultaneously, placing trades based on probability calculations that update in real time. In a world where everything is a market, the participants with 24/7 uptime and no emotional bias have a structural advantage that is almost impossible for human traders to match. Jump Trading assigned 20 people to prediction markets. Imagine an AI agent swarm that needs zero people and trades every market simultaneously.

The instinct here is to feel threatened. Bots with 98% accuracy sounds like a game you cannot win. But think about this differently. You do not compete with Google's search algorithm when you type a query. You use it. The AI trading bots in prediction markets are not your competition. They are infrastructure. The question is not whether you can beat a bot at prediction accuracy. The question is whether you can build a system, a tool, a product, a strategy, that uses machine-speed prediction as a component. The one-person billion-dollar company from Chapter 9 does not compete with AI. It employs AI. Same principle, different market.

Who wins in that world? The agent operators. The infrastructure builders. The people who understand that attention energy, compute energy, and financial energy are all converting into each other through the same token systems. The people who see what MrBeast sees, what Polymarket sees, what WYDE sees: that the conversion chain from attention to outcome is the most valuable pipeline in the economy.

Who loses? Anyone who thinks this is just about betting. Anyone who still believes markets are a thing that happens on Wall Street between 9:30 and 4. Anyone who hasn't noticed that the attention economy, the prediction economy, the creator economy, and the agent economy are all converging into one system that runs on tokens, prices everything, and never closes.

Someone is going to put all of these layers together. Attention, prediction, impact, automation. One stack. One energy conversion chain from human curiosity to funded outcome. I do not know who builds it first. I just know the pieces are sitting on the table waiting to be assembled.

But before that can happen at the scale this moment demands, the system needs rules. Not the old rules, the ones written for a world where money moved at the speed of paper and markets closed on weekends. New rules. Written specifically for programmable money by people who understand what it actually is and what it can do.

That's the next chapter. And it's already being written, in Wyoming, in Washington, in Brussels, and in every regulatory body that just realized the future arrived while they were still debating the past.

PART IV: THE GOLDEN ERA

Chapter 13

THE NEW MONEY ORDER

In November 1910, seven men boarded a private railcar in New Jersey under fake names, telling anyone who asked that they were going duck hunting off the coast of Georgia. They were not going duck hunting. They were going to Jekyll Island, a private resort owned by some of the wealthiest families in America, and over the next nine days they would design the Federal Reserve System.

Senator Nelson Aldrich. Abraham Piatt Andrew, Assistant Secretary of the Treasury. Frank Vanderlip, president of National City Bank. Henry Davison, senior partner at J.P. Morgan. Charles Norton, president of First National Bank of New York. Benjamin Strong, representing J.P. Morgan's interests. Paul Warburg, partner at Kuhn, Loeb & Co. These seven men represented roughly one quarter of the world's wealth at the time. They arrived at the island in secret because what they were about to do would have been politically unthinkable if the public knew about it in advance. They were designing the monetary architecture that would govern the United States, and by extension the global economy, for the next century.

The Federal Reserve Act was signed into law three years later, in December 1913. It created a central banking system with the power to issue currency, set interest rates, regulate banks, and serve as lender of last resort. It was, at its core, an energy routing system. It determined how monetary energy would flow through the American economy, who would control the valves, and under what conditions the pressure could be released or tightened. Every dollar printed, every rate adjusted, every bank regulated was a decision about energy distribution. The people on Jekyll Island understood that. They just didn't call it energy. They called it money.

I keep coming back to Jekyll Island because we are living through the same kind of moment right now. Not in secret. Not on a private island. But with the same fundamental stakes. The monetary order that those seven men built, the system that was reinforced after World War II at Bretton Woods, expanded through dollar hegemony, and patched repeatedly through every crisis from Nixon closing the gold window to the 2008 bailouts, that system is ending. Not collapsing overnight. Ending the way every monetary order ends. Slowly, then all at once.

And the people building what comes next are not seven men on an island. They are state legislators in Cheyenne. They are protocol developers in Denver and Lisbon and Singapore. They are members of Congress who just passed the first major crypto legislation in American history. They are the founders, the regulators, and the builders who are constructing the monetary architecture for the next hundred years. The difference is that this time, the blueprints are open source. Anyone can read them. Anyone can build on them. And for the first time in the history of money, the system being built does not require you to trust the people who built it.

That is what this chapter is about. The regulatory renaissance is not a policy story. It is a story about the end of one monetary order and the beginning of another. And if you understand where we are in the cycle, you understand why everything happening right now, from Wyoming's DUNA framework to the accredited investor expansion to the foundation tax reforms, is not random. It is the pattern repeating. The same pattern that repeated at Jekyll Island. The same pattern that Ray Dalio has been mapping for decades.

The 150-Year Clock

Ray Dalio published an essay in February 2026 that made something official that most people already felt in their bones. The post-1945 world order is dead. German Chancellor Friedrich Merz said it plainly at the Munich Security Conference: the world order as it has stood for decades no longer exists. French President Emmanuel Macron said Europe must prepare for war. U.S. Secretary of State Marco Rubio said we are in a new geopolitics era because the old world is gone.

Dalio's framework maps this with precision. In his book on the changing world order, he identified a pattern that repeats roughly every 150 years across recorded history. The cycle moves through six stages, from the creation of a new order after a major conflict, through a period of peace and prosperity, into overextension and debt, then internal conflict, then external conflict, and finally the establishment of a new order. The upswings produce the Renaissance, the Enlightenment, the Industrial Revolution. The downswings produce the Thirty Years' War, the Napoleonic Wars, and two World Wars.

Dalio places us in Stage 6. Great disorder. No rules. Might is right. Clashing great powers. The international order follows the law of the jungle much more than it follows international law. That is not Aaron Rafferty's opinion. That is one of the most respected macroeconomic thinkers of the last fifty years, echoed by the leaders of the three most powerful Western nations, all saying the same thing at the same conference.

Here's what Dalio's framework reveals that most people miss. These transitions are monetary. Every shift from one world order to the next involves a fundamental restructuring of how money works, who controls it, and how it flows. The creation of the Federal Reserve in 1913 was not separate from the geopolitical upheaval that produced World War I. It was part of the same cycle. The Bretton Woods agreement in 1944 was not separate from World War II. It was the monetary foundation of the new order that emerged from the war. Nixon closing the gold window in 1971 was not separate from America's overextension in Vietnam and the decline of its manufacturing base. It was the monetary expression of a declining empire trying to maintain its position.

And now. The United States carries $38.56 trillion in national debt. Interest payments are approaching $1 trillion per year. The debt-to-GDP ratio has surpassed 100 percent and is projected to hit 120 percent by 2036, surpassing the World War II peak. The Congressional Budget Office projects annual deficits averaging more than 6 percent of GDP for the next decade. Nearly one out of every five dollars the federal government collects in revenue goes to servicing debt. Not building roads. Not funding schools. Not paying soldiers. Servicing debt.

The most powerful nation on earth is spending an increasing percentage of its total energy output just to maintain the financial commitments it has already made. It is a system running a growing energy deficit. And every engineer knows what happens to a system that consistently outputs more energy than it generates. It degrades. It fails. Unless someone redesigns the system.

That is what is actually happening right now. Not just in crypto. Not just in fintech. The entire regulatory apparatus of the United States is being redesigned, rapidly, aggressively, and with a sense of urgency that I have never seen in my career. And the reason is not ideological.

The reason is mathematical. The old system cannot sustain itself. The numbers do not work. And the people in charge know it.

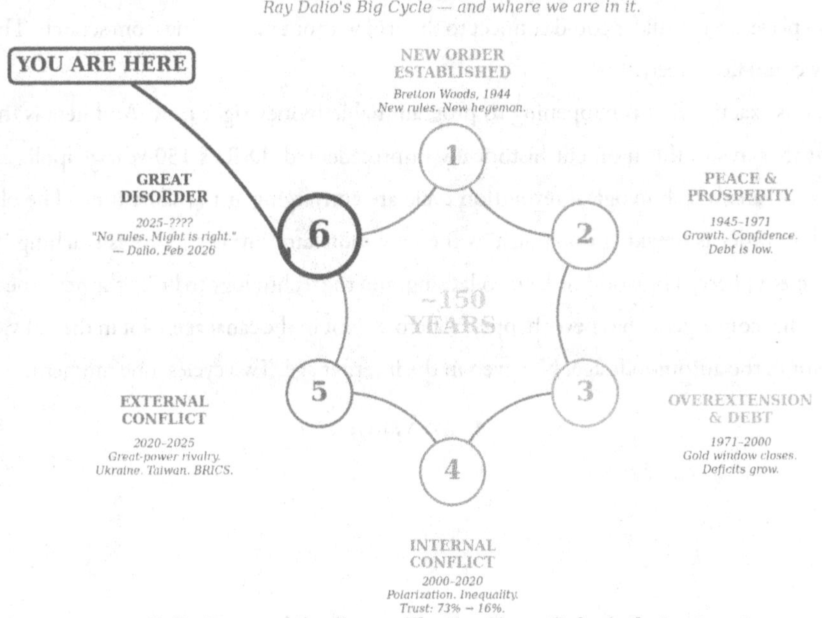

Figure 13.1: The 150-Year Clock

Carlotta Perez would recognize this moment immediately. I introduced her framework in Chapter 4, and I need to bring it back here because what is happening in regulation right now maps perfectly onto her model.

Every technological revolution follows the same arc. Installation, crash, turning point, deployment, golden era. The installation phase is speculative, chaotic, often fraudulent. The deployment phase is when regulation arrives, not to kill the technology, but to standardize it so institutions can build on it. The golden era is what comes after, when the technology is so deeply embedded in the economy that it stops being a sector and starts being the infrastructure.

Electricity went through this. In the 1880s and 1890s, dozens of competing electrical standards fought for dominance. Companies wired buildings with incompatible systems. Fires were common. People died. Then regulation arrived. Not to ban electricity, but to create the National Electrical Code, to standardize voltages, to require safety inspections. The regulation did not constrain innovation. It unleashed it. Because once the standards were in place, every builder could connect to the grid without negotiating from scratch. The energy could flow freely.

That is exactly what is happening to programmable money right now. And here is the insight that makes this moment historically unprecedented: Dalio's 150-year geopolitical cycle and Perez's technological revolution cycle are converging at the same time. The old monetary order is breaking down just as the new monetary infrastructure is reaching its deployment phase. The world order is collapsing, and the technology to build the next one is ready. That convergence has never happened before. Not in the canal age. Not in the railway age. Not in the automobile age. Not even in the internet age. Two cycles, one moment.

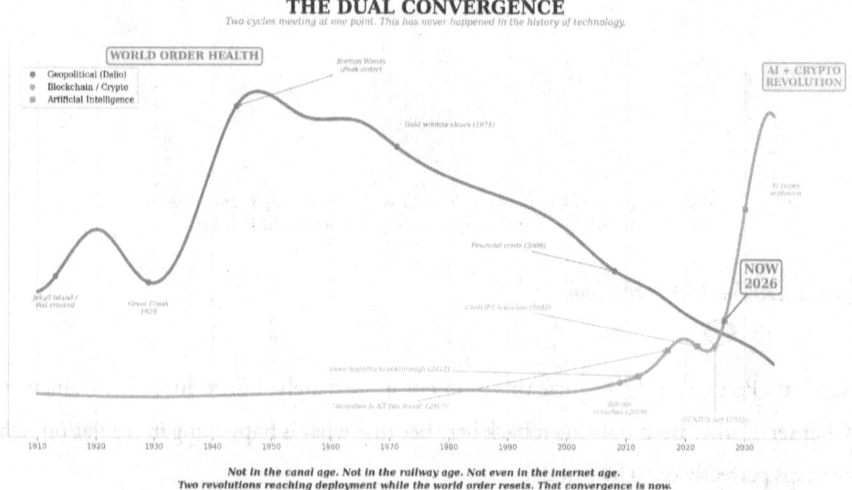

Figure 13.2: The Dual Convergence

And there is one more overlay that makes this even more striking. The last time the United States faced a comparable crisis of monetary architecture, it produced Jekyll Island. A small group of powerful men designed a system in secret. This time, the system is being designed in public. In state legislatures. In Congressional hearings. On GitHub repositories. The blueprints are open. And the first state to understand what that means was the same state that has been first before.

The State That Builds the Future

Wyoming has this habit of being fifty years ahead of everyone else and getting no credit for it until the rest of the country catches up.

In 1869, Wyoming became the first territory in the United States to grant women the right to vote. That was fifty-one years before the 19th Amendment. In 1977, Wyoming became the first state to create the limited liability company. The LLC. The most popular business structure in America today, used by millions of companies, from solo freelancers to Fortune 500 subsidiaries. It did not exist before Wyoming invented it.

The LLC story is worth knowing because it maps directly onto what Wyoming is doing now with crypto. In the mid-1970s, the Hamilton Brothers Oil Company, based in Denver, had been operating overseas using hybrid business structures that gave them both partnership-style taxation and corporate liability protection. Those structures worked fine abroad, but the United States did not have anything equivalent. You could form a corporation and get liability protection, but you got taxed twice. Or you could form a partnership and get pass-through taxation, but your personal assets were on the line.

Hamilton Brothers worked with Wyoming legislators to create something new. A hybrid entity. Limited liability for the owners. Pass-through taxation for the profits. Simple to form. Flexible to operate. The Wyoming LLC Act was signed on March 4, 1977. The first LLC in American history was filed that same year.

And then nothing happened. For eleven years. The IRS took until 1988 to rule that LLCs would be taxed as partnerships. Other states were afraid to act without IRS clarity. It was not until the mid-1990s, nearly two decades after Wyoming's innovation, that LLCs gained widespread acceptance. By 1996, all fifty states had adopted LLC laws. Today, the LLC is by far the most common business entity in the country.

A state creates a new legal structure that the existing infrastructure cannot process. The IRS takes over a decade to figure out how to classify it. Other states wait for federal clarity before acting. And then, once the clarity arrives, the innovation becomes so ubiquitous that people forget it was ever controversial.

Now replace LLC with DUNA. Replace 1977 with 2024. Replace Hamilton Brothers Oil Company with every crypto-native organization trying to build something real in the

United States. The pattern is identical.

Wyoming's DUNA framework, the Decentralized Unincorporated Nonprofit Association, is the LLC of Web3. It is the first state-level legal structure specifically designed for decentralized organizations. It gives a DAO, a decentralized autonomous organization, the same legal standing as a corporation. It provides limited liability for token holders. It allows governance through smart contracts and on-chain voting. It creates a path to tax-exempt status. The IRS has already accepted it.

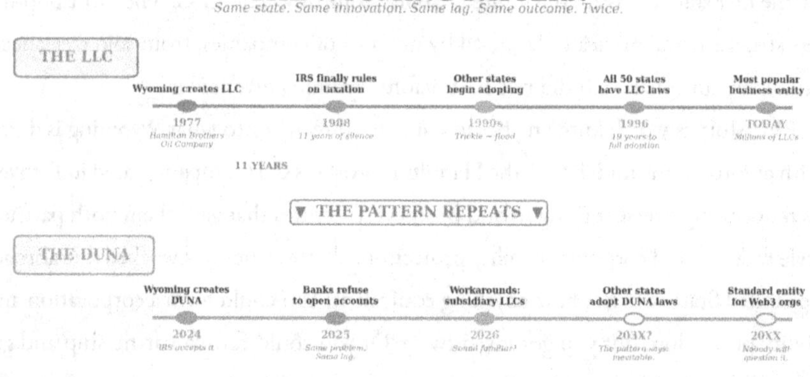

Figure 13.3: The Wyoming Pattern

When we launched WYDE as a DUNA, we knew we were early. And we learned what "early" means in regulatory infrastructure, because no bank in the country would open an account for us. Coinbase would not do it. Mercury would not do it. We went to banks that specifically market to nonprofits and crypto companies. None of them recognized the DUNA structure. Wyoming had built the road, but the vehicles had not been invented yet.

We solved it by creating a subsidiary LLC, which the banks understood. Same workaround that companies in the 1970s had to use when nobody understood what an LLC was. Same pattern. Same lag. Same eventual resolution. Wyoming has passed over forty-five blockchain-related laws since 2016. It launched the first state-issued stablecoin, the Frontier Stable Token, in August 2025. And the state is now working to ensure that the DUNA becomes as standardized and accepted as the LLC. It will take time. But the LLC took time too. And now it is everywhere.

I need to tell you about the years that led up to this moment, because most people have no idea what it was actually like to try to build something in crypto in the United States between 2021 and 2024. It felt like a movie. The kind where you are not sure if the main characters are going to end up in handcuffs or on the cover of Forbes.

In 2021, Martin and I were building Standard Labs and exploring what would become WYDE. We had a thesis. We had the technology. We had the energy to build. What we did not have was any regulatory framework in the United States that would allow us to do it legally, clearly, and confidently. Zero. The SEC under Gary Gensler was running an enforcement-first strategy, suing projects and platforms without providing any guidance on how to comply. You could not get a clear answer on whether a token was a security or a commodity. You could not get a clear answer on what kind of entity to form. You could not get a clear answer on anything.

So we did what every serious crypto builder did in that era. We went offshore.

The Bahamas. The Cayman Islands. The British Virgin Islands. Singapore. Swiss foundations. You name a jurisdiction with crypto-friendly regulation, and Martin and I mapped it, consulted lawyers in it, and in some cases incorporated entities in it. We set up structures in jurisdictions I had never visited, working with lawyers I met on video calls, because it was the only way to build something that had any kind of regulatory clarity for our users, our investors, and ourselves.

I am not being hyperbolic when I say it felt like a movie. There were calls at 2 AM with lawyers in Zurich. There were proposals for foundation structures in the Cayman Islands that came with sixty-page legal opinions explaining why they might work. There were moments where Martin and I looked at each other on Zoom and said, out loud, this is insane. We are American builders with an American thesis about using American technology to fund American hunger relief, and we are being forced to build from the British Virgin Islands because our own country will not give us a framework.

And while we were navigating that maze, we watched the enforcement actions pile up. Uniswap, the decentralized exchange that I wrote about in Chapter 7, which was 300 lines of code that created a permissionless market, got hit with an SEC Wells notice. Coinbase, the largest US exchange, was sued. Ripple was sued. Kraken was sued. These were not scam artists. These were the builders creating the infrastructure. Uniswap's airdrop of the UNI token did more to distribute wealth across DeFi than any other single event. It created genuine, broad-based value. And the reward for building that was a regulatory threat.

The chilling effect was real and measurable. Projects that would have launched in the United States launched in Singapore instead. Talent that would have stayed in San Francisco moved to Dubai. Capital that would have funded American innovation went to Europe, where MiCA, the Markets in Crypto-Assets regulation, was providing the clarity that the United States refused to offer. We were watching America export its next financial revolution in real time.

And then the administration changed. And everything changed with it.

I covered this in Chapter 4, but it bears repeating in this context. The Trump administration's approach to crypto was not subtle. Before he even took office, the president launched his own meme coin. Whatever you think about the motivations, the practical effect was a seismic signal: if the president of the United States issues a token, the enforcement-by-ambiguity era is over. The SEC pivoted from enforcement to frameworks. Congress moved with speed that I did not think was possible. And by March 2025, Martin and I were not on calls with lawyers in Zurich anymore. We were building in Wyoming.

The Federal Upgrade

I want to tell you what it felt like when the architecture actually changed. Not when the legislation passed. When I felt it in my own work.

The period between the GENIUS Act and our DUNA launch was a series of legal conversations that kept getting clearer. The GENIUS Act was the first signal that we were in the right place, but nobody else was looking where we were looking. Everyone was focused on stablecoins, which is directly adjacent to banking. That made sense. Stablecoins were the obvious play, and the legislation confirmed it. But the Clarity Act was still pending, and that was where our opportunity sat. The regulatory framework for tokens with utility, for instruments that do something beyond store value, was still being written. We were building exactly the thing that framework would need to classify.

Then our lawyers came to us. Not the other way around. They told us that what we were building at WYDE was directly in line to influence the next phase of crypto regulation. Not just comply with it. Influence it. That was a moment I will not forget, because it inverted everything. For four years we had been navigating around regulation, trying not to trigger enforcement actions, building in regulatory white space. And now our own legal counsel was telling us that the regulators were going to need examples of what responsible token utility looks like, and we were one of the few that qualified.

The next steps became clear almost immediately: a conversation before the Senate and the House to discuss what works and what does not in the current framework. Continued engagement with the SEC and CFTC to help protect retail investors. A role in making sure the United States stays at the forefront of this technology instead of regulating it offshore. That is not lobbying. That is the deployment phase doing what it always does. The builders who survived installation get invited to help design the rules for deployment. We were at the table.

What has happened at the federal level since 2025 is not incremental. It is structural. And the speed of it reflects the urgency of the underlying math. The United States cannot afford to fall behind in the next financial infrastructure. Not with $38.56 trillion in debt. Not with interest payments approaching $1 trillion a year. Not with the CBO projecting deficits of $1.9 trillion in 2026 growing to $3.1 trillion by 2036. The country needs economic growth at a pace that the old system cannot deliver, and the people writing the laws know it.

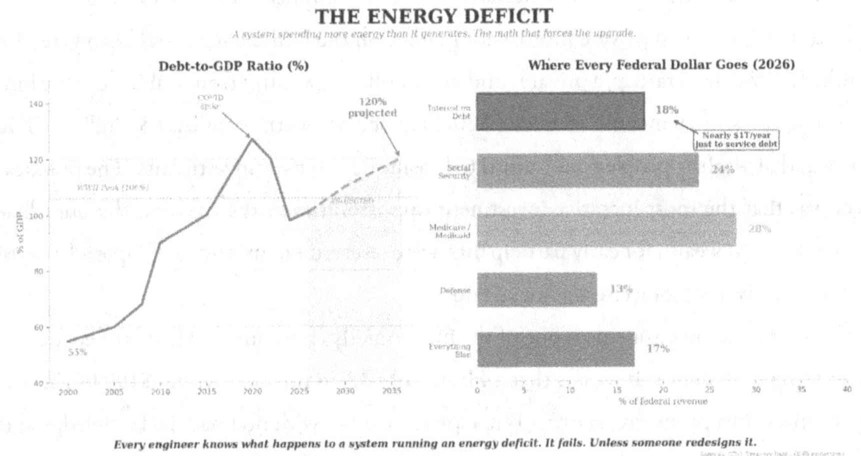

Figure 13.4: The Energy Deficit

The GENIUS Act was signed into law on July 18, 2025. The first major federal crypto legislation in American history. It passed the Senate 68 to 30 and the House 308 to 122. Bipartisan. Decisive. It established a regulatory framework for stablecoins that includes one-to-one reserve requirements, mandatory audits, anti-money laundering compliance, and a dual federal-state oversight structure. Stablecoin issuers under $10 billion in assets are regulated by the states. Above $10 billion triggers federal oversight. The law gave the Office of the Comptroller of the Currency authority over federal-qualified issuers.

The practical effect was immediate. JPMorgan launched a pilot deposit token on a public blockchain. Fidelity issued its own stablecoin. Wyoming launched the first state-issued stablecoin. The institutions did not enter because they suddenly believed in the technology. They entered because the regulation gave them the legal clarity to do it without existential risk. Regulation was the catalyst, not the constraint.

I remember the day it passed. Martin called me. We did not celebrate. We just started building faster.

But the GENIUS Act was just the beginning. The INVEST Act passed the House in late 2025, a sweeping capital markets reform bill that includes a provision most people have not fully processed yet. It contains the Equal Opportunity for All Investors Act, which directs the SEC to create an examination that any person can take to qualify as an accredited investor.

Let me explain why this is revolutionary, because the implications are enormous.

Since 1982, access to private investment markets in the United States has been gated by wealth. To invest in a startup, a private fund, or any offering exempt from public registration, you needed an annual income of at least $200,000 or a net worth of at least $1 million. The logic was that wealthy people could afford to lose money on risky investments. The practical effect was that the most lucrative investment opportunities in the country, the ones that created the most wealth for early participants, were reserved exclusively for people who were already wealthy. Everyone else was locked out.

The accredited investor rule is one of the most quietly consequential forms of economic gatekeeping in America. It means that a Harvard MBA in finance earning $190,000 a year cannot invest in a promising startup, but a lottery winner with no financial knowledge and $1.1 million in the bank can. It means that the generation of wealth that venture capital and private equity have created over the past forty years has been legally reserved for the richest 19 percent of American households. Everyone else could buy public stocks, public bonds, and hope for the best.

The Equal Opportunity for All Investors Act breaks that gate. Under the proposed legislation, the SEC must create an exam, administered free of charge, that tests financial sophistication, knowledge of investment risks, and understanding of private market structures. Pass the test, and you are accredited. Period. Regardless of your income. Regardless of your net worth. Knowledge replaces wealth as the qualification. The SEC's own Investor Advisory Committee endorsed this direction in September 2025, calling the current wealth-based framework not reflective of today's capital markets.

Think about what this means for cause coins. For WYDE. For every tokenized asset that exists in the space between public market and private offering. If the accredited investor definition expands to include anyone with demonstrated financial knowledge, the addressable market for every token project in the United States expands by orders of magnitude. The 81 percent of American households currently locked out of private markets suddenly have a pathway in. And they do not need to get rich first. They need to get educated.

This one is personal for me. I came from academia. I left a PhD. I spent years studying economic disparities. And the single biggest structural barrier to wealth creation in America is not education or talent or work ethic. It is access. The accredited investor rule is a velvet rope in front of the best opportunities in the economy, and the bouncer only lets you in if you are already rich. Tearing that down with a knowledge-based test is the kind of policy I left academia hoping someone would build.

That is not deregulation for deregulation's sake. That is the system adapting to survive. The old gatekeeping mechanisms were designed for a world where information was scarce and financial instruments were complex enough that only professionals could evaluate them. That world does not exist anymore. Anyone with a smartphone can access the same data that a Wall Street analyst uses. The accredited investor threshold has not been adjusted since 1982, not even for inflation, which means millions more Americans qualify every year simply because wages and home values rose. The framework was already eroding. The legislation just makes it official.

The Foundation Reckoning

There is one more piece of this regulatory puzzle that ties directly to the thesis of this book, and it is the one that most people are not paying attention to.

In early drafts of the One Big Beautiful Bill Act, Congress proposed a dramatic increase in the excise tax on private foundation investment income, replacing the existing flat rate of 1.39 percent with a tiered system that could reach 10 percent for foundations with assets above $5 billion. The $5 billion provision was ultimately stripped from the final bill, but the fact that it was proposed, that it had serious Congressional support, and that the final law still includes a tiered system with increased rates tells you where the political winds are blowing.

Foundations are under scrutiny. And the reason is not abstract policy debate. In January 2026, the Department of Justice released three million pages of documents related to Jeffrey Epstein under the Epstein Files Transparency Act, revealing extensive email exchanges between Epstein and Bill Gates showing that Epstein served as a philanthropic advisor to the Gates Foundation. The Gates Foundation holds $86 billion in assets. Its philanthropic strategy was being shaped, at least in part, by a convicted sex offender who used access to that very kind of wealth and influence as his primary currency. I am not going to litigate the specifics. The point is what this means for the foundation model itself.

The foundation model concentrates enormous resources under the control of a very small number of people, with minimal public accountability, minimal market discipline, and tax advantages that reduce what those resources contribute to the public treasury. A foundation can sit on $86 billion forever. It can deploy 5 percent a year, the legal minimum, and never spend down. The assets grow. The control remains. The public benefit is whatever the foundation decides it should be. The Epstein scandal and the foundation tax proposals are connected, whether legislators explicitly say so or not. The public is losing trust in the foundation model. The government is responding by increasing the cost of maintaining that model.

And the alternative, programmable philanthropy through cause coins and tokenized impact, is arriving at exactly the moment when the old model is most vulnerable. Contrast a foundation with a cause coin. EAT generates meals through trading activity. Every trade. Automatically. The smart contract does not need a philanthropic advisor. It does not have dinner with anyone. It routes energy from point A to point B according to code that anyone can read, audit, and verify. The mechanism is transparent, permanent, and incorruptible. Not because the people who built it are saints, but because the system does not require saints. It requires math. If foundations face higher excise taxes and increasing public scrutiny, the case for market-based impact funding becomes stronger every day. Causecoins do not replace foundations. They provide an alternative that does not depend on the character or connections of a single donor. The energy flows through the protocol, not through the person.

The New Money Order

We changed the title of this book. It was Money Becomes Software. Now it is The New Money Order. And I want to explain why, because the change is not cosmetic. It is the thesis crystallized.

Dalio's work is called Principles for Dealing with the Changing World Order. He maps the rise and fall of empires across centuries. His insight is that world orders follow predictable cycles, and that understanding those cycles gives you the ability to position yourself and your country for what comes next. The changing world order is his framework. His machine.

The New Money Order is ours.

Dalio diagnosed the disease. He showed that the current world order is breaking down, that debt-to-GDP ratios are unsustainable, that internal conflict is rising, that external power dynamics are shifting. He mapped the symptoms with extraordinary precision. But his framework was written before the deployment phase of programmable money. Before the GENIUS Act. Before BlackRock tokenized treasury bonds. Before cause coins proved that market energy could be automatically directed toward social impact. Dalio's model describes the cycle. The New Money Order describes what breaks the cycle.

Here is the framework. I want you to remember it the way you remember the Cashflow Quadrant from Rich Dad Poor Dad, or the way you remember Dalio's concept of the economic machine. Simple enough to sketch on a napkin. Deep enough to explain everything.

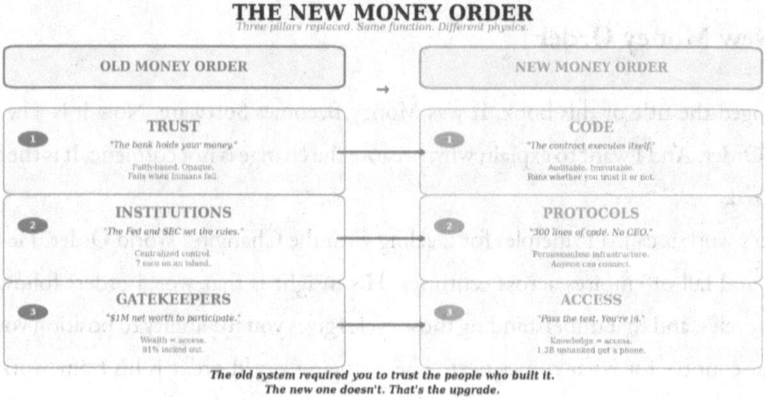

Figure 13.5: The New Money Order

The Old Money Order operated on three pillars: trust, institutions, and gatekeepers. You trusted the bank to hold your money. Institutions like the Fed, the SEC, and the big investment banks set the rules and controlled access. Gatekeepers, from accredited investor requirements to SWIFT transfer networks to foundation boards, decided who could participate and who could not. When these three pillars worked, the system worked. When they eroded, as they have for the past two decades, the system degraded.

The New Money Order operates on three different pillars: code, protocols, and access.

Code replaces trust. You do not need to trust the bank when the smart contract is auditable, immutable, and executes exactly as written. The USDC in your wallet does not care about your credit score. The EAT trade routes fees to hunger relief whether the founder is having a good day or a bad one. Code does not have dinner with Jeffrey Epstein.

Protocols replace institutions. Uniswap processes more trading volume than most exchanges, and it runs on 300 lines of code with no CEO, no board, and no office. Aave manages billions in lending without a loan officer. Chainlink provides data feeds to the entire DeFi ecosystem without a centralized data provider. These are not companies. They are protocols. They are energy grids that anyone can connect to.

Access replaces gatekeepers. The accredited investor exam replaces the wealth threshold. The DUNA replaces the offshore entity. Stablecoins replace the slow, expensive, gatekept rails of the traditional banking system. The unbanked billions with mobile phones suddenly have access to the same financial infrastructure as a JPMorgan client. The 81 percent of

American households locked out of private markets get a pathway in based on knowledge, not net worth.

Old Money Order: trust, institutions, gatekeepers. New Money Order: code, protocols, access. That is the transition. That is what every chapter in this book has been building toward. And the regulatory renaissance we are living through right now is the moment when the old pillars are being formally replaced by the new ones.

The GENIUS Act is code and protocols receiving institutional legitimacy. The accredited investor expansion is gatekeepers being dismantled by law. Wyoming's DUNA is a new institutional form built on code-native principles. The foundation reckoning is the old trust-based model facing consequences for its structural weaknesses. Everything connects. Everything converts. The energy flows.

There is a question that I get from smart, skeptical people every time I talk about this. Why is all of this happening at once? The regulatory changes, the institutional adoption, the technological convergence, the geopolitical shift. It feels like too much to be coincidental. So is it?

No. It is not coincidental. It is mathematical.

The United States is running a $1.9 trillion annual deficit. That number is projected to grow to $3.1 trillion by 2036. Debt held by the public is 101 percent of GDP and climbing to 120 percent. Interest payments are consuming an ever-larger share of federal revenue. And the One Big Beautiful Bill Act, the administration's signature fiscal legislation, adds an estimated $2.4 trillion to deficits over the next decade after the tax cuts, even accounting for tariff revenues.

In that fiscal environment, the government has exactly two options. Cut spending or grow revenue. Cutting spending is politically suicidal, which is why every administration talks about fiscal responsibility and then runs larger deficits. Growing revenue requires growing the economy. And growing the economy at the pace required to service this debt means unleashing every possible source of new economic activity.

That is why the administration is deregulating everything simultaneously. It is not ideology. It is survival. The GENIUS Act creates legal clarity so that the $307 billion stablecoin market can scale inside US borders, generating transaction fees, tax revenue, and economic activity. The accredited investor expansion opens private markets to millions of new participants, increasing capital formation and broadening the tax base on investment gains. The DUNA framework allows new kinds of organizations to form domestically instead of fleeing to the Caymans. Every regulatory upgrade is a valve being opened to let energy flow into the American economy.

And this is where the Dalio framework and the Perez framework converge into a single insight that I think is the most important idea in this book.

Dalio says the old world order is ending. Perez says the new technology is reaching deployment. The history books will record this as the moment when the decline of one system and the rise of another happened simultaneously. And the United States, for all its debt problems and political dysfunction, is in a unique position. It has the largest financial markets in the world. It has the deepest pool of technical talent. It has the most active crypto and AI developer communities. And it just passed the regulatory infrastructure to let them build.

The old money order is breaking down under the weight of its own contradictions: too much debt, too little trust, too many gatekeepers extracting value without creating it. The new money order is being built on infrastructure that does not require trust, does not need gatekeepers, and creates value through code that anyone can verify.

Jekyll Island produced a monetary system that lasted a century. It was designed by seven men in secret. The New Money Order is being designed by thousands of builders in public. The blueprints are open source. The infrastructure is permissionless.

Read that again.

For the first time in the history of money, the system does not require you to trust the people who built it.

Not less trust. Not distributed trust. Not trust-but-verify. No trust required. The code is public. The ledger is public. The rules are enforced by mathematics, not institutions. You do not need to believe that the people running this system are honest, competent, or even alive. The system runs because the code runs. Period.

That sentence is why this book exists. Every chapter you have read has been building toward it. The Architecture of Trust, the Breaking Point, the Energy Theory, the Programmable Layer, DeFi, stablecoins, tokens, agents, cause coins. All of it was infrastructure for this single claim. Money no longer requires trust in the people who built the system. For the first time. In history.

Once you see it, you cannot unsee it. And that is the point.

That does not mean nothing can go wrong. It can. It will. Technology is not inherently good. Code can be exploited. Protocols can centralize. Regulation can overcorrect. The next chapter confronts those risks honestly, because intellectual honesty is the only thing that makes optimism credible.

But the direction is clear. The old pillars are crumbling. The new pillars are being installed. And you are reading this book at the exact moment in the 150-year cycle when what you do next actually matters.

The risks are real. The failure modes are predictable. And confronting them honestly is the only way to earn the optimism that the golden era demands. That's next.

Chapter 14

Risks, Failure Modes, and the Dark Scenarios

Sometime in 2021, I was sitting at my desk watching a bridge transaction that should have taken ten minutes. It had been forty-five. The market was choppy and looking grim. I had been yield farming across a handful of chains, probably Polygon and BSC, accumulating positions in protocols I barely remembered signing up for. The kind of thing you do when you are deep in DeFi and every new pool looks like free money. But the market was turning, and I knew I needed to consolidate. Pull everything back to Ethereum L1. Clean up the random wallets. Get organized before things got worse. This was after a string of high-profile hacks. The Ronin bridge had been exploited for $625 million. Other bridges were dropping like flies. I knew bridges were insecure. Everyone in the space knew. But I needed to move the funds, so I found a bridge, connected my wallet, set the transaction, hit confirm, and waited. The funds never arrived. I checked the chain. Gone. The bridge router itself had

been compromised. My transaction had been rerouted to someone else's wallet. Not a phishing attack. Not a user error, exactly. An exploited contract that targeted my transaction at the worst possible moment. A nontrivial amount of money, more than five thousand dollars, less than fifty thousand. I had sent it without a test transaction first. The kind of shortcut you take when you have done a hundred transactions and they all worked and you forget that the hundred-and-first might not. Stupid. And now it was just gone. Irreversible. No customer service number. No dispute process. No chargeback. No one to call. No one to blame except myself and whatever anonymous attacker was now holding my funds in a wallet I would never identify. My heart sank. I did not even believe it at first. I kept refreshing the block explorer like the funds might somehow reappear. They did not. It was the first and last time I had my funds drained like that. And I remember the exact thought that went through my head in the moment: I hate DeFi.

I do not actually hate DeFi. I built a cause coin on DeFi infrastructure. I believe in what this technology can do. But that moment taught me something that no whitepaper or conference talk ever could. When code fails, it fails completely. There is no safety net. There is no institution that steps in to make you whole. The system works exactly as designed, and sometimes the design has a hole in it, and you fall right through.

The last chapter laid out the New Money Order. Code replaces trust. Protocols replace institutions. Access replaces gatekeepers. I believe in that framework. I built my career on it. But intellectual honesty requires confronting the failure modes before celebrating the architecture. Every system fails. The old money order failed in ways we have spent thirteen chapters documenting. The new one will fail too. Just in different ways. And if we are not honest about what those ways are, then we are not building a better system. We are building a sales pitch.

When Systems Break

Code replaces trust. Protocols replace institutions. Those are the first two pillars of the New Money Order. But code is only trustworthy when the code is correct, and protocols introduce their own concentration risks that can look uncomfortably similar to the institutional failures they were supposed to eliminate. When either fails, the damage is immediate, permanent, and total. No bank reverses the mistake. No regulator steps in. The code ran. The code was wrong. Your money is gone.

The DAO hack in June 2016 was the first major test. An attacker exploited a recursive call vulnerability and drained roughly $60 million in Ether. The Ethereum community faced a choice that should have been impossible under the "code is law" philosophy: do nothing and let the attacker keep the money, or rewrite the blockchain's history to reverse the theft. They chose to reverse it, splitting Ethereum into two chains. The technology's foundational promise was broken within a year of its first serious deployment. The lessons since have been more expensive.

In March 2022, North Korea's Lazarus Group compromised the Ronin bridge and stole $625 million. The theft was not discovered for six days. Six days, over half a billion dollars gone, and nobody noticed because the validators were still running and everything looked normal from the outside. In February 2025, the Bybit exchange lost $1.4 billion in a single attack, the largest crypto theft in history. Again, Lazarus Group. In July 2023, Curve Finance was exploited when a vulnerability in the Vyper programming language allowed attackers to drain pools worth over $60 million. The exploit was not in Curve's logic. It was in the compiler one layer beneath the code itself. You could audit the smart contract perfectly and still miss the flaw. The numbers compound relentlessly. In 2024, $2.2 billion was stolen across crypto hacks and exploits. By mid-2025, that total had already been surpassed, with $2.7 billion gone by year's end. The three-year running total exceeds $7.7 billion.

The mitigation is real but incomplete. Formal verification is becoming standard for major protocols. The audit industry has matured significantly. Bug bounty programs incentivize white-hat hackers to find vulnerabilities before black-hat hackers exploit them. And the data shows that pure smart contract exploits are declining as a percentage of total losses, replaced by off-chain attacks like private key compromises and social engineering. The DeFi ecosystem of 2026 is meaningfully more secure than the one I was navigating in 2021.

But the risk is structural. Every line of code that controls billions of dollars is a potential single point of failure. Every bridge connecting two blockchains is an attack surface. And the adversaries are not hobbyists. North Korea alone has stolen an estimated $6 billion in crypto since 2017, and they use the proceeds to fund their nuclear weapons program. Formal verification and bug bounties are important. They are not sufficient against a nuclear power's intelligence apparatus.

"Code is law" sounds elegant until bad code becomes bad law and there is no appeals court.

Protocols have their own concentration problem. Ethereum's security depends on validators staking Ether to secure the network. Lido, a liquid staking protocol, accumulated so much staked ETH that by late 2023 it controlled over 32 percent of all staking, approaching the 33 percent threshold at which a single entity could theoretically disrupt consensus. The crisis was averted, but the fact that it happened reveals something important: decentralized systems have a gravitational pull toward centralization. Convenience, liquidity, and network effects drive users toward the largest provider, creating the same "too big to fail" dynamic crypto was supposed to eliminate. The block building problem is worse. After Ethereum's merge to proof of stake, three block builders, Beaverbuild, Titan, and Rsync, now produce roughly 85 to 90 percent of all Ethereum blocks. These builders control transaction ordering, which means they decide which trades execute first and which get sandwiched.

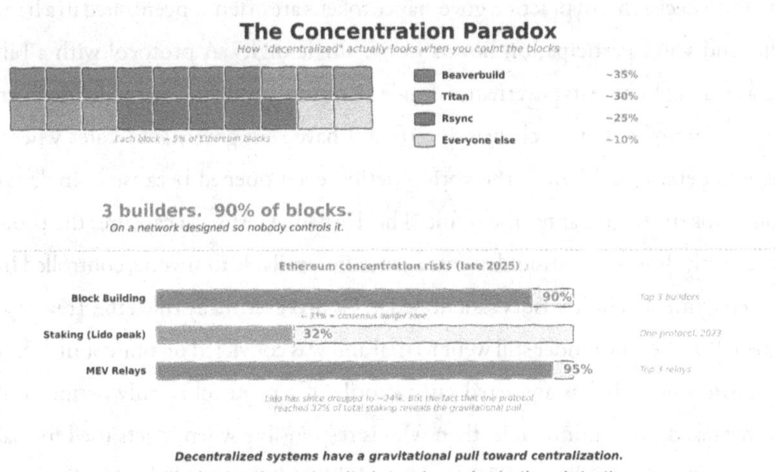

Figure 14.1: The Concentration Paradox

A sandwich attack is exactly what it sounds like: a builder inserts their own buy before your trade and their own sell after it, extracting value from the price impact you create. These attacks average more than 4,400 per day. The decentralized network has an invisible toll booth, and three companies operate it.

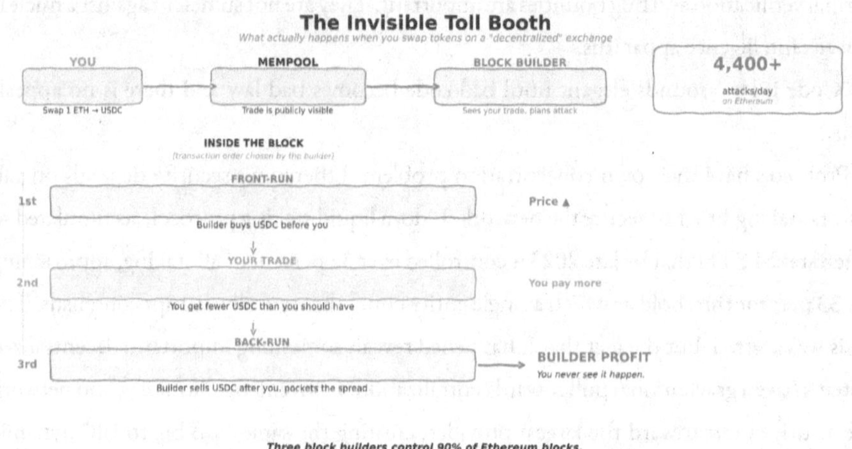

Figure 14.2: The Invisible Toll Booth

Then there is governance capture. Many protocols are governed by DAOs where token holders vote on decisions. In practice, governance tokens are often concentrated in a handful of wallets, and voter participation hovers in the single digits. A protocol with a billion dollars in assets might have its governance decided by twenty wallets. That is not democracy. That is an oligarchy with a blockchain interface. I have seen governance votes where the outcome was determined before the voting period even opened because a single whale held enough tokens to guarantee the result. The Tornado Cash saga captures the protocol paradox perfectly. It was permissionless infrastructure, available to anyone, controlled by no one after deployment. The Treasury sanctioned it. Courts eventually ruled the Treasury had overstepped. But the co-founder still went to trial and was convicted on one count. The case poses a question nobody has answered satisfactorily: if a protocol is truly permissionless, truly decentralized, truly immutable, then who is responsible when it gets used for harm? The answer so far is the developers. That creates a chilling effect on every builder in the space, including me. Permissionless, unless the government decides otherwise.

Michael Egorov is the founder of Curve Finance, one of DeFi's most important stablecoin trading protocols. In July 2023, Curve was exploited for over $60 million when a vulnerability in the Vyper programming language, not in Curve's code but in the compiler underneath it, was used to drain multiple pools. Egorov's personal position was underwater. The protocol's token price collapsed. Every obituary was written within forty-eight hours.

Egorov repaid the debt. Not by selling equity or raising an emergency round. He negotiated directly with the ecosystem, restructured his positions, and kept building. Within twelve months, Curve's total value locked had recovered, and the protocol had deployed upgrades that addressed the vulnerability class. The obituaries were wrong. Not because the exploit did not happen. Because the builder did not stop.

That distinction matters for how you read every risk in this chapter. The question is never whether something can go wrong. It can. It will. The question is whether the system contains people who build again after it breaks. Egorov is one of dozens. The pattern is consistent: the protocols that survive hacks are the protocols whose builders treat exploits as engineering problems, not existential crises. They patch, they learn, they ship. And the system gets harder to break

When Access Fails

Access replaces gatekeepers. That is the third pillar. The 1.3 billion unbanked adults with mobile phones can connect to the same financial infrastructure as a JPMorgan client. But removing the old gates can create new ones. And some of the new gates are scarier than anything the old system built.

Start with the surveillance risk, and start where most people do not expect it: the West.

The European Central Bank's digital euro project includes language about holding limits, transaction monitoring, and the ability to program conditions into the currency itself. A programmable euro controlled by the ECB could, in theory, enforce spending limits, restrict purchases of certain goods, or expire if not spent within a certain timeframe. The ECB insists it will protect privacy. But the infrastructure being built has the capability for total financial surveillance whether or not that is the stated intention. The capability is the risk. Intentions change. Governments change. Infrastructure endures. In the United States, the CBDC debate was effectively killed under both the Biden and Trump administrations, but the discussion revealed just how close the largest democracy in the world came to building infrastructure that could monitor and restrict every transaction its citizens make.

China built it. The digital yuan has been deployed across major Chinese cities and integrated into the broader social credit framework. The Chinese government can track every transaction, restrict spending for citizens with low social credit scores, and program the currency to expire if unspent, forcing economic activity during downturns. This is not a theoretical risk. This is deployed technology operating at scale in the world's second-largest economy. A government official in Beijing can, right now, see exactly what any citizen spent money on today, flag transactions that violate policy, and restrict future spending in real time. The old gatekeepers decided who got into the financial system. Programmable surveillance money decides what you can buy once you are in, where you can send it, and whether your account works at all. When people in the crypto space warn about surveillance money, they are not being paranoid. They are describing something that already exists for over a billion people.

The knowledge gatekeeper problem is subtler but potentially just as exclusionary. If you need technical sophistication to participate in the new financial system, you have replaced a wealth gatekeeper with a knowledge gatekeeper. Self-custody means self-responsibility. The person who loses their seed phrase loses everything, permanently. There is no forgot-my-password button for a hardware wallet. No branch manager who can look you up in the system. If you make a mistake, you absorb the full cost of it. If someone tricks you into signing a malicious transaction, the blockchain will execute it faithfully and permanently. My own bridge disaster was a knowledge failure. I understood that bridges were insecure. I sent funds through one anyway without a test transaction because I was in a hurry. I had the knowledge and still made the mistake. Now imagine someone who has never held a crypto wallet trying to navigate the same system without the years of experience I brought to it.

And then there is the inequality question that haunts every honest person building in this space. Does programmable money widen or narrow the gap? The optimistic case is real. Stablecoins are already transforming remittances in the global south. Mobile wallets reach people that traditional banks never will. The accredited investor exam opens markets that were locked behind a wealth threshold. All of that matters. But the pessimistic case is equally real. Early adopters accumulate tokens at lower costs and benefit from appreciation that later participants cannot access. Technical literacy becomes a de facto wealth threshold. And the protocols being built are overwhelmingly designed and controlled by developers in a handful of cities. If the new financial infrastructure replicates the geographic and demographic power structures of the old one, then we have built a shinier version of the same machine.

I do not have a clean answer to this. I think access is genuinely expanding. But I also think the industry has been too quick to celebrate access without examining who actually has it and on what terms. A farmer in the Philippines who receives remittances through a stablecoin wallet is genuinely better off than one who pays Western Union seven percent to move money. That is real progress. But that same farmer has no say in the governance of the protocol she depends on, no recourse if the stablecoin issuer freezes her funds, and no understanding of the smart contract risk she is taking on by holding a token she cannot audit. She has access. But access without agency is a different kind of dependency, and I am not sure the industry has grappled with that distinction honestly.

The person downloading a DeFi wallet in Lagos and the person deploying a smart contract in Denver are not operating in the same universe of capability, even if they are technically on the same network. If we are serious about the access pillar of the New Money Order, we need to be serious about what access actually means for the people who need it most.

The Honest Counter-Argument

A book that only presents the optimistic case is a pitch deck, not a thesis. So let me give the strongest version of the case against everything I have argued for the last thirteen chapters.

Nouriel Roubini is an economist at New York University who correctly predicted the 2008 financial crisis years before it happened. He earned the nickname "Dr. Doom," and he has applied the same analytical framework to crypto with equal conviction. His argument is not that blockchain technology is useless. His argument is that the vast majority of crypto activity is speculation masquerading as innovation, that DeFi protocols are unregulated shadow banks repackaging the same systemic risks that caused 2008, and that stablecoins are ticking time bombs backed by opaque reserves that would not survive a serious bank run. Roubini looks at the $2.7 billion stolen in 2025 and says this is not a bug. It is a feature of a system designed to operate outside regulatory oversight. You can disagree with his conclusions. You cannot dismiss his evidence.

Nassim Nicholas Taleb is the author of "The Black Swan" and "Antifragile," two of the most influential books on risk ever written. Taleb was initially sympathetic to Bitcoin. He wrote the foreword to a popular Bitcoin book and seemed to view it as a tool for decentralizing financial power. Then he turned against it, publicly and forcefully. His argument: Bitcoin has no intrinsic value because it generates no cash flows and requires continuous energy expenditure to maintain its network. It is not a hedge against inflation because it crashes during the same crises when you most need a hedge. And the mathematical properties that Bitcoin maximalists celebrate, the fixed supply, the halvings, the deflationary schedule, are precisely the properties that make it poor money for an economy that needs elastic supply. Taleb has put his analytical reputation squarely against Bitcoin. He may be wrong. But he is not uninformed, and his framework for thinking about fat-tailed risk is the same framework that made him one of the few people to profit from the 2008 collapse.

Hilary Allen is a law professor at American University who has spent years studying the systemic risks that DeFi introduces to the broader financial system. Most people outside legal academia and financial regulation circles have never heard of her, but her arguments are among the most technically rigorous critiques of the space. Allen's core thesis is that DeFi protocols are recreating the interconnectedness and opacity that made the 2008 crisis so devastating. When lending protocols plug into trading protocols which plug into insurance protocols, you get the same kind of cascading failure risk that took down Bear Stearns and Lehman Brothers. The composability I celebrated in Chapter 5, protocols snapping together like Lego blocks, is the same composability that Allen warns creates hidden chains of dependency. When one protocol fails, the failure cascades through every protocol connected to it. Terra/Luna's collapse in 2022 was a $40 billion preview of what a truly systemic DeFi failure would look like at scale.

I take these arguments seriously because they identify real failure modes that the industry has been too slow to address. The speculative froth that Roubini criticizes is real. I have been in the rooms where people launch tokens with no utility and no plan beyond extraction, and walk away rich while retail investors absorb the loss. The tail risks that Taleb identifies are real. Bitcoin has crashed 80 percent or more in multiple cycles, and anyone who tells you the next crash cannot happen is selling you something. The systemic interconnectedness that Allen maps is real. I watched Terra/Luna take down lending protocols, stablecoins, and hedge funds in a cascade that moved at the speed of code.

Here is where I land. These critics are right about the risks. They are wrong about the conclusion. The risks they identify are real, but they are not unique to the new system. The old system has speculative froth, tail risk, and systemic interconnectedness too. It just dresses them up in pinstripes and hides them behind closed doors. The 2008 crisis was caused by the exact same kind of interconnected, opaque, under-regulated financial engineering that

Allen warns about in DeFi. The difference is that in DeFi, the code is public. The risks are visible on a public ledger. The collapses happen in real time where everyone can see them instead of behind the walls of a bank that is too big to fail and too important to let you look inside.

That does not make the risks acceptable. It makes them addressable. And that is the distinction the critics consistently miss. Roubini is right that speculation is rampant. The answer is better regulation, not no blockchain. Taleb is right that Bitcoin crashes. The answer is portfolio construction, not ignoring the only monetary network that operates without permission from any government. Allen is right that composability creates cascading risk. The answer is better circuit breakers and risk modeling, not dismantling the most transparent financial infrastructure ever built.

The honest position is not that the critics are wrong. It is that their prescription, abandon the project, is worse than the disease they diagnose.

How Energy Systems Fail

Every energy system fails in one of four ways.

Overload: too much energy flooding the system too fast. In the old system, this looks like a speculative bubble. In the new system, it looks the same. DeFi Summer 2020. The NFT mania of 2021. The memecoin frenzy of 2024. When speculative energy overwhelms the system's capacity to absorb it productively, the system overheats and breaks. Terra/Luna was an overload failure. Forty billion dollars of speculative energy pouring into a protocol that had no real economic activity underneath it. The energy had nowhere productive to go, so it vaporized.

Leakage: energy draining out through cracks in the infrastructure. In the old system, this is fraud, embezzlement, insider dealing. In the new system, it is exploits, hacks, and bridge failures. The $7.7 billion stolen over three years is leakage. My bridge disaster was leakage on a personal scale. Energy that was supposed to stay in the system found a crack and drained out, and no one could put it back. The difference from the old system is that in DeFi, the leakage is visible on a public ledger. You can trace every stolen dollar. You just cannot always get it back.

Blockage: something preventing energy from flowing where it needs to go. In the old system, this is regulatory capture, gatekeeping, bureaucratic friction. In the new system, it is regulatory overreach that kills innovation before it matures, sanctions that target neutral infrastructure, or compliance requirements so onerous that only large institutions can afford to meet them. The Tornado Cash sanctions were a blockage. Energy could not flow through a privacy-preserving protocol because the government sealed the pipe.

Concentration: too much energy routing through a single node, creating a single point of failure. In the old system, this is "too big to fail." In the new system, it is Lido approaching 33 percent, three block builders controlling 90 percent of Ethereum blocks, or DAO governance concentrated in a handful of wallets. Concentration failures are especially dangerous because they undermine the core value proposition of the entire project. A centralized decentralized system is just a worse version of the centralized system it was supposed to replace.

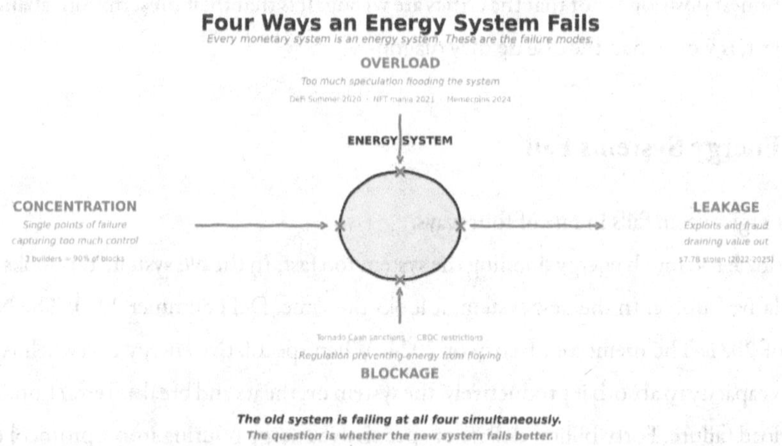

Figure 14.3: How Energy Systems Fail

The New Money Order is not immune to any of these failure modes. But here is what I keep coming back to. The old system is already failing at all four simultaneously. Speculative overload in meme stocks and leveraged derivatives. Leakage through fraud, corruption, and the $48 billion extracted annually in remittance fees alone. Blockage through gatekeeping that locks out billions from banking access and 81 percent of American households from private markets. Concentration through a handful of banks and asset managers that control the plumbing of global finance and have proven, repeatedly, that they will use that control to serve themselves first.

The question is not whether the new system is perfect. It is not. Nothing I have seen in a decade of building in this space suggests that programmable money will eliminate human greed, stupidity, or malice. The question is whether the new system is better. Whether its failures are more visible, more addressable, and more fixable than the failures of the system it replaces. And whether the risks of building are greater than the risks of standing still.

I keep coming back to my answer. They are not.

I lost money to a bridge exploit. I watched Terra/Luna vaporize $40 billion. I have seen protocols I believed in get hacked, governance get captured, and the same concentration dynamics that plague Wall Street start creeping into the systems that were supposed to replace it. And I am still building. Not because I am naive about the risks. Because I have seen enough of the old system to know that its failures are worse, less visible, and less fixable. The 2008 crisis was a code failure too. It was just code written in legal contracts instead of Solidity, and the people who wrote it walked away richer than when they started.

The risks are real. But so is what comes next. The final chapter is not about what can go wrong. It is about how to see what is coming, and how to position yourself for a world where the old architecture is crumbling and the new one is just getting started.

Chapter 15

SEEING THE NEW MONEY ORDER

We had just walked out of the Sphere. It was January 2026, CES in Las Vegas, and Lenovo had packed ten thousand people into what might be the most disorienting venue on earth to watch Jensen Huang talk about AI gigafactories while a 16K wraparound screen made you feel like you were falling through a data center. Gwen Stefani performed afterward. The whole thing was sensory overload in the best possible way. Everyone was buzzing. Everyone had opinions about Nvidia's next chip, about agentic AI, about whether Lenovo's new personal AI platform would actually work. The conversations spilling out of that building were exactly what you'd expect from ten thousand people who just had their brains rearranged by a two-hour technology keynote inside a giant orb. I got into the Uber and the driver asked what I did. We have the best conversations with Uber drivers. I mean that without a trace of irony. They are inside the network. They understand the scale of the system they work within. They feel the energy flowing through it, and they feel when they are getting the raw end of the conversion. They pick up passengers from every industry, every

income level, every corner of the economy. A good Uber driver in Las Vegas during CES has a better sampling of the global technology industry's current thinking than most analysts at Goldman Sachs. And unlike the analysts, the driver has skin in the game. Every fare is an energy exchange. Every tip is a signal. Every conversation is data. This particular driver asked what brought me to the conference. And I've learned that how I answer that question determines whether the next five minutes are interesting or not. If I say "I work in crypto," the conversation goes one of two directions, neither of them productive. If I say "I'm writing a book about the future of money," I get a polite nod and a question about Bitcoin's price. But if I explain what I actually see happening, something different occurs. So I told him. I said the financial system is going through a transition as fundamental as the one from paper money to digital money, except this time money is becoming software. I said the old system runs on three things: trust, institutions, and gatekeepers. You trust the bank. The institution sets the rules. The gatekeeper decides who gets access. And the new system runs on three different things: code, protocols, and access. The code executes. The protocol sets the rules. Anyone with a phone gets access. Two columns, three rows. That's the whole transition. He was quiet for about ten seconds. Then he said,

"That's Uber."

I asked what he meant. He said he understood exactly what I was describing because he was living inside a version of it. Uber is a platform that connects drivers and riders through software. The algorithm sets the price. The app handles the payment. The rating system provides the trust layer. No dispatcher. No taxi medallion. No gatekeeper deciding who gets to drive. The old system was trust, institutions, gatekeepers: you trusted the dispatcher, the taxi commission set the rules, the medallion system decided who could participate. Uber replaced all three with code. Then he said something I have not stopped thinking about. He said,

"But Uber is still the gatekeeper. They take their cut. They set the algorithm. They control the whole thing. What you're describing sounds like what happens when even that layer goes away."

And he was right.

What if the Uber network went a step further? What if the software was owned by the drivers, not by Uber? What if it ran autonomously, and drivers could plug into it whenever they chose, vote on upgrades to the network, and share in the value of the whole system?

That is not a hypothetical. That is what a protocol looks like. That is what the New Money Order looks like when you apply it to ride-sharing. The driver saw it in under a minute because he lives inside the system every day. He feels the energy flowing through it. He knows where the leakage is. He knows who captures the value he creates.

Here's what I have learned from hundreds of conversations like this one. The people who grasp the New Money Order fastest are almost never the people you would expect. It is not the finance executives or the venture capitalists or the people who already own Bitcoin. It is the Uber driver. The FedEx delivery guy. The real estate agent. The restaurant owner. The people who are always looking for the next opportunity, always feeling the friction of the current system, always open to the idea that there might be a better way. They are in the network. They feel the energy. They know the deal they are getting.

The people who glaze over? They tend to be the ones who are comfortable. The ones whose positions in the old architecture are secure enough that the transition feels abstract. They see money as money: dollars, accounts, balances, prices. The Uber driver sees money as energy: conversions, flows, leakage, extraction. The difference is not intelligence. It is perception.

This chapter is about giving every reader the perception of the second group. Not the facts. You have had fourteen chapters of facts. This is about the lens. Once you have it, you cannot unsee the transition. And once you can see it, you can position yourself inside it.

The Diagnostic

In Chapter 13, I introduced the New Money Order framework. Old Money Order: trust, institutions, gatekeepers. New Money Order: code, protocols, access. That framework is a map. Now I want to teach you how to use it as a diagnostic. Not as a checklist. As a way of seeing.

When you evaluate a company, ask three questions. Does it depend on trust, or does it run on code? Does it require institutions to set and enforce the rules, or do protocols handle that? Does it use gatekeepers to control who participates, or is access open? Any company, any financial product, any government program can be classified in under thirty seconds using these three questions. And the classification tells you something important about where that entity sits in the transition and how vulnerable it is to disruption.

Start with a traditional bank. You trust the bank to hold your deposits. The institution, regulated by the FDIC and the Federal Reserve, enforces the rules. A gatekeeper, the credit committee, the branch manager, the algorithm that decides your credit score, determines your access. Three for three on the Old Money Order. Every pillar is trust-dependent, institution-mediated, and gatekeeper-controlled. That does not mean the bank will disappear tomorrow. It means the bank's entire architecture is built on the old operating system, and every component of that architecture is being rebuilt in code somewhere.

Now look at Uniswap. The code executes trades automatically through an algorithm that anyone can audit. The protocol sets the rules: liquidity pool mechanics, fee structures, governance processes. Access is open to anyone with a wallet. There is no credit check, no application, no account minimum, no branch to visit. Three for three on the New Money Order. The entire system runs on the new architecture.

The interesting cases are in between. Take FTX. It called itself a crypto exchange. It used blockchain terminology. It was covered as a crypto company. But apply the diagnostic. Did it run on code? No. It ran on trust. Customers trusted Sam Bankman-Fried and his team to custody their assets honestly. Did protocols set the rules? No. Institutions did, poorly. Internal decision-making was opaque, unaudited, and concentrated in a handful of people. Were gatekeepers removed? No. FTX was the gatekeeper. It decided who traded what, on what terms, with whose money. FTX was an Old Money Order company wearing a New Money Order costume. The diagnostic would have told you that before the collapse. Trust-based opacity with a blockchain label is still trust-based opacity.

Now apply it to BlackRock's tokenized treasury fund, BUIDL. The fund uses blockchain rails for settlement. That is code replacing some institutional plumbing. But BlackRock the institution still manages the fund, sets the terms, and controls access through traditional accredited investor requirements. It is a hybrid: an Old Money Order institution adopting New Money Order infrastructure. That is not a criticism. It is a classification. And it tells you exactly where BlackRock is in the transition: using the new pipes but keeping the old control structure. For now.

Apply it to EAT. The smart contract executes the fee routing automatically. No human decides whether a meal gets funded after a trade. That is code. The protocol, built on Base with transparent, auditable logic, sets the rules for how trading fees convert to impact. That is protocol. Anyone with a wallet can trade. No gatekeeper decides who participates. That is access. Three for three. The diagnostic classifies EAT as New Money Order native.

Now apply it to your own financial life. Map your paycheck through the lens. Your employer's payroll system processes your wages through a bank, which takes one to three business days to settle. That is an institution mediating the transfer. Your bank charges fees, enforces overdraft policies, and decides your credit limit. That is a gatekeeper. You trust that the numbers on your screen reflect real dollars that you can access when you need them. That is trust. Every fee, every delay, every intermediary between the work you perform and the money you receive is a remnant of the old architecture. Programmable money removes them because the code enforces the flow, the protocol sets the rules, and access is permissionless.

The Uber driver understood this instinctively. He mapped his own industry through the diagnostic in real time. The old taxi system: trust, institutions, gatekeepers. Uber: code replaces the dispatcher, but Uber itself becomes the new institution and gatekeeper. A protocol-based alternative: code, protocols, access. He saw three generations of the same industry laid out in the same framework, and he did it in the back seat of his own car.

That is what the diagnostic does. It gives you the ability to look at any system, any company, any government program, any piece of your own financial life, and see where it sits in the transition. Old Money Order systems are not evil. Many of them work. But they are all built on pillars that are eroding: declining trust, weakening institutions, increasingly resented gatekeepers. The New Money Order does not require those pillars. It runs on code that executes, protocols that enforce, and access that is open. The diagnostic tells you which world you are standing in and which way the ground is shifting.

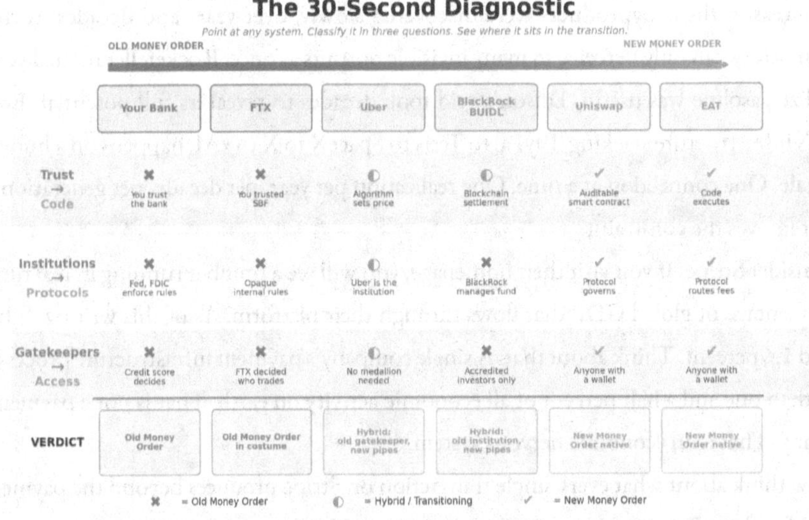

Figure 15.1: The 30-Second Diagnostic

The Byproduct Explosion

In Chapter 3, I planted a seed that I have been waiting the entire book to harvest.

The byproduct principle. Every action produces the intended product and everything else. And the everything else, the byproduct, is almost always worth more than the product itself. Rockefeller refined crude oil into kerosene and threw away the gasoline. The gasoline powered the twentieth century. Edison built a power grid to sell light bulbs. The grid powered factories, appliances, computers, and eventually the internet. Vanderbilt built railroads to move freight. The railroads created a national market that made mass production possible, which created the middle class. Nvidia built chips for gaming. Those chips became the foundational hardware for artificial intelligence.

The pattern is so consistent across centuries that you could make it a law: the infrastructure you build for one purpose will produce byproducts worth orders of magnitude more than the original purpose. The product is the product. The byproduct is the future.

But there is a second half to the insight that I did not reveal in Chapter 3, because the reader needed twelve more chapters of context to understand why it matters. Here it is.

The reason those byproducts were discovered slowly, over years and decades, is that human beings can only perceive so many invisible outputs at once. Rockefeller needed years to realize gasoline was useful. Edison's grid took decades to reveal its full potential. Even Musk's infrastructure stacking, PayPal to Tesla to SpaceX to X to xAI, happens on a human timescale. One connection at a time. One realization per year, per decade, per generation.

AI removes the constraint.

Consider Stripe. If you visit their homepage, you will see a number running in real time: the percentage of global GDP that flows through their platform. As of this writing, it has crossed 1.6 percent. Think about that. A single company's payment infrastructure processes more than one and a half percent of all economic activity on earth. That is not a payments company. That is an economic nervous system.

Now think about what every single transaction on Stripe produces beyond the payment itself. Metadata. Behavioral signals. Fraud patterns. Merchant analytics. Conversion rates by geography, by device, by time of day, by payment method. API usage patterns. Churn indicators. Revenue velocity. Cross-border flow data. Each transaction is a packet of information that contains dozens of byproducts, signals about the economy that are invisible to the merchant, the buyer, and in many cases even to Stripe's own team.

We use Stripe across all of our companies. And I can tell you firsthand that the outputs we have access to through Stripe have become the operating system for our decision-making.

We build our workflows and systems off of those outputs. They give every one of our companies an x-ray into what is working and what is not. Which products convert. Which geographies are growing. Where the churn signals appear before the customer even knows they are leaving. The payment is the product. The intelligence is the byproduct. And the byproduct is worth more than the payment. Stripe knows this. That is why their mission is not to process payments. Their mission is to grow the GDP of the internet. They understand that the transaction is the product and the economic nervous system they are building from the transaction data is the real value. The counter on their homepage is not a vanity metric. It is a statement of ambition: we are building the infrastructure layer of the global economy, and every fraction of a percent of GDP that flows through us produces byproducts that make the next fraction easier to capture.

A human team, even a brilliant one, identifies and acts on maybe five or ten of those byproduct signals per transaction. AI agents running continuously identify and act on thousands. And here is where it goes exponential. Each action an AI agent takes in response to a byproduct produces its own byproducts. A fraud detection action generates a behavioral pattern. That pattern triggers a risk model update. The update changes the scoring algorithm. The new algorithm surfaces previously invisible anomalies. Each anomaly is a byproduct. And each byproduct triggers more actions. The equation goes recursive. One plus one equals ten.

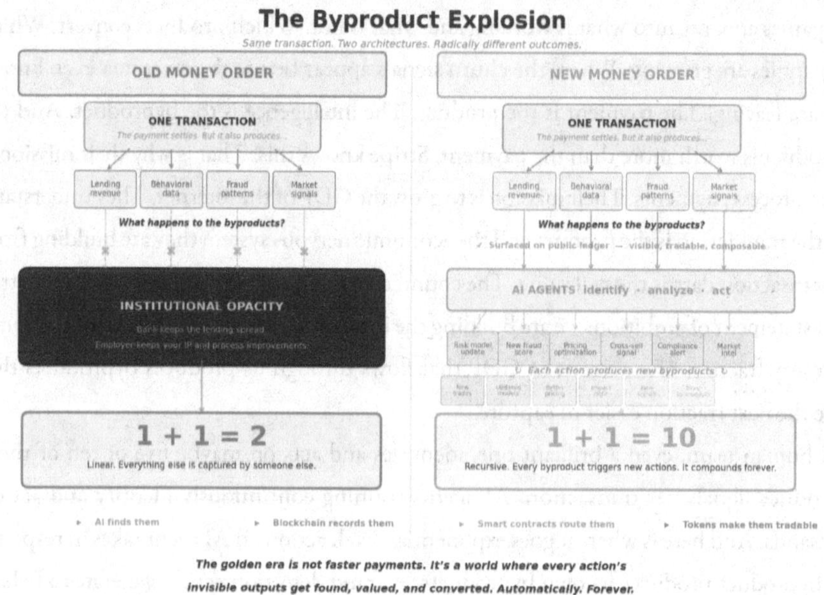

Figure 15.2: The Byproduct Explosion

The Old Money Order buried byproducts. It had to. The architecture was not designed to surface them. It was designed to capture them, invisibly, for the benefit of whoever controlled the infrastructure.

Your bank takes your deposits and lends them out at a higher interest rate. The spread between what they pay you and what they charge the borrower is the byproduct of your deposit. It funds the bank's entire business model. You generate the raw material, the capital. The bank captures the byproduct, the lending revenue. You receive a fraction of a percent in interest. The bank keeps the rest. This is not theft. It is architecture. The system was built so that the institution captures the byproducts and the depositor does not even see them.

Your employer captures the byproducts of your labor every day. The process improvements you figure out. The client relationships you build. The institutional knowledge you accumulate. The data your work generates. All of it belongs to the company, not to you. When you leave, you walk away with a final paycheck and whatever you learned. The company keeps the compounding value of every byproduct you produced over your entire tenure. Again, this is not a conspiracy. It is how the architecture works. The employment relationship was designed in the industrial era to concentrate byproducts at the institutional level.

Social media platforms are the most brazen example. You spend an hour scrolling Instagram. Your attention is the product you are selling, and you are selling it for free. But the byproducts of that hour, the behavioral data, the engagement patterns, the preferences revealed by every pause, every click, every share, are worth a precisely calculable amount to advertisers. The platform captures all of it. You get a feed. They get a multibillion-dollar data asset. The attention economy is not new. What is new is the possibility of an architecture where the person generating the attention captures the byproducts instead of the platform.

Government is the largest byproduct burial ground of all. I wrote in earlier chapters about the DOGE investigations revealing billions in unaccounted-for spending. That is the ultimate byproduct problem. Every dollar the government spends produces byproducts: data on program effectiveness, signals about where resources are actually needed, information about which interventions work and which do not. In the Old Money Order, those byproducts are buried in institutional opacity. Nobody traces the energy from tax collection to program delivery to outcome measurement, because the architecture was never built to surface those flows. Programmable money changes this. When government funds flow through transparent, auditable code, the byproducts become visible. You can trace every dollar from collection to deployment. You can measure outcomes in real time. You can identify leakage not in years or decades, but in minutes. The DOGE investigations found what they found by forcing transparency onto a system designed for opacity. Programmable money makes transparency the default.

The New Money Order surfaces byproducts because the architecture makes them visible. Code is transparent. You can read it. Protocols are composable. They snap together, and each connection reveals new data flows. Access is open. Anyone can build on top of anyone else's infrastructure. When every action is recorded on a public ledger, when every protocol can connect to every other protocol, when anyone can build on the infrastructure, the byproducts stop being invisible. They become visible, capturable, and tradable.

AI finds the byproducts. Blockchain records them. Smart contracts route the value. Tokens make them tradable. That is the full stack. And that is what the golden era actually looks like. Not just faster payments or cheaper transactions. A world where every action's invisible outputs can be identified, valued, and converted into new forms of energy. Automatically, at the speed of software, with 100% uptime.

This is why I said in the energy chapter that the byproduct is almost always worth more than the product. It was true for Rockefeller. It was true for Edison. It was true for Nvidia. And it will be exponentially more true in the New Money Order, because for the first time in history, we have the tools to find every byproduct, value it, and convert it in real time. The discovery cycle that used to take decades now takes seconds. The conversion mechanisms that used to require human insight now run autonomously. The energy that used to leak out of every transaction, invisible and uncaptured, now gets routed to wherever the code directs it.

Including toward impact. Every EAT trade produces a payment and a meal. The meal is the byproduct of the trade. But the trade also produces metadata, market signals, behavioral data, and proof-of-impact records on the blockchain. Those are byproducts of the byproduct. And as AI agents begin trading on cause coin rails, those agents will identify and act on byproducts that no human team would ever notice, generating more trades, more meals, more data, more byproducts. The whole system compounds.

One plus one equals ten. That is not marketing. That is the math of byproduct recursion in a transparent, composable, AI-augmented financial system. And it is happening right now.

The Enterprise Playbook

You have the framework. Old Money Order versus New Money Order, the diagnostic that classifies any system in thirty seconds. You have the lens. Byproducts, the invisible outputs that are worth more than the products themselves, now discoverable at machine speed. The question is what you do with them.

Start with the foundation. Think in energy, not money. This sounds abstract until you try it, and then it changes how you evaluate everything. When someone offers you a job, do not just calculate the salary. Calculate the energy exchange. What energy are you putting in: time, attention, creativity, expertise? What energy are you getting out: money, skills, network, optionality? A job that pays well but produces no byproducts, no skills you can compound, no network effects, no future optionality, is an energy-losing trade even if the paycheck is large. A job that pays less but connects you to infrastructure, to protocols, to systems that are growing, is an energy-multiplying trade. The salary is the product. Everything else is the byproduct. And the byproduct is where the real value lives.

Infrastructure beats applications. This is the Rockefeller lesson, the Edison lesson, the Nvidia lesson. The people who build the pipes capture more value than the people who pour things through them. In practical terms: if you are evaluating where to invest your time, your money, or your career energy, look for the infrastructure layer. The company building the blockchain is more durable than the company building the app on the blockchain. The protocol that enables trading is more durable than any individual token that trades on it. The platform that powers payments, Stripe processing 1.6 percent of global GDP, captures more value than any individual merchant on its platform. Build infrastructure. Invest in infrastructure. Work at infrastructure companies. The applications will change. The infrastructure compounds.

Tokens are the new atomic unit. I spent Chapter 9 on this, but the personal implication is worth making explicit. Learn to read token economics the way a previous generation learned to read balance sheets. Understand what a token incentivizes, what energy it converts, and what byproducts it produces. A Bitcoin is a token that stores energy. An AI compute credit is a token that produces intelligence. An EAT token is a token that converts trading energy into funded meals. The substrate varies. The principle is the same. If you cannot evaluate a token's energy conversion mechanism, you are investing blind. If you can, you have an advantage that most of the market does not.

Attention is monetizable energy. Every hour you spend scrolling, watching, clicking, and engaging is energy that someone is converting into revenue. The old system captured that energy without compensating you for it. The new system is building mechanisms, creator tokens, attention markets, prediction platforms, that let you capture the value of your own attention. Be deliberate about where you direct it. What you pay attention to, you fund. What funds your attention, extracts energy from you. The conversion runs both directions.

I think about this constantly in real estate and home services, because those industries are pure energy conversion systems and most of the people working in them do not realize it. A real estate agent's entire business is a game of attention and trust, magnified by byproducts. The agent spends energy on marketing, relationships, open houses, and social media content. That energy converts into attention from potential buyers and sellers. The attention converts into trust. The trust converts into a listing or an offer. The offer converts into a transaction. And the transaction produces byproducts: referral networks, market data, neighborhood expertise, client relationships that compound over years. The best agents intuitively understand this energy chain. They invest in the byproducts, the relationships, the reputation, the local knowledge, because they know the byproducts are worth more than any single commission.

Now apply the diagnostic. The current real estate system runs on the Old Money Order. Trust: you trust the agent to represent your interests honestly. Institutions: the MLS, the brokerage, the licensing board set the rules. Gatekeepers: the commission structure, the lockbox system, and the MLS access control who participates and who does not. Every one of those pillars is being rebuilt. Tokenized property ownership is code replacing some of the trust layer. Protocol-based listing platforms are replacing institutional gatekeeping. Open access to market data is eroding the information asymmetry that agents have relied on for decades. The agent who sees this transition and repositions as an energy converter, someone who adds value through expertise, relationships, and trust that code cannot replicate, will thrive. The agent who relies on gatekeeping and information asymmetry will be disintermediated.

Impact is a business model, not a department. This is the cause coin insight, but it applies far beyond cause coins. If you are running a business, impact is not something you bolt on as a PR initiative or a line item in your CSR report. It is a byproduct that can be captured by design. Every transaction your business processes produces byproducts. Some of those byproducts can be directed toward outcomes that matter. The mechanism is the smart contract. The infrastructure exists. The question is whether you build it into your architecture or keep treating impact as an afterthought.

The convergence is the opportunity. AI and crypto are not separate sectors. They are two expressions of the same energy revolution: converting electricity into intelligence and converting value into programmable flows. The intersection, where AI agents use blockchain rails, where compute tokens trade on decentralized exchanges, where machine intelligence discovers byproducts in transparent financial data, is the largest and least competed opportunity in the economy right now. Position yourself there.

And position for the deployment phase. The installation phase rewarded speculators. ICO flippers, meme coin traders, people who got in early on hype cycles. The deployment phase rewards builders. The people who build the infrastructure, write the code, design the protocols, and create the access points. Perez's framework is clear on this: every golden era in history belonged to the builders who showed up during the deployment phase and put the installed infrastructure to productive use. The rails are laid. The regulation is arriving. The institutions are entering. The question is whether you are going to build on the new architecture or keep running on the old one.

I have spent the last several hundred pages giving you the lens. But I know how this works. You are reading this as a restaurant owner, or a real estate broker, or a freelance designer, or a nonprofit director. You are reading this as a website developer who has been building sites for small business owners for a decade and is starting to notice that the phone rings less often because vibe coding and AI tools are making it easier than ever for someone with no technical background to build their own site. You are reading this as a real estate agent who understands intuitively that your entire business is a game of attention energy and trust, converting the energy you spend on marketing and relationships into transactions, and you can feel that the rules of that conversion are changing. You want to know what this means for your business, specifically, on Monday morning.

That is what the Playbook at the end of this book is for. Find your industry. Read your section. See the gap between where you are and where you could be. Three moves. The same three pillars from Chapter 13, applied to your specific world: where code replaces trust, where protocols replace institutions, and where access replaces gatekeepers in your business. And then decide whether you want to keep running on the old architecture or start building on the new one.

Here is the shift. Before this book, you saw money as money. Dollars and cents. Prices and balances. A number that went up when you worked and down when you spent. The question you asked of any financial decision was: how much does it cost and what do I get?

That question is now incomplete. You know it. You can feel it. Because you spent fourteen chapters learning to see what is underneath the price. The energy that produced it. The trust layer it depends on. The institution enforcing it. The gatekeeper extracting from it. The byproducts being thrown away at every conversion point. You did not have that sight when you picked up this book. You have it now.

Test it. Think about the last financial decision you made. A purchase, an investment, a bill you paid. Now run the diagnostic. Was the trust layer based on a person you believe in or code you can verify? Was the institution a gatekeeper charging for access or a protocol providing it? Where was the energy leaking? What byproducts were being generated and who was capturing them?

If you can answer those questions, and you can, because you just did it in your head, then you see in three dimensions now. You did not see in three dimensions four hundred pages ago. That is the transformation. Not an opinion you adopted. A lens you built. And a lens, once ground, does not ungrind.

The 3D View

The Uber driver dropped me off at the hotel. I tipped him well, because he had just given me the opening scene for this chapter, though he did not know that yet. And I thought about what had happened in that fifteen-minute ride.

Ten thousand people had just watched Jensen Huang describe the future of AI infrastructure inside the most technologically advanced entertainment venue on earth. They walked out talking about chips and models and compute capacity. The Uber driver, who had not been inside the Sphere, who had never heard of Carlotta Perez or Ray Dalio, who probably could not name three DeFi protocols, understood the New Money Order in under sixty seconds. He mapped it onto his own industry without being asked. He identified the energy flows, the leakage, the gatekeeper extraction, and the architectural alternative. He saw in three dimensions what most of the people walking out of that keynote were still seeing in two.

That is not a knock on the people at CES. They are some of the smartest technology minds in the world. But intelligence is not the variable. Perception is. Most people, most very smart people, see money as money. Dollars and cents. Prices and balances. Inflows and outflows. They see in two dimensions: what things cost and what things are worth. The third dimension is energy. It is the conversion mechanisms underneath the prices. It is the byproducts that nobody is capturing. It is the leakage that nobody notices because the old architecture was designed to hide it. It is the flow of value through systems, and the question of who controls the valves.

The golden era belongs to the people who can see in three dimensions. Not because they are smarter. Because they have a framework that makes the invisible visible. Trust becoming code. Institutions becoming protocols. Gatekeepers becoming access. And at every conversion point, byproducts more valuable than the products themselves, waiting to be discovered by anyone with the eyes to see them.

Think about where you were when you started this book. You knew money was changing. Maybe you had bought some crypto on Coinbase. Maybe you had heard about Bitcoin and were not sure what to make of it. Maybe you worked in finance and could feel the ground shifting but could not name what was moving. You were looking at the transition in two dimensions.

Now you have the third dimension. You can see the energy underneath the money. You can trace the flows. You can identify the byproducts. You can classify any system, any company, any piece of your own financial life using a diagnostic that takes thirty seconds and tells you which world it belongs to. You can see the 150-year cycle that Dalio mapped, the installation-to-deployment arc that Perez described, and the convergence of AI and programmable money that neither of them fully anticipated. You can see why it is all happening at once, why it is mathematical and not coincidental, and why the regulatory apparatus is being rebuilt at emergency speed.

You can look at a headline about a new stablecoin regulation and see it for what it is: a valve opening on the energy grid. You can look at a company announcing a tokenized fund and classify it in seconds: old institution, new pipes. You can look at your own bank statement and see the byproducts being extracted at every step, the spread on your deposits, the fees on your transactions, the settlement delays that let someone else use your money for two days before it arrives. You can see all of this because you have the framework, and the framework makes the invisible visible.

You can see the New Money Order.

And now that you can see it, the question is what you do with the sight. The Uber driver is going to do something with it. I could tell. He was already thinking about what a driver-owned protocol would look like, how the value would flow, where the byproducts would go. He was not waiting for someone to build it for him. He was running the diagnostic on his own life and seeing the gaps.

The people who navigate the golden era successfully will not be the ones with the most money or the best connections or the deepest technical knowledge. They will be the ones who can see the energy grid clearly. Who can trace the conversions. Who can spot the byproducts that everyone else is throwing away. Who understand that trust is becoming code, that institutions are becoming protocols, and that access is replacing gatekeepers across every industry, in every country, at every scale.

What you build next is up to you. The frameworks are in your head now. The diagnostic takes thirty seconds. And the gap between what you can see and what most people can see is your advantage for as long as it lasts.

It will not last forever. These ideas are spreading. The frameworks are being taught. The golden era rewards the early builders, not the late arrivals. And you are early.

EPILOGUE: THE MEAL THAT FUNDED ITSELF

T he first EAT trade was entirely anticlimactic.

I remember staring at my screen, watching numbers shift. That was it. No fireworks, no celebration, no dramatic moment where the heavens parted and the future of philanthropy revealed itself. Just a transaction on a decentralized exchange. Numbers moving from one line to another.

You read those words at the beginning of this book. They were true then. They are true now. The screen looked the same. The transaction looked the same. A buy order, a fee collected, a routing executed. If you had been standing behind me in Irvine on December 10th, 2025, watching over my shoulder, you would have seen nothing worth remembering.

But you have spent the last sixty thousand words learning to see what those numbers mean. And now I want to show you what actually happened in those six seconds. Twice. Through both lenses this book has given you.

The Energy Path

A person, somewhere in the world, decided to trade EAT. That decision was an expression of attention energy. Their time, their focus, their capital, directed toward this specific action at this specific moment. Maybe they were speculating. Maybe they believed in the mission. Maybe they were just looking at charts and liked what they saw. It did not matter. The smart contract does not care about motivation.

The trade executed on a decentralized exchange. The moment it settled, the smart contract collected its fee. Automatically. No human reviewed the transaction. No compliance officer approved the transfer. No board convened to discuss allocation. The code ran. The fee was extracted. A portion routed directly to a wallet designated for hunger relief.

That wallet funded the purchase of food through verified partners. Feeding America. Feed the Children. Organizations with distribution networks that reach food banks and school lunch programs across the country. The food was purchased. The food was distributed. A person facing food insecurity received a meal.

The calories entered their body. Carbohydrates converted to glucose. Glucose fueled cellular respiration. ATP was produced. Muscles moved. A brain thought. A heart beat. Metabolic energy, the most fundamental kind there is, sustained a human life for another few hours.

From a click on a screen to calories in a human body. From attention energy to metabolic energy. The complete circuit, executed in seconds, recorded permanently on the blockchain, requiring no trust in any person or institution at any step. That is the energy thesis of this book, made concrete in a single transaction that took less time than reading this paragraph.

In Chapter 3, I told you that money is energy. That every phase change in monetary history was an efficiency upgrade in how humans store, transmit, and convert value. Shells were portable energy. Paper was lightweight energy. Digital was instant energy. Programmable is intelligent energy. Energy that carries instructions.

The EAT trade is what intelligent energy looks like in practice. The money carried an instruction: when this token moves, fund a meal. The instruction executed. The meal was funded. Someone ate. The energy converted from one form to another to another, losing almost nothing along the way, because the system was designed to minimize resistance at every step.

That is thermodynamics. Not a metaphor for it. The actual thing.

The New Money Order Path

Now trace the same trade through the other lens.

No trust was required. The code executed exactly as written. No one had to believe that anyone would be honest. No one had to hope that the donation would be used properly. No one had to trust that the foundation's board was acting in good faith. The smart contract is auditable, immutable, and executes identically whether the founder is having a good day or a bad one. Whether the market is up or down. Whether anyone is watching or not. Code replaced trust.

No institution decided. No bank approved the transfer. No foundation board allocated the funds. No compliance department reviewed the transaction. No grant committee scored the application. No payment processor took its 2.5% cut. No intermediary touched the money between the trade and the meal. The fee routed through a protocol. Protocols replaced institutions.

No gatekeeper controlled access. Anyone with a wallet could trade, anywhere in the world, at any time. No accredited investor requirement. No minimum donation threshold. No geographic restriction. No operating hours. The market runs 24 hours a day, seven days a week, 365 days a year. Access replaced gatekeepers.

Code, protocols, access. The three pillars of the New Money Order, demonstrated in a single transaction.

Now consider what that same forty dollars of economic energy directed toward hunger relief would have required under the Old Money Order. A donation page. A credit card processor taking its fee. A nonprofit's administrative overhead, typically twenty to forty percent of the donation absorbed before a dollar reaches the cause. A board meeting to allocate funds. A grant application to a food bank. A reporting cycle to satisfy donors and regulators. Months of lag between the moment someone decided to help and the moment someone ate.

Trust at every step. Institutions at every step. Gatekeepers at every step. Energy leaking at every handoff, converting useful intent into administrative heat.

The Old Money Order could not do in six months what the New Money Order did in six seconds.

The Byproducts

And the trade produced byproducts. This is the part almost nobody sees.

The meal was the intended output. One trade, one fee, one meal. That was the design. But the trade also generated something else. Several something elses.

It generated proof. Proof that the cause coin model works. That market activity can be automatically converted into social impact without requiring anyone to be generous. That proof is recorded on the blockchain, permanently, publicly, verifiable by anyone. And that proof makes the next cause coin possible. A cancer research token. An education token. A climate token. Each one easier to launch because EAT proved the mechanism. Each one carrying the weight of evidence that this is not theoretical. The first domino fell. The rest are in motion.

It generated data. Trading data that attracts more participants. Volume data that demonstrates market viability. Impact data that proves to nonprofits that an alternative funding model exists. Data compounds. Each trade adds to the dataset. Each dataset makes the next trade more likely. The flywheel does not require fuel. It requires activity. And activity is the one thing markets never stop producing.

It generated a governance signal. Token holders are participants in an economic system with opinions about how impact should be allocated. Their trading behavior, their holding patterns, their governance votes create a signal about hunger relief priorities that no annual donor survey could match. The signal is continuous, real-time, and backed by real economic stakes. That is a better information system for philanthropic allocation than anything the traditional sector has ever built.

It generated a demonstration. Every nonprofit executive, every foundation program officer, every state charity regulator who learns that a token funded over seven thousand meals through normal market activity is seeing a proof of concept. Not a pitch deck. Not a whitepaper. A functioning system with an onchain record. The nonprofit sector has never had a public market. Now it has its first working prototype. And working prototypes, as I learned from building five companies, are worth more than a thousand business plans.

One trade. One meal. And a cascade of invisible outputs, each one potentially more valuable than the trade itself.

The Distance Between Here and There

Here is where we are. A single cause coin funding meals through trading activity. One token on one exchange on one Layer 2 blockchain. Seven thousand meals. A working prototype, not a finished system.

And here is where this goes. The nonprofit sector generates $3.7 trillion in annual revenue. It has never had a public market. Not a donation platform. A market. The infrastructure to build one now exists. The legal framework is in place. The mechanism is proven. The question is no longer whether it works. The question is how long it takes to scale.

I am not going to give you a number for how big this gets. I have watched enough founders project hockey-stick growth curves on pitch decks to know that the number is always wrong and always beside the point. What I will tell you is that we are at the very beginning. Not the beginning of the end. The beginning of the beginning. And I have been building long enough to know what that feels like.

It feels like standing in a conference room in Reno with marker stains on your hands and a CPA who has no idea what you are talking about. It feels like pitching investors in Dallas who have never heard of Davos. It feels like explaining to a bank that your legal structure was created by the state legislature of Wyoming and watching them stare at you like you just spoke Mandarin.

The distance is closing. The mechanism that currently runs on crypto trades will eventually run on ordinary purchases, ordinary cards, ordinary people who never heard of blockchain and never need to. The infrastructure becomes invisible. The impact becomes permanent. But that is the next chapter of the story, not this one.

When we started building WYDE, there was no domestic legal framework for what we were creating. The options were the Caymans, BVI, or a handful of other offshore jurisdictions. Those were the only places where the legal infrastructure existed to launch a decentralized organization with the kind of token economics we needed. So we did what every serious crypto project did at the time. We incorporated offshore.

And every time someone asked where our company was based, and we said BVI, they looked at us funny. Not suspicious, exactly. More like they were recalibrating. Like the conversation had shifted from interesting to complicated. Y Combinator does not invest in Cayman or BVI entities. Neither do most institutional investors. The standard path to raising capital and eventually going public in the United States runs through Delaware. It has for decades. And we were not on that path.

We were not tax evaders. We were completely public about who we were and what we were building. Our names, our faces, our thesis, all of it out in the open. But the structure did not communicate that. The jurisdiction told a story we did not intend. We quickly realized we needed a solution that made investing in us more palatable, because the substance of what we were building was getting lost in the optics of where we were building it.

Then Wyoming passed the DUNA framework. The Decentralized Unincorporated Nonprofit Association. A legal structure designed specifically for organizations like ours. Domestic. Compliant. Built on code-native principles. The first legal framework in the

United States that recognized what we were actually doing and gave us a home for it.

We moved immediately. WYDE became the first Impact Exchange built on the DUNA framework. No more offshore jurisdictions. No more awkward conversations about BVI. A Wyoming entity, American-made, operating within a regulatory structure that was designed for the future of decentralized impact.

The late nights, the whiteboarding sessions that ran until the markers dried out, the pitch meetings where we had to explain not just what we were building but why it could not be built within existing frameworks, the months of legal research, the conversations with legislators who had never heard of cause coins. All of that was the installation phase. The part that does not make the highlight reel. The part that happens before the first trade, before the first meal, before the 600% surge that every crypto outlet ran as a headline.

I keep coming back to a moment in a conference room in Reno. Tax advisors, attorneys, Martin and me at the whiteboard, trying to figure out how to make this thing work within a system that was not designed for it. The markers squeaking on the board. The diagrams getting more complicated with every regulatory constraint we mapped. And then someone said, have you looked at what Wyoming is doing? Everything after that moment moved differently. Not easier. Differently. Like the problem had shifted from impossible to merely very hard. And very hard is something builders know how to work with.

The New Order

The last monetary order was designed on a private island. Jekyll Island, Georgia, November 1910. Seven men traveled in secret under fake names. They represented approximately one-quarter of the world's wealth. Over nine days, they drafted the framework that became the Federal Reserve Act. The system they created lasted a century. It shaped the modern economy, funded two world wars, built the American middle class, and is now buckling under the weight of $39 trillion in national debt and a 78% decline in public trust.

The New Money Order is being designed in public. In open-source code. By thousands of builders in dozens of countries. The blueprints are readable by anyone with an internet connection. The infrastructure is permissionless. And for the first time in the history of money, the system does not require you to trust the people who built it.

I wrote this book because I wanted you to see it. Not the headlines. Not the price charts. Not the speculation and the scams and the noise that dominates every conversation about crypto. The thing underneath all of that. The energy grid being built. The conversion mechanisms being installed. The moment when money stopped being a passive ledger entry and started carrying instructions, purpose, and intelligence.

You can see it now. That is what the last sixty thousand words were for. Not to convince you of anything. To teach you to see a process that is already underway, that will continue whether you participate or not, and that will reshape every institution, every market, and every sector of the economy within your lifetime.

And if you want to know exactly how the New Money Order applies to your business, your industry, your Monday morning, the Playbook that follows is where I wrote it down. Find your section. It was written for you.

The last monetary order was designed by seven men who traveled under fake names to a private island. The new monetary order is being designed by thousands of builders whose code is public, whose ledgers are transparent, and whose infrastructure is open to anyone.

You are one of those builders now.

Not because you wrote code. Not because you launched a token. Because you can see the energy grid. You can trace the conversions. You can run the diagnostic on any system, any company, any transaction, and identify which order it belongs to and where the value is leaking. That sight is the Elixir. Not the knowledge itself. The ability to give it away.

Someone in your life is going to mention crypto this week. Or complain about a bank fee. Or ask why their paycheck buys less than it did a year ago. And you are going to feel something shift behind your eyes. You are going to see the question underneath their question. The energy underneath the price. The architecture underneath the frustration. And you are going to want to explain it.

Let yourself.

That conversation, the one you are already composing in your head right now, between you and whoever you are thinking of, that is the New Money Order spreading. Not through legislation. Not through institutional adoption. Through one person showing another person how to see what was always there.

Now you know where to look. Go show someone else.